CLASS CONFLICT

CLASS CONFLICT

THE PURSUIT AND HISTORY OF AMERICAN JUSTICE

GREGORY C. LEAVITT

Transaction Publishers
New Brunswick (U.S.A.) and London (U.K.)

This book is printed on acid-free paper that meets the American National Standard for Permanence of Paper for Printed Library Materials.

Library of Congress Catalog Number: 2012031049
ISBN: 978-1-4128-4979-1
Printed in the United States of America

Library of Congress Cataloging-in-Publication Data

Leavitt, Gregory C.
Class conflict : the pursuit and history of American justice / Gregory C. Leavitt.
p. cm.
Includes bibliographical references and index.
ISBN 978-1-4128-4979-1
1. Law--United States--History. 2. United States--Social conditions. I. Title.
KF352.L43 2013
349.73--dc23

2012031049

Dedicated to the memory of
Gary Ival Gaer

Contents

Preface

You, gentlemen, the preachers up of the new Constitution, will not surely contest a fact proved by the records of all ages and of all nations, that the liberties and rights of the people have been always encroached on, and finally destroyed by, those whom they have entrusted with the power of government (unknown Antifederalist in Rakove 1996: 152).

The above words, written by an unknown Pennsylvania Antifederalist, reflected the attitude of many common Americans when the Constitution was being debated after the conclusion of the Philadelphia Convention. These Americans opposed the creation of a more powerful federal government because centralized power had always meant the disfranchisement of common people and a neutering of their rights. As such, common Americans wanted to keep government close at hand in the towns and villages where they lived. The desire for local government became known as "states' rights" before the term was sullied by slavery and Jim Crow.

The men who met in Philadelphia in 1787 were charged with amending the Articles of Confederation, not with writing a new constitution. Their product was suspect because they were predominately men of wealth who wanted a stronger federal government to enhance and protect their commercial activities and property rights, the latter being the first principle of the Constitution as Chief Justice Taney declared in the Dred Scott decision in 1857. In this respect, the class of people who opposed the Constitution and those who wrote and supported it constituted at least the partial ingredients of a class struggle.

Although benign in its presentation, and taken for granted today, property rights and commerce as encouraged by the wealthy have been the bane of common Americans throughout most of US history. It was not until the Great Depression and the construction of the Roosevelt Court that we see a marked shift from the primacy of property rights to that of human rights as related to work and employment. The condition of common Americans began to take some political priority over private property rights and the commercial interests of the elite.

The American Revolution, with its inspiring promises of "inalienable rights" and "government by and for the people," encouraged common Americans with the promise of a better day. Behind this promise common Americans supported the Revolution and the Articles of Confederation and continued a fight to construct a structure of liberties, rights that predated the American colonies in Anglo-Saxon history.

From the early struggles over the access to land to the labor struggles of the nineteenth and twentieth centuries, average Americans challenged the hegemony of elite Americans at times with a substantial cost in blood. With the appearance of a large middle class, the nature of class conflict began to change. The middle class, which had more wealth and education than other common Americans, perceived an unjust world in need of change. This played out, in part, through middle-class participation in the abolition movement, the women's movement, the prison-reform movement, the Temperance movement, juvenile justice reform, the passage of child labor laws, and labor reform itself, among other activities.

By the early and mid-twentieth century the farm and labor movements and their political coalitions began to peak. Behind much turmoil, violence, and the threat of serious political-economic changes, common Americans began to improve working conditions and create a government more responsive to their needs. Social programs like Social Security and regulatory agencies enhanced living conditions and standards for common Americans. In 1935 the Wagner Act legitimized labor unions and collective bargaining giving working Americans the political clout needed to help shape their own lives.

After World War II, and with the maturity of the Industrial Revolution, the American middle class came to majority status and expected a more just society reflecting their core values. This mood for greater liberty and freedom via the creation of a more just society was enhanced by the American victory over tyranny in Europe and Asia in World War II. This mood manifested itself in a number of social movements and social changes. Often overlooked in this context was middle America's demand for higher education. Encouraged by a rapidly growing middle class that strongly valued education and the GI Bill after WWII, higher education in American society quickly expanded. More education meant a growing population of middle-class persons exposed in-depth to American republican values and rights as expressed in the Constitution and founding documents like the Declaration of Independence.

The American middle class cannot be credited with the integration of the races and the Civil Rights Movement but its support and growing political influence were certainly an important factor in the Movement's success. As middle-class values of fairness and justice permeated the society, fertile ground for civil rights, the women's movement, gay rights, cultural diversity, and Constitutional reform were improved. Growing demands for economic justice helped create a more substantial welfare state and an insistence on a more equitable distribution of wealth and income. These demands have helped reveal both historically and currently a class tension in American society between common and elite Americans.

In the discussion that follows the author traces the thread of class conflict and the struggle for a broader justice for common Americans from pre-revolutionary America through the Due Process Revolution of the twentieth century. In the final chapter there is an examination of the continuing American class struggle. It is not the argument here that class conflict accounts for most or all of American social problems but rather that it is a significant factor that has commonly been excluded or deemphasized in past scholarship.

1

American Justice and Social Class: An Introduction

It may be expedient but it is not just that some should have less in order that others may prosper. But there is no injustice in the greater benefits earned by a few provided that the situation of persons not so fortunate is thereby improved. The intuitive idea is that since everyone's well-being depends upon a scheme of cooperation without which no one could have a satisfactory life, the division of advantages should be such as to draw forth the willing cooperation of everyone taking part in it, including those less well situated. The two principles mentioned seem to be a fair basis on which those better endowed, or more fortunate in their social position, neither of which we can be said to deserve, could expect the willing cooperation of others when some workable scheme is a necessary condition of the welfare of all (Rawls 1999[1971]:13–14).

Class Tensions and Justice Today

The *New York Times* ran a story recently entitled "Survey Finds Rising Perception of Class Tension" (Tavernise 2012). The survey, conducted by the Pew Research Center, found that, "conflict between rich and poor now eclipses racial strain and friction between immigrants and the native-born as the greatest source of tension in American society." Continuing, the survey noted that the "perception of class conflict surged the most among white people, middle-income earners and independent voters." For independent voters this perception has increased from 23 percent to 68 percent and includes both Republicans and Democrats. "The survey attributed the change, in part, to 'underlying shifts in the distribution of wealth in American society,' citing a finding by the Census Bureau that the share of wealth held by the top 10 percent of the population increased to 56 percent in 2009, from 49 percent in 2005."[1]

The recent Occupy Wall Street demonstrations are another indication that many Americans are finding the lopsided distribution of wealth and income unfair. Currently, such discussions seem to be coming up regularly encouraged by the present deep recession. The flat or declining income and wealth of common Americans over the past several decades—while the wealthy have made substantial gains—have been an ongoing public concern.

What is unknown to many Americans is that class tension has been a part of the American fabric since before the American Revolution. American history readily reveals that class conflict has often been violent and of a large scale. This may be most apparent when examining the long labor strife of the nineteenth and early twentieth centuries. This labor and class friction also included large numbers of American farmers and involved the American middle class in various facets of the labor reform movement. The central issues in this conflict, while often depicted as monetary, also significantly involved various kinds of injustices: the on-the-job treatment of men, women, and children; the lack of compensation for the many and various types of injuries received in the work place; access to medical care; and the generally poor living conditions of common Americans.

As noted above in the *New York Times* article, issues of class and justice are very timely subjects today and the history that follows should provide a context from which to understand how these matters have evolved over time. In the sections that follow the basic concepts of this discussion will be examined, giving the reader tools to understand the history covered in the subsequent chapters.

An American Sense of Justice

There are few values as sacred to Americans as those embraced in the principle of "justice," or the "first virtue" as Rawls (1999[1971]:4) describes it. The bedrock of the American social contract is the precept that since "all men are created equal" they should likewise receive equal justice. "In a just society the liberties of equal citizenship are taken as settled" (Rawls 1999[1971]:3). In this depiction, we find not only the basic elements of American justice but its enduring dilemma: can the essential equality of all persons exist alongside the unequal distribution of wealth and income and the establishment of social classes?

More particularly, the existence of social divisions has led to class conflict, and a significant aspect of this discord affects how American justice has been historically shaped. In early American history "social class" referred chiefly to a structural dualism with a small wealthy gentry on the one hand and a large body of modest and poor citizens in contrast. The Revolutionary War era also recognized the beginnings of a small middle class, which over time became increasingly important for understanding class conflict as it fashioned American justice. For this reason, considerable discussion will be devoted in Chapter Six to the development and influence of American middle-class culture.

Americans are, of course, diverse in their specific understandings of justice, a fact readily appreciated when examining such issues as war, civil rights, abortion, women's legal status, gay rights, pre-marital sex, and firearm rights, to name but a few of the more apparent (see Wolfe 1998; Kuo 2006:26–27). But no matter their particular diversity, Americans have been almost unanimous in agreeing that "fairness" should be a fundamental ingredient in the foundation of the society. Americans have inherited a sense of justice that considerably predates the birth of the United States and has often been considered as originating with the signing of the Magna Carta.[2] Guaranteed liberties in the advancement of justice are historically common and deeply rooted in the Anglo-American tradition.[3]

As Wood (1998[1969]:268) observes, it is important to appreciate that justice in the Anglo-American experience is defined on a background of "encroaching power." The desire for justice by ordinary Americans has often and historically been a reaction to the privileges and abuses of the sociopolitical and economic elite. Americans have historically recognized that the affluent and influential in their midst not only experience justice differently than ordinary people, but in the pursuit of elite interests, have often denied justice to common Americans. In other words, understanding American justice, presently and historically, involves understanding class conflict.[4]

The core documents of American justice—the Declaration of Independence and the U.S. Constitution, especially its Bill of Rights and Fourteenth Amendment—were conceived and fashioned in the context of class tensions. Noting that Anglo-American history reveals many documents meant to preserve rights and privileges in the pursuit of a just society, the number of recurring efforts strongly suggests ongoing class friction. Repeatedly, ordinary citizens have reasserted rights that were thought to be well established. This reassertion has been necessary not only because of persistent opposition but because it is very difficult to completely and unambiguously expound all such liberties.

The very act of enumeration can result in limiting those rights, as noted by the Supreme Court's historical reluctance to find new rights in the Constitution. We might reasonably conclude that if ordinary citizens feel the need to repeatedly write down their rights and privileges it is because there is a powerful group attempting to obstruct those same liberties. Consequently, and in assorted ways since the inception of the American republic, common Americans have continued their struggle for justice against a wealthy and powerful establishment as similarly revealed in earlier Anglo history.

More specifically, because Anglo-American justice has been appreciably shaped by the fear of encroaching power, there has evolved in jurisprudence a tradition that emphasizes a jury of peers: that one will be judged by common citizens not the whims of the powerful. It has long been the belief that a jury of peers protects all rights, liberties, and justice more broadly (Rakove 1996:293–295; Conrad 1998:4). Americans have confidence that a jury of peers will, more often than not, produce a fair judgment when a fellow citizen's behavior comes under the scrutiny of government or, in civil cases, where a citizen must challenge or seek protection from a powerful entity.

In truth, juries can rise above the law and the facts of a case to deliver a sense of community justice they feel may not be adequately expressed in the law or delivered by the courts and legislature. The act and right of jury nullification (see Conrad 1998:5–6) is regularly kept from jurors by judges and prosecutors. Likewise, in civil cases, it has not been uncommon for the appellate courts to overturn the damages and penalties assigned by juries. Regardless of these impediments, the jury has been an important safeguard of rights and liberties for common citizens in the maintenance of justice.

The concept of American justice also includes the idea of "just desserts," a forceful part of the justice principle. This value has been decidedly tied to both criminal punishments and civil penalties with the idea that an offender should receive punishment or pay redresses that corresponds to his or her transgressions. This idea of justice also impels class tensions as when those with wealth escape criminal punishment or civil penalties (see, for example, Michalowsi and Kramer 2006) or the poor are over represented in arrests and correctional confinement.

Justice, then, though multifaceted, is primarily composed of the American sense of evenhandedness or fairness. Justice refers to one's realization of appropriate participation in the social contract; that is, we all participate in the common good with the anticipation of an equitable return in the pursuit of basic needs, even if that return has not been distributed equally. On its ideal side, justice has a strong egalitarian edge; equality under the law, equality of opportunity, and the fair distribution of resources in exchange for labor that results in a life free of unmet basic needs. Additionally, justice prescribes the avoidance of excessive wealth, a factor that can neutralize justice's other requirements.

Class and Class Consciousness

An appreciation of American social class is apparent when discussing justice and yet it is a difficult concept to define. Americans, who are often depicted as rejecting class distinctions, are, nevertheless, constantly assessing the social characteristics of those around them. In this assessment, people attempt to determine their social position vis-à-vis others; that is, does one defer, interact as an equal, or expect deference from another in social interactions?

Material accoutrements and income are perhaps the most obvious cues of social standing. Perceiving someone dressed as the homeless do as opposed to another wearing an expensive imported suit will generally evoke different kinds of social evaluations, interactions, and relationships. Beyond immediate appearance, people constantly monitor others' behaviors, manners of speech, gestures, and activities to place one's self in relationship to others in the social hierarchy. Such discernment can also involve race, ethnicity, foreignness, religion, gender, and other factors. But even in these latter instances, social class is frequently an active presence. These social class evaluation activities not only determine the nature of interactions between individuals but also result in a stratified society very conscious to Americans.

Sociology has traditionally employed three basic empirical measures to define social class and determine an individual's or group's placement in the social strata. These measures are income and wealth, occupation, and education—three highly correlated factors (Domhoff 2010[1967]:1–7). On the other hand, history and the humanities have more often defined social class through the observation of values, beliefs, life styles, and life chances (Bledstein and Johnston 2001; Blumin 1989). Though different, these two approaches are complementary and together give us a fuller understanding of social class.

Definitional problems most often occur when trying to separate one class from another and in determining how many class categories are useful. While these difficulties cannot be dismissed, this text is not meant to engage this definitional problem as a central point. Rather, we are concerned here with the relationship between the American elite (Domhoff 2010[1967]) and ordinary, average, or common Americans (Wolfe 1998). In the latter case, we find over the span of American history a developing middle class that has had an increasing impact on the ordinary American's sense of justice. It is through this class presence and history that the current text will examine the broad sense of American justice.

It is not unusual for the issue of class consciousness to emerge when social class is offered to explain social behavior. Do people act consciously as individuals and groups in pursuit of particular class interests? Lengthy essays and contentious discussions have appeared around this subject, especially since Marx raised the issue, but that debate will largely be avoided here. The history and social events discussed in this text did not often occur because a particular social class of persons mindfully recognized their self-interest and contrived to act as a group. Rather, people in similar class circumstances often coalesce in some manner and interact within a social environment that affects the social surroundings in particular ways without a conscious effort. In other words, the degree and kind of class consciousness varies by circumstances and has varying effects on the surrounding social behavior.

Class consciousness is not the rigid phenomenon that many mistakenly attribute to Marx—a kind of either/or state of mind. Indeed, consciousness itself, as a general state, occurs in varying degrees. People may think and act unconsciously in certain ways because of the social class circumstances of their life. People who live in particular dwellings in particular neighborhoods, who drive particular automobiles, and think particular thoughts while joining particular activities may be doing so because of their social class circumstances without being class conscious. At other times, similar activities may raise class consciousness to a subconscious level as when a person drives through an area either more or less affluent than their own and becomes vaguely aware of the dissimilarity with their own situation. At still other times, people may have class interests at the front of their mind as when the US Congress contemplates lowering taxes on the wealthy and the public at large becomes engaged.

There seems to be little doubt that Americans have a fairly strong sense of their own socioeconomic situation and can evaluate their circumstances vis-à-vis those who are similar or different. Likewise, Americans are commonly aware of class differences at an aggregate level as when they note the economic differences among neighborhoods in their community. Whether they make these observations and to what degree they do so will depend on the situation they confront. There is awareness among Americans, even in stereotype, of the "rich" and the "poor." Admittedly, these notions can at times be nebulous but not so vague as to be impotent.[5]

Likewise, there is little uncertainty amongst most social scholars that the American upper class has the strongest and most persistent class consciousness (Domhoff 2010[1967]:56–71, 83–84). In other words, the American upper class is very aware of their "classness," and they have actively organized around their common interests, especially those interests related to their wealth (Domhoff 2010[1967]; 1983; 1970; 1978a, b; 1975; 1972). It will become clearer upon examination that this class consciousness existed from the very beginning of American society in an elite earlier referred to as the "American gentry." For early Americans these upper-class members came to be associated with the Federalists, first as an ideological group and then as a political party. Throughout American history, the depth of class consciousness among the elite has been due to their small size and their need to preserve their interests. In that sense they have a common understanding in preserving governmental and economic systems that perpetuate and sustain their wealth and power.

The American middle class, which is now the largest social class, was in its infancy during the American Revolutionary period. Though at that time it was a small amorphous class, it still played a substantial role in the Revolutionary War (see Ryerson 1978). The middle class' self-awareness came about not only because of their common occupational situations but also because of the derogatory attitude the gentry took toward the "middling sorts." Genteel Americans, emerging as the Federalist elite, had different notions from ordinary Americans on how the new society and government should be institutionalized. These differences were significant and commonly provoked tension and violence, which in turn provoked class consciousness.

Critical Social Theory and Charles Beard's "New History"

To appreciate American justice requires a fuller understanding of the history and social context that led to the American revolt and the subsequent formation of American society. Not usually discussed in standard American histories are the evident class frictions that were frequent in eighteenth-century colonial America. Notably, these conflicts had a major impact on the establishment of constitutional government.

It may be that the current class analysis will be viewed and criticized by some as "Marxist." However, no matter the similarities that might be drawn, the analysis in this book, while involving social class as a critical factor in understanding American society, is not Marxist. While many of Marx' understandings of economics, history, and social affairs have compelling insights, Marxian analysis (in its many modern and varied forms) is often dogmatic, narrow, and insistent upon a simple social class dichotomy (e.g., working class vs. capitalists), which is inadequate for a clear socio-historical examination of the American class structure and the justice that results.

More accurately, the analysis in this text follows what is commonly called critical social theory. Critical social theory is perhaps better understood as an academic and philosophical perspective rather than a formally specified theory. C. Wright Mills' (2000[1959]) *The Sociological Imagination* has been a common and traditional reference for understanding critical social theory as rendered in sociology.

In his first chapter, "The Promise of Sociology," Mills (2000[1959]: 3–24) begins by noting that people correctly feel "that their private lives are a series of traps" and consist of troubles they feel helpless to overcome. While they perceive these troubles as individual issues, they are in many instances the manifestations of societal and historical forces. In recognizing this widespread condition, critical social theory often states that its purpose is liberation: "to liberate human beings from the circumstances that enslave them" (Horkheimer 1982:244). Put less dramatically, its purpose is to reveal to people the social and historical forces that bind their lives. In sociology, social class is recognized as one of the most important socio-historical forces controlling human behavior.

Conceptually, social class acknowledges a society divided hierarchically by material, social, and psychological factors, which of necessity requires subordinate and superordinate relationships. Such relationships are by definition fractious in nature as those at the top of the hierarchy exploit and control those who are secondary in social standing. In American history resolution of this class conflict has importantly been sought by common Americans in cultural notions of justice.

American justice is broadly realized on the insistence of certain basic principles and values understood as natural rights, that is, God-given privileges believed to be inherently provided and equitably distributed. Originally acknowledged in Anglo-Saxon customs and traditions, these rights have a history of written expression traced to the Magna Carta but re-expressed several times through history in various documents including more recently the Declaration of Independence, the US Constitution, the Bill of Rights, and the Fourteenth Amendment. Such expressions of rights stand as a buffer between common people and the elite that govern the society. An assertion of rights is not only an attempt to forestall exploitation but can be an expression of conflict in class relations.

An early precursor and subsequent important part of critical social theory is the "new history" first introduced by Charles A. Beard. When Beard published his work *An Economic Interpretation of the Constitution of the United States* in 1913, it was met with great hostility from the American establishment, not so much for what he said but that he had said it at all. An early advocate of the new history, Beard proposed that the personal economic interests and wealth of the members of the Constitutional Convention strongly affected the document they created. Beard went on to document, in a manner never done before, the individual wealth and resources of each Convention member. Beard concluded that the founding patriarchs wrote a constitution that primarily enhanced their economic interests and protected their rights of private property. Consciously, the Framers went to some lengths to constitutionally ensure that ordinary Americans could not seriously compromise the gentry's wealth, commercial activities, and property interests.

Any honest reading of Charles Beard's life and writings will not lead to the conclusion that he was a radical of any kind. Indeed, it is clear on reading his work that Beard was a supporter and admirer of the Constitution and many of its authors, even of Alexander Hamilton who represents, perhaps, one of the most conservative, autocratic, arrogant, and aristocratic-minded members of the group. Simply, Beard was only trying to present materials that had been forgotten. All of Beard's materials can be found in government archives, which at the time included information often left out of American and Constitutional histories.

In a new introduction to Beard's (1963[1913]) book written in 1986, Forrest McDonald reveals the reception Beard's book received at the time of its publication. As McDonald notes, Beard's book did receive some positive comment but most of the praise came only years later from academics whose laudatory comments are obscured from public view. What follows is a partial rendering of the comments McDonald presents in characterizing the reception Beard's book received at its publication.

> It is difficult . . . to understand the vehemence of the hostility with which *An Economic Interpretation* was greeted by many. Ex-president William Howard Taft, speaking at the Waldorf-Astoria before an audience of 1,100, which included governors, senators, and Supreme Court justices, lambasted "these God-forgetting Progressive days" for producing an associate professor at Columbia who dared to make a "muckraking investigation" that besmirched the cherished memory of the Founders. Former secretary of state Elihu Root expressed similar outrage. Future president Warren G. Harding, publisher of the Marion, Ohio, *Star*, denounced Beard in a story whose headline read: SCAVENGERS, HYENA-LIKE, DESECRATE THE GRAVES OF THE DEAD PATRIOTS WE REVERE. The book, the story said, was filled with "filthy lies and rotten perversions"; it was "libelous, vicious, and damnable in its influence." A reviewer in *The Nation* called the book "a pioneer work" of "first-rate importance," but afterward the journal ran a scathing editorial denunciation of it. Nicholas Murray Butler, president of Columbia, attacked the work of his faculty colleague for charging the Framers with writing the Constitution to satisfy their "economic appetites". . . and suggested that Beard, in assigning unworthy motives to the Framers, revealed that he himself would have acted unworthily in similar circumstances. In Seattle, Washington, Beard's book was banned from public schools and placed on "closed and restricted reserve" in the public library. . .Constitutional historian E. S. Corwin denounced Beard in *The History Teacher's Magazine* for being "bent on demonstrating the Socialist theory of economic determinism and class struggle." (in Beard 1963[1913] [Forrest McDonald *New Introduction*]:vii–xl)

The most important point here is not that Beard received unfair and hyperbolic criticism for reporting shocking information. Indeed, some of the comments Beard received were true; he did, in fact, attribute greedy motives to many of the Framers. The critical point is that these ad hominem and derogatory practices are still employed to stifle information that challenges American nationalistic myths.

Charles Thomson, for many years secretary of the early Congress, illuminated the laundering of historical information when describing his personal motives and behavior. "[Thomson] probably knew more about the administration and politics of the Revolutionary War than any other American, but he refused to publish a history of the Revolution: 'I could not tell the truth without giving great offense. Let the world admire our patriots and heroes. Their supposed talents and virtues (where they were so) by commanding imitation will serve the cause of patriotism and our country . . . I shall not undeceive future generations.' Before he died, Thomson burned his papers" (in Raphael 2001:6). And so, the common practice of hiding the less than glamorous nature of the Framers and their accomplishments behind nationalistic myths was established early. When Beard's research took some of the gloss off of these nationalistic myths he was villainized.

The influence of American nationalistic mythology should not be underestimated. Even new historians find it difficult to completely escape such practices. For example, in discussing Beard's work, Irons (1999:55–56)[6], a new historian himself, stated:

> In a book that shattered the conventional view of the Framers, historian Charles Beard of Columbia University argued . . . that the Philadelphia delegates were motivated primarily by economic self-interest. He computed—down to the last dollar—the amount of wealth that each delegate held in public securities, land speculation, "mercantile, manufacturing, and shipping" businesses, and ownership of slaves. Beard claimed that the "overwhelming majority" of the Framers were "economic beneficiaries from the adoption of the Constitution." His book . . . came at the height of the "progressive" era in American politics, a time in which "muckrakers" . . . exposed the greed and corruption of American capitalism.
>
> Historians, much like politicians, move with the currents of public opinion. Beard's depiction of the Framers as self-interested capitalists was countered in 1928 by Charles Warren of Harvard, who had already won the Pulitzer Prize for his three-volume work, *The Supreme Court in United States History.* Warren, a lawyer and scion of a patrician Boston family, argued in his book, *The Making of the Constitution,* that the Framers were farsighted statesmen who abandoned their parochial interests to forge a Grand Compromise that created a strong national union as the only alternative to the disunity of the confederated states. Basing his research largely on the correspondence of the Framers, Warren wrote that the "patriotic sincerity" of these men was based on "principles which were distinctly American and little connected with economics." Warren, of course, wrote in a decade that celebrated the achievement of American capitalism, which soon crumbled in the Great Depression that followed the Crash of 1929.

> Which historian—Beard or Warren—correctly identified the underlying motivations of the men who framed the Constitution? There is no question, as Beard concluded, that most of the Framers had some personal stake in the outcome of their deliberations. But evidence of economic motivation does not necessarily contradict Warren's claim that the Framers also acted from "such motives as patriotism, pride in country, unselfish devotion to the public welfare, desire for independence, inherited sentiments, and convictions of right and justice."

In a more understated manner than Beard's earlier critics, Irons questions Beard's work or, at least, lets us know that even though Beard may be correct about the economic interest of the Framers, it is not particularly significant but a product of the "muckraking" Progressive Era. For Irons to say that Beard calculated the Framers wealth "down to the last dollar," leaves the impression that Beard is an overzealous partisan. (In fact, Beard did not make such a calculation and makes it clear that early records from the Revolutionary War period are incomplete.) Irons then contrasts Beard's work with the Harvard scholar and Pulitzer Prize winner Charles Warren who, in 1928, wrote *The Making of the Constitution.* As Irons quotes above, Warren tells us that the Framers were statesmen and patriots who abandoned their parochial interests to forge a "Grand Compromise that created a strong national union." Irons does qualify Warren's assertion by stating that he wrote in a period that celebrated the achievements of American capitalism tempered later by the Great Depression.

Irons (1999:56) then asks rhetorically, "Which historian . . . correctly identified the underlying motivations of the men who framed the Constitution?" Irons concedes that certainly the Framers had some personal economic stake in the Constitution but this does not contradict the claim that the Framers were patriots who took pride in country, devoted themselves unselfishly to public welfare, desired independence, and had convictions of right and justice. More accurately, being patriotic does not mean that these men were not looking out for their own selfish interests.

What Beard fails to realize is that individual wealth or interest is not the only important point. What is important for our understanding is that this document was crafted by men of wealth who largely shared a common worldview and social philosophy. For the "nationalists" or American Federalists, McDonald (1979[1965]:32–33) says that they believed that "[a]ll men were ruled by avarice and ambition, and so must they be . . . in government, one filled public office out of esteem for a public trust, but all the while pursued personal gain. Those who pretended otherwise could never be trusted . . . and were either knaves . . . or fools. . . . On their manner: they spoke and carried themselves with a too easy, too natural grace that suggested pride, vanity, arrogance. They imposed harsh discipline on underlings, but were likely to be . . . ill-disciplined themselves."

Common Americans of the Revolutionary War period were aware of these elite attitudes and therefore opposed the Constitution the Framers offered. In American history the opponents of the Constitution have been referred to as "Antifederalists." Although a group of mixed interests and not nearly as cohesive and organized as their Federalist counterparts, the Antifederalists were very suspicious of the centralized government framed in the Constitution. For good reasons they feared that a wealthy Federalist government would act in much the same way as the British had.

And this fear was no small matter. Most historians agree that the Antifederalists outnumbered the Federalists, and in a one-man one-vote system they would have defeated the Federalists and their constitutional agenda. But this was not to be. By one means or another, the Federalists succeeded in implementing a constitution of their making. In very real ways, the Federalist/Antifederalist conflict was a struggle between the haves and have-nots, a class conflict.

Before, during, and after the Revolutionary War and then the Constitutional Convention, the American elite discussed and understood the American circumstance in social class terms. And, certainly, they were not Marxists. The Framers worried that the common American majority would trump the privileges of the elite minority. The American gentry strongly believed that the average American could not handle responsible democratic government, that common people were ultimately a mob bent on self-interest at the expense of the successful. Indeed, many in the American gentry, including some Framers, opposed democracy in principle. With such beliefs the Federalist-dominated Constitutional Convention took pains to remove common Americans from governmental processes.

This was done partially through state property requirements for voting and for running for public office. More importantly, the Framers created a republican government where a restricted population of white men could vote directly only for representation in the House of Representatives. Democracy was further thwarted by a system where the Senate was appointed by state legislatures that were dominated by wealthy men and the Supreme Court was appointed by the President with the advice and consent of the Senate. The President was appointed by Electors who, in turn, were appointed by state legislators. This Constitutional structure, Federalists reasoned, would avert democratic rule by the common people, who they feared, while protecting elite interests.

A central feature of class struggle in the post-Revolutionary era involved the Bill of Rights. The first ten amendments reflect common class interests: what the Federalist gentry feared and the Antifederalists required. The Antifederalists wanted assurances of certain basic rights to guard citizens from abusive centralized power. The Federalists argued that such rights were not needed as part of the federal Constitution and privately feared that an assertion of rights might compromise property interests.

As history records, a bill of rights was passed after the Constitution was approved. The Father of the Bill of Rights, James Madison, a wealthy planter who also opposed a bill of rights, wrote the Bill into the first ten amendments to the Constitution. Because of the Bill of Rights average Americans may have felt more protected from governmental tyranny, but, as we will see, only forty-four years later, Chief Justice John Marshall, an ardent Federalist himself, all but neutered the Bill of Rights and its protections for ordinary Americans in their daily lives.

The New History (and the Old)

Traditional history, which many Americans received in primary and secondary school, as well as in many college courses, is the history of "great men" (mostly of European descent), "great wars," and "great innovators" presented through a nationalistic theme that largely lauds the country and its elite establishment. Beard (1963[1913]:1) outlined a number of traditional approaches to history that are familiar to most American readers. A common one still frequently heard "explains the larger achievements in our national life by reference to the peculiar moral endowments of a people acting under divine guidance." The social sciences have long recognized the power of religion in justifying government and history. Once government—including the Constitution and early leaders—becomes sacred, it is very difficult for anyone to question it or provide criticism. In some guise this may be the strongest opposition to the new history. History that is not so glorious and that contains many dark features is difficult to subscribe to a higher power.

A second, and often related, theme is a variation on what most Americans know as Manifest Destiny, or what Beard (1963[1913]:2–3) refers to as the Teutonic school. "Without distinctly repudiating the doctrine of the 'higher power' in history, it finds the secret to the 'free' institutional development of the Anglo-Saxon world in innate racial qualities."

Specific to the history of law, Beard (1963[1913]:8) observes,

> In the absence of a critical analysis of legal evolution, all sorts of vague abstractions dominate most of the thinking that is done in the field of law. The characteristic view of the subject taken by American commentators and lawyers immersed in practical affairs is perhaps summed up as finely by Carter as by any writer. "In free, popular states . . . the law springs from and is made by the people; and as the process of building it up consists in applying, from time to time, to human actions the popular ideal or standard of justice, justice is the only interest consulted in the work . . . The law of England and America has been a pure development proceeding from a constant endeavor to apply to the civil conduct of men the ever advancing standard of justice." In other words, law is made out of some abstract stuff known as "justice."

In this traditional school, the Constitution is described in a similar fashion; the Constitution was born of freethinking people and comes from the whole people who ultimately give it legitimate authority (see Dahl 2003[2002]). McDonald (1979[1965]:18–21) critically describes traditional American history this way:

> The nationalists won [the American Revolution], and their victory established as truth a pentad of fictions: (1) that the war for independence had been a united war for national independence, not for the independence of the several states; (2) that the question facing the new nation was not whether it should have a national government, but what form that government should take; (3) that the first form, that of the Congress under the Articles of Confederation, was unworkable and consequently public and private morality collapsed just after the end in 1783; (4) that in the ensuing political chaos and commercial stagnation Americans came to realize that the Confederation was inadequate to promote the national ends that all desired; and (5) that the wisest group of men ever assembled in a single body, a group of demigods, came to the rescue by writing a Constitution that would assure the blessings of liberty to themselves and their posterity. For a hundred years historians of this epoch

> dutifully performed the function that was the universal function of historians; they preserved the myths.

Howard Zinn (in Raphael 2001:xi) adds:

> [Traditional history] is an approach to history which, in every society, serves the interests of the privileged and powerful, because, by ignoring ordinary people, it reinforces their feelings of powerlessness. We are not surprised when the narratives given to the public in totalitarian states deify the leaders and reduce the citizenry to ciphers. But we are startled when it is suggested to us that in liberal democratic states such as ours, boasting freedom of expression and a pluralism of ideas, there is similar exaltation of leaders, with everyone else barely visible.

In recent times[7], the veneer of traditional history has begun to crack and allow the flaws and imperfections of "great" Americans and American society and culture to be revealed. As McDonald (1979[1965]:19) observes, "[T]he followers of the New History unearthed an array of long-forgotten facts—most notably, facts demonstrating the Fathers had been a cantankerous lot who fought . . . for power and wealth." The American quincentennial observation in 1992 of Columbus' "discovery" of the Americas in 1492 brought the new history to the wider attention of Americans. Many Americans were shocked to find that Columbus was far from the glorious saint we had been led to believe in our schools, while others were outraged that the information was made public at all. Accurate information about the slave-owning and slave-abusing Founders soon followed. Americans were also exposed to the genocide of Native Americans, the abuse and displacement of Hispanic peoples, the internment of Japanese Americans, the lawful abuse of women and children, and so on.

Macrological Studies

Employing the sociological imagination in pursuit of a critical understanding of society, Mills (2000[1959]) requires the pursuit of a number of questions. Imperative are the questions: "Where does this society stand in human history?. . .How does any particular feature we are examining affect, and how is it affected by, the historical period in which it moves?" Specifically, what has often been missing in the study of social class and justice is a "macrological perspective" to which Mills alludes.

We can understand this broader perspective in two ways. As Durkheim (1982[1895]) proposed, we can compare class and justice in American society with other societies, thus deriving general propositions that place American society in a larger societal context. Or we can look at American class and justice in the broad context of American history. Kai Erickson (1966), in *Wayward Puritans,* gives us an excellent example of this kind of study. Peter Irons' book *A People's History of the Supreme Court* does another admirable job of helping us to understand not only the American Supreme Court but also American justice in its broader historical context.

This text follows a similar macrological approach and aims at providing a historical context for American class and justice from roughly the pre-Revolutionary War era through the Due Process Revolution of the Warren Court (1953–1969). A macrological approach in this instance refers to a broad historical context that identifies those societal and cultural factors that influenced history's direction, and yet it is not meant to be a complete and comprehensive discourse. One of the most important features of this kind of study is to identify sociocultural consistency in the historical current. In this case we are most interested in class conflict and its effect on American justice.

Because sociology has traditionally taken a more micrological approach, many social scholars are perplexed and uncomfortable with macrological positions. They may argue that concepts like class and justice are not defined the same across expanses of time or that behavior, whether individual or societal, is relative to their own particular moments and cannot be compared across time. To the unaccustomed eye, forces and factors at the macro-level often appear as unrelated. However, Erickson (1966) provides a good example of this kind of analysis when he relates the societal need for *boundary maintenance* to the crime waves in the Puritan settlement. Certainly, the crimes and social boundaries of Puritan society are not the same as those of contemporary America. Erickson (1966) never pretends that they are, but, rather, he hoped to identify general factors applicable across time. In this same manner, this text is interested in how socioeconomic class interests and factors of the past continue to shape the notions and institutional establishments of justice in American society today.

As already suggested, a macrological examination is not particularly concerned with immediate details or understandings, which might leave the impression that history is being oversimplified.

Oversimplification is by no means the intent of this volume. Simple sociocultural explanations do not exist at any level of social analysis and, even though academic scholars like to digress to cover such deficiencies, endless qualifications are never sufficient. In this sense, all methodologies and theories lead to incomplete understandings.

The "Big Picture": The Agricultural Revolution, Social Inequality, and Justice

The kind of macrological analysis suggested above does not have a particularly deep tradition within the discipline of sociology. Kai Erickson is acknowledged in criminology and many may be familiar with Nolan and Lenski's (2009[Lenski 1970]) macro-analysis of human society or Lenski's (1966) macrological study of social class and stratification. In the social sciences this kind of analysis has been found more commonly in cultural anthropology. Since this examination of American justice is immediately concerned with social inequality, social class, and justice, we can set an even broader context to view American society's place in societal existence using comparative historical and pre-historical knowledge.

The following description of the development of human society since the Agricultural Revolution is admittedly brief and must necessarily leave out much rich and complex detail. But social class and class conflict were born in agricultural societies as was the developing struggle by common people for a just society. The Paleolithic hunting and gathering communities that preceded agriculture were not class divided and many would agree those communities had the most democratic justice of all the known types of societies. Examining them and the evolution of sociocultural systems allows us perspective as we examine the American case below.

Prior to the appearance of agriculture, all humans lived in small hunting and gathering bands of twenty-five to forty people who were usually related by blood and marriage. Humans and their ancestors had lived exclusively in some variation of this social form for hundreds of thousands of years. Bands in a particular geographical location that spoke the same language and shared a common culture would normally have a loose association referred to as a "tribe" that, on average, would include about five hundred individuals. These human bands were nomadic, moving when wild game and foods became depleted in an area. Their only real institutional social form was the family, and it was from this family organization that most other behaviors were anchored and orchestrated. There were no written rules or laws, no enforcement agencies, courts, or correctional institutions. Behavioral problems were usually minor and handled informally by family and friends who would arrive at some consensus. Serious disputes that could not be settled would normally result in one of the parties in the dispute leaving the band and joining another.

Hunters and gatherers had no government or anyone with societal authority. There might be persons with greater or lesser influence, like the headman or shaman but no one was in a position to compel another's behavior. Likewise, there was no institutionalized social inequality or social classes. In fact, many of these peoples consciously insisted on social equality (Lee 1990:150–153) and actively took steps to maintain it. Because they were nomadic and had to carry their belongings on their backs, there was little, if any, accumulation of wealth or private property.

Living in small nomadic bands had the effect of spreading populations over vast geographical areas. Though bands might occasionally meet other bands in their yearly migration patterns or regularly gather as a tribe (usually on an annual or semi-annual basis), population density was normally very low—on average about one person per square mile. Living on wild foods, almost by definition, meant that there were plenty of resources, all renewable and shared. Cooperation was at a premium, a necessity in this kind of lifestyle. As a result there was little warfare (i.e., organized social violence) or crime of any serious nature whether violent or property. Anthropologists argue about the amount of violence in these societies, both within and between them, but, certainly, by any modern standards, violence was unusual and lacked intensity.

Some scholars have over-idealized the human aboriginal life pattern; certainly life in these societies could have hardships, both individually and for the group. On the other hand, the traditional stereotype has these people living a brutish life, which is just as incorrect. Under normal conditions, these people had little disease because they did not live in highly dense populations; were healthy because of their high protein, low fat, low sugar diets and active physical lives; and have consistently been reported to be happy with their way of life. Most important for our notice is that for the overwhelming amount of time of human existence social inequality did not exist or play a role in human behavior. There were no social classes or ruling elites and justice was egalitarian and democratic.

About ten thousand years ago, as the last ice age was ending, this small-band nomadic lifestyle began to end and be replaced by simple forms of agriculture.[8] Agriculture changed the old universal human way of life drastically. Ironically, though we commonly learn that agricultural societies are the birthplace of "civilization," with all its positive attributes and connotations, "civilization" actually meant that most humans would come to live in very poor and violent conditions, a situation that still exists today for many of the humans on earth. Almost immediately with the appearance of agriculture we have the emergence of institutionalized social inequality and an escalating rise in violence, both inter- and intra-societal. Agricultural land was far scarcer than hunting and gathering areas—which included the entire landed earth except for the Antarctic—and not all agricultural lands were equally fertile. Aggravating the scarcity of this essential resource was a simultaneous explosion in human population. Because agriculture was labor intensive until the twentieth century, large families were economically encouraged.

In this situation very fierce competition for arable land escalated and was expressed in progressively more vicious and deadly warfare between societies. Likewise, the violent suppression of common people in the society by a developing warrior class also occurred. The warrior class was also stratified and, of necessity, encouraged the rise of the most ruthless and cunning people to the top of the society. If the society were to survive in an environment surrounded by warlike neighbors a particular kind of leadership would be encouraged. After ten thousand years of this kind of competition, we would not expect to find peaceful kindly people at the top of human community power.

In the earliest agricultural societies, the headman of hunting and gathering societies was replaced with the "Big Man" who led by influence derived from his fighting prowess and economic leadership abilities. In a relatively short time, we find the appearance of local (village) chiefs who have authority and who have institutionalized their families in a hereditary elite (royal clan). As the social and technological complexity of societies continued to be driven by population pressures and competitive violence, we observe the appearance of paramount chiefs who brought several chiefdoms under centralized control through warfare. Because much of the arable land on earth produces more under irrigation, these areas were more easily ruled by a small ruling elite (Carnerio 1970) who controlled the flow of water. Subsequently, we find the development of large irrigation empires such as China, Mesopotamia, and the Inca.

As societies grew larger in land mass, they also grew in population size, population density, and social complexity. By the time agrarian societies emerged (i.e., plow and field agriculture—see Nolan and Lenski 2009) large towns and cities had also appeared. While cities served as centralized markets of exchange and as religious centers, they also housed tyrannical governments and masses of malnourished and disease-ridden people. Life in the countryside was little better. Human life expectancy and the standard of living for average humans plummeted and most human life became essentially worthless.

Even today Americans can glimpse some of these conditions in their own society and certainly in the developing world. Most immigrants (refugees) to the Americas in the past five hundred years have come to escape these kinds of conditions. Besides the dire poverty, Americans can still witness the most horrific dictatorial regimes as in Iran, North Korea, and Sudan to name some of the current brutal dictatorships. In all of these advanced agricultural societies, we find a privileged elite who are advantaged in wealth and power and commonly believe that their positions are inherent and blessed by God. They maintain their positions through the most inhumane and cruel tactics and are frequently overthrown by some group within or without that is even more brutal. In those instances where revolt by the masses has been successful, elite leadership quickly reappears.

At the height of worldwide agrarian development American society emerged. Part of the myth of the American Revolution is that Americans not only freed themselves from the British, but, through democracy, also freed themselves from elite control and a class-divided society. Any objective observation of human society since the Agricultural Revolution would cast serious doubt on the claim that American republicanism resulted in the demise of a small and powerful elite social class. While industrial or post-industrial societies are new to the human scene and we may not have a good fix on the types or variations elite control will take, in American society elite control is certainly evident.

American social class and justice is not a separate, isolated, or unique history in the scheme of human existence. It would be difficult to argue that any society is not heavily influenced by the history and circumstances that have affected all human societies. The difficulty is getting past self-aggrandizement, for example, "that we are not only a democratic society but the most democratic; that American justice may have its faults but it is still the best in the world." In other words, we need to get past the ethnocentrism that prescribes that Americans are exceptional and the best case of a society in societal development.

Notes

1. For example, a *Time* magazine article (October 29, 2007, p. 18) reported that "48% . . . of Americans surveyed . . . say the country is divided along economic lines. The number was 26% in 1988. Thirty-four percent think they belong to the have-nots, double the percentage of 1988.
2. The "Magna Carta was regarded at the time as a charter of baronial privilege, detailing the rights of feudal lords. It also had provisions guaranteeing the freedom of the church and local autonomy for towns. It came out (in vague terms) against the oppression of any of the king's subjects. Over time the document was interpreted more broadly by English judges, turning it into a quasi constitution that enshrined certain individual rights" (Zakaria 2003:38).
3. "Like all English people the colonists were familiar with written documents as barriers to encroaching power. 'Anxious to preserve and transmit' their liberties 'unimpaired to posterity,' the English people had repeatedly 'caused them to be reduced to writing, and in the most solemn manner to be recognized, ratified and confirmed,' first by King John, then Henry III and Edward I, and 'afterwards by a multitude of corroborating acts, reckoned in all, by Lord Cook, to be thirty-two, from Edw. 1st. to Hen. 4th. and since, in a great variety of instances, by the bills of right and acts of settlement.' Moreover, America's own past was filled with written charters to which the colonists had continually appealed in imperial disputes—charters or grants from the Crown which by the time of the Revolution had taken on an extraordinary importance in American eyes" (Wood 1998[1969]:268; also see Levy 1999).
4. Obviously, class conflict is not the only form of major social discord in American society. Notably there are racial, ethnic, religious, and gender conflicts—to name some of the more obvious—and these, too, have had notable impact on American justice. However, the scope of this text is focused on class conflict.
5. In the 2008 presidential election, social class issues, especially with regards to economic issues and taxes, aired commonly. In stating that he would give the middle class a tax break, President Obama defined middleclass as those making less than two hundred fifty thousand dollars a year. There was also populist talk that pitted the middle class ("Main Street") against the wealthy ("Wall Street") and certainly such discussion helped raise class consciousness. This appears to be having a relatively long-term effect. As of this writing, financial institutions have recently been on the verge of failing and the government (i.e., the taxpayer) has stepped in to prop them up. With these failings in market institutions and with a feeling of ownership because their tax dollars are being used to finance these corporations, ordinary Americans are becoming more aware of the "us" versus "them" of the class structure. Recently, it was revealed that institutions that have

received billions of dollars in government loans are still giving large bonuses to their top executives, and these executive are still using private jets for transportation to conferences at expensive resorts on the government's dime. This, for the moment at least, has created a class consciousness that is moving the government toward taking punitive actions against such corporate behavior.

6. The author of this text is an admirer of Iron's book (1999) *A People's History of the Supreme Court.* The example used from Iron's work is not meant to discredit Iron's excellent history, which I use frequently in class, graduate seminars, and research, but rather to demonstrate how we are all victims of the old nationalist history.
7. Historians generally make the claim that the new history appeared at the turn of the twentieth century. See McDonald 1979[1965]:19).
8. For those readers who are interested in pursuing this subject in greater depth I would suggest Marvin Harris, 1977, *Cannibals and Kings*; Jared Diamond, 1997, *Guns, Germs, and Steel*; Allen W. Johnson and Timothy Earle, 1987, *The Evolution of Human Societies; From Foraging Group to Agrarian State;* Patrick Nolan and Gerhard Lenski, 2009, *Human Societies: An Introduction to Macrosociology.*

2

Eighteenth-Century America: The Pre-Revolutionary Era

He seems not to have reflected that there can be no true liberty without security of property; and where property is secure, industry begets wealth; and wealth is often productive of a train of evils naturally destructive of virtue and freedom! (William Smith Moore in Wood 1998[1969]: 65).

The pre-Revolutionary period, when American colonists began to chafe under British rule and to contemplate separation, is generally identified with that moment in time beginning after the French and Indian War (1754–1763). The cost to Britain of fighting that war had been substantial. Maintaining an army after the war to discourage further French aggression, contain Indian attacks, and stem the illegal expansion of American colonists into Indian Territory was a continuing financial burden on the British treasury. To offset these costs, the English Parliament was resolved to tax Americans and create an ongoing stream of supportive revenue.

The early taxes imposed by the Parliament were the Sugar Act of 1764 and the Stamp Act of 1765. The first Act taxed molasses, a major American staple, and the second Act taxed a number of items requiring parchment and paper. Whether rich or poor, the people universally opposed these taxes because of their broad impact on daily life. Most Americans found they had little money for paying new taxes since species (coinage) was rare and most Americans were of modest means.

The Stamp Act, especially, became intricately related to and symbolic of the American confrontation with England. History tells us that American concerns were not only taxes but how these taxes were imposed. Increasingly, colonial assemblies wanted the authority to tax themselves or, at the very least, to have a stronger involvement in colonial taxation. The Stamp Act was quickly followed by other taxes adding to American discontentment.

Governmental leadership in the American colonies was primarily comprised of men with substantial property and financial means. These elite Americans saw themselves as English citizens deserving a form of governance that would help deflect British meddling in American market affairs. To achieve this end, American leadership began identifying itself with the progressive republicanism of the English Radical Whigs. The pre-Revolutionary American leaders calculated that by identifying themselves with the Whigs they could generate pressure on the Crown and Parliament to reconsider the taxes and economic policies directed at the colonies. For many American leaders it was never the plan to actually separate from Britain but simply to posture in a manner that would bring favorable political and economic considerations from British authorities.

The taxation issue with England went a long way in overriding prevalent American factionalism. Growing animosities in the colonies were not just over taxes imposed by England but they also existed within the domestic affairs of the American population. Wood (1998[1969]:76; also see Domhoff 2010[1967]:12) notes:

> [B]y the middle of the [eighteenth] century there were increasing signs, even in so stable a colony as Virginia, that more and more groups, with more broadly based grievances and more deeply rooted interests than those of the dominating families, were seeking under the prodding of popular spokesmen a larger share in the wielding of political authority, a process that would in time work to shape a fundamentally new conception of American politics.

Factionalism in the American colonies was further veiled by the growing problems Americans were having with British troops. There was harassment in the streets and intrusion in American homes where the law allowed British soldiers to board free of charge and search American homes and businesses on broadly written warrants. British soldiers were also taking jobs that would otherwise go to Americans because military pay was inadequate. Such activities pulled Americans together in common cause.

As other English taxes were levied, colonial leadership began enlisting common Americans to enhance opposition to Crown and Parliament through strength in numbers. To recruit average Americans in a common cause, the colonial leadership elevated the republican rhetoric, an approach that appealed to a broad spectrum of the American population (Domhoff 2010[1967]:2). As a result, a largely pragmatic action to change tax policy was turned into a broader, more impassioned, and popular philosophical engagement for "freedom" and "liberty." Indeed, ordinary Americans got out ahead of their leadership and began taking collective and violent actions, which, once started, were difficult to control.

When American Whig leaders did join the shooting revolt, they often did so reluctantly, some arguing that the colonies should rejoin the British Empire even after the Revolution had ended with an American victory. By joining the revolt, American Whigs were able to maintain leadership as the Revolution began and thus were able to position themselves to remold republicanism to suit their interests once the Revolution ended.

As pre-Revolutionary troubles with Britain passed from practical issues over taxation to ideological issues over "liberty," the community's emotional height and the degree of violence grew quickly. In roughly ten years, America went from grumbling over taxes to shooting over freedom. A people's everyday life is typically explained and justified through their beliefs, values, and encompassing cosmology (see Keller 2007:12–13). It is threats to these ideational matters that most inflame a people's passions and, historically, has been a tactic regularly used by leadership to motivate common people to action. Today, Americans remember the Revolutionary War mainly as a conflict over ideals related to rights and liberties as represented in the Declaration of Independence.

Understanding this social psychology, the American Whigs used progressive republican rhetoric to emotionally stir the population to action. Revealing this tactic and its problems, Wood (1998[1969]:83) observes that "even the most aristocratic of southern Whig planters . . . were pushed into creating an egalitarian ideology that could be and, even as early as 1776, was being turned against themselves." When this method worked, it was tempting to inflame the situation with even more radical language. In so doing, American Whig leadership created a popular movement that often went farther ideologically than its own position. It seems clear that in the beginning of the troubles with Britain, most Whigs did not want violence or war. Rather, they wanted a show of strength, an implicit threat that would convince the British to provide the American colonies with a significant voice in their daily affairs and economic activities.

Escalating the republican oratory brought common Americans into action so that by the time the shooting started there was a powerful republican philosophy that was beginning to institutionalize itself. From this thinking a number of sacred American myths have arisen—that this philosophy represented the beliefs of the Founders and that the Founders used this progressive republicanism to shape a Constitution. As a result, so the myth continues, common Americans supported the Constitution, which provided them with democratic government and guarded their hallowed liberties.

The Evolution of Republicanism: From the Merchant to the Common People

"Republicanism" is a broad philosophy and ideology that can be reasonably equated with Western polity. American and English Whigs commonly identified classical antiquity as the source of their republicanism. Modern Americans are also enamored with this ancient past. The recent Hollywood film *300*, which depicts the Spartan republic's defense at the Pass of Thermopylae against the Persian invaders, frequently had the Spartan King exclaiming their position as "free men" defending their way of life from tyranny. Such sentiments are a common reflection of an underlying Western republicanism. But these and related republican terms are uncertain without a specific context. Concepts like natural rights, freedom, liberty, democracy, and equality, while seemingly apparent, often reserved the benefits of republicanism for elite and propertied men and not for the poor, women, slaves, or minorities, whether in Spartan or American society.

Western republican government was born in the environment of maritime societies (Nolan and Lenski 2009[Lenski 1970]:181–183), some of the earliest being the Mycenaeans or pre-Hellenic Greeks from which Western culture was born. As Nolan and Lenski (2009[Lenski 1970]:182–183) observe,

> [M]aritime societies were usually republics. . . . The explanation for the republican tendency in maritime societies seems to be that commerce . . . was the chief interest of the governing class. . . . An oligarchy of wealthy merchants could do the job [of government], since their primary responsibilities would be to regulate commercial competition and to provide naval forces to defend their access to foreign ports.

Later European maritime societies included Venice, Genoa, Danzig, Lubeck, and the Netherlands. "Britain moved far in this direction in the seventeenth, eighteenth, nineteenth and early twentieth centuries" (Nolan and Lenski 2009[Lenski 1970]:187). From the ancient Greeks to the British Empire, the heritage passed to Americans contained a strong maritime republican tradition. As has been suggested, the traditional republican philosophy and government was a government for people of commercial wealth. In other words, we need to be careful not to equate traditional Western republicanism with a broad-based democracy. Republicanism did become more democratic as it became increasingly progressive, and it became increasingly progressive as common people—and especially the middle class)—demanded greater participation. This progression came from and created a social class tension and competition for power that continues in American society today.

Anglo-Saxon tradition and history frequently portrays the Magna Carta (1215) as the original foundation for republican constitutional liberties.[1] Though in abbreviated summation its constitutional liberties are often exaggerated, the Magna Carta was actually an agreement to end a civil war between King John and his barons. The English barons found King John's rule unacceptable in a number of respects, and thus they forced him to sign an agreement ending frequent abuses. The Magna Carta is a foundational document of Anglo-Saxon republicanism in that it limited the Crown's arbitrary powers and required the king to obey the law. The Magna Carta also used much ink in preserving property rights and created a council to approve taxes proposed by the King. King John, like those monarchs succeeding him, found such restraints annoying and he did his best to ignore and side step them.

Less than fifty years after the signing of the Magna Carta—which itself was revised several times—disgruntled barons compelled Henry III to sign the Provisions of Oxford (1258), considered by many to be the first English constitution. When this also failed to work and the Pope declared the Provisions invalid, Simon de Montfort again raised an army of barons and in 1265 called for the first partially-elected Parliament that included Freeholders of a certain wealth, from which the current British Parliament evolved. In Britain, a republic for common people (or Commonwealth) was first realized in 1649 after the English Civil War. This conflict, led by Oliver Cromwell, defeated King James

II who, like his predecessors, was viewed as abusive and frequently acting outside of the law.

Cromwell emerged from the growing middle class of England, a class closely associated with progressive republicanism. Cromwell's family had the means to send him to study law at Cambridge. Both a lawyer and member of the English Parliament, Cromwell also carried the influences of the Reformation and Puritanism in his thinking. The Reformation and the Puritan movement promoted individual value by emphasizing a person's equality with others and their free volition in dealing directly with God. This posture in relation to the Supreme Being straightforwardly translated into a greater worth of the individual within the polity and social surroundings. Furthermore, this rising socioreligious culture was realized in both Britain and America as a broader republicanism concerned with the rights of average citizens, not just the privileges of the propertied and commercial class. By 1689, some thirty years after Cromwell's death, the English Parliament passed the English Bill of Rights (*An Act Declaring the Rights and Liberties of the Subject and Settling the Succession of the Crown)* that granted broad protections and liberties to all British citizens.

It is clear when reading the English Bill of Rights that there was great concern about the abuses of power suffered earlier under King James II. To avoid such mistreatment the Crown's powers were limited. The English Bill of Rights begins by identifying the practices of King James II that would no longer be tolerated by the Parliament, practices the new king and queen agreed to abandon by their oath of office. It is also apparent that the English Bill of Rights was meant to restore the "ancient rights and liberties" specified in thirteen statements. Preceding the US Bill of Rights, the English version gives English subjects the right to petition the executive (i.e., king), the right of Protestants to bear arms, the right to free speech, the right to be free of excessive bail and fines, the right to be free of cruel and unusual punishments, and the right to a jury.

By the eighteenth century in both Britain and America, an even more progressive republicanism began to emerge with a philosophy that more directly included the needs and rights of average citizens. As described previously, when the American colonial elite became dissatisfied with the constraints placed on their market activities by the English Crown and Parliament and when their lobbying efforts with the English Parliament failed, they gained the support of common Americans by appealing to a more progressive republicanism, a republicanism that reflected substantial individual rights. With the success of the American Revolution, the American elite collaborated to create a more conservative and centrally powerful constitutional republic that would preserve their property rights while structurally protecting these interests from the more radical republicanism popular with common Americans. This clash of interests expressed itself in historical American society by the heated debate between Federalists and Antifederalists over the passage of the Constitution, a rivalry that cleaved society strongly along class lines.

Ultimately, republicanism is a continuum with conservative republicanism on one end and progressive republicanism on the other. Conservative republicanism is typified by rule of a propertied segment of the society—usually men of a small wealthy commercial class—that is primarily concerned with private property rights, including market activities free from governmental rule. This governing body may be elected or in some manner selected from this privileged class. They desire a government where the propertied or wealthy have a commanding voice in looking after their interests through the instruments of government, especially including the military.

On the other end, progressive republicanism is more concerned with a constitutional government that is created by and for the people, a government that constitutionally guarantees certain rights and liberties. Progressive republics espouse equality and the common welfare of all people and are involved with the development of democratic institutions and universal suffrage. Economically, republicanism of this tenor is reflected in a statement such as that made by Thomas Perkins Abernethy at the Kentucky convention of 1784–85. On the American frontier there existed few social class distinctions and most landowners had similar wealth. This egalitarianism was something frontier people desired to maintain. "That to grant any Person a larger quantity of Land than he designs Bona Fide to seat himself or his Family on, is a grievance, Because it is subversive of the fundamental Principles of a free republican Government to allow any individual, or Company or Body of Men to possess such large tracts of Country in their own right as may at a future Day give them undue influence" (Abernethy, Thomas Perkins, in Main 1961:1).

Only a few years later, in the urban areas of the country, Phillips (2002:5) observes a similar progressive republican attitude. "The egalitarian-minded working classes of New York and Philadelphia . . . quickly rallied against the Federalist merchants and financiers of the

1790s, with their predilection for British manners and contempt for the common man."

The American Gentry

In a truly republican society the artificial subsidiary distinctions would never be extreme, not as long as they were based solely on natural distinctions. It was widely believed that equality of opportunity would necessarily result in a rough equality of station, that as long as the social channels of ascent and descent were kept open it would be impossible for any artificial aristocrats or overgrown rich men to maintain themselves for long (Wood 1998[1969]:72).

As already noted, the American gentry was composed of large land- and slave-owning farmers, prosperous merchants and traders, manufacturers, entrepreneurs, financiers, speculators, and rentiers who owned large estates and rented parcels to small tenant farmers (see Main 1961:3–4). This gentry-elite was but a very small percent of the population whose disproportionate share of the wealth grew continuously through the eighteenth century. For instance, near the end of the century 4 percent of the wealthiest Philadelphians owned over half the city's wealth (Phillips 2002:6). Their numbers included some English aristocracy with whom the American elite intermarried, shared a worldview, and whose manners and lifestyles they emulated.

The American gentry accepted the notion that class divisions, called "ranks," largely reflected inherent traits: that common persons were by birth less intelligent, more uncouth, and more violent and criminal in nature. The American gentry habitually flaunted their wealth and treated their perceived inferiors with tiresome disregard.[2]

Ellis (2004:158) discusses this issue in his biography of George Washington, a planter and one of the wealthiest men in the colonies, who retained traditional attitudes about social distinctions. Washington's views on "ranks" found him in the midst of a controversy only a few months after his retirement as commanding General of the Continental Army. Continental army officers had formed an organization they designated the "Society of the Cincinnati" and asked Washington to be their first president. The Society "was an avowedly elitist enterprise designed to sustain the aristocratic ethos of superior virtue the officers in the Continental army had been harboring since Valley Forge. Most ominously, membership was defined in hereditary terms" (Ellis 2004:158). Washington initially ignored the public outcry that scorned the Society because he maintained an elitist attitude himself. Although Washington did not support a monarchy, he likewise did not believe that the Revolution had "destroyed the world of privilege, rank, and deference in which he had risen to prominence" (Ellis 2004:158).

Rank, then, was a vestige of the old aristocratic society that viewed social positions as having largely inherent qualities so that higher-ranking people were "superior" to lower ranking persons. Today we think of ranks in terms of military organizations and they, indeed, make for a good analogy. Military ranks are divided between officers and non-officers or the lower ranks. While ranks are not castes, the mobility between lower or non-commissioned ranks and commissioned officer ranks is rare and supposedly occurs only with exceptional personal qualities and performance. Even today, upper ranks in the American military are commissioned by the Congress as "Officers and Gentlemen," a remnant of the old social ranking system.

Social class hostilities were certainly apparent in pre-Revolutionary America and played a major role in the events that followed. While the war submerged these hostilities to a certain extent, they were to re-emerge after the Revolution—as we see in the case of the Society of the Cincinnati—and play an important part in the formation and implementation of the Constitution.

In the pre-Revolutionary period, the American elite could be more or less divided into two groups for purposes of understanding the Revolutionary War era. The first were the Whigs, gentlemen who ascribed to some form of republicanism and separation from England. The other well-known group was the Tories or Loyalists, those persons we think of as remaining loyal to the British Crown and who were also often conservative monarchists. The fact, however, is that the divisions between these two groupings of elite peoples were often blurred. Indeed, one could not always tell a Whig from a Tory until the Revolutionary War began and people were forced to take sides. Even then, there was a fair amount of switching positions.

Although history has placed the Whigs on the people's side and the Tories on the Crown's side, except in rare instances, American Whigs and Tories were often disagreeing over narrow points. Primarily, Whigs and Tories could not agree on how much power should be invested in the people and how much in the executive (Wood 1998[1969]:49). Where American Whigs and Tories colluded was in opposing the Crown's corruption and unfairness as it applied to American interests (Wood 1998[1969]:28–36). Most American Whigs and Tories thought that a show of discontentment with the policies of the British Crown and Parliament would lead to a suitable resolution (Keller 2007:32). The Whigs were generally more willing to take the agitation further, such as employing boycotts of British goods and enlisting a broader base of common Americans. The Tories were more comfortable with lobbying the Parliament and dealing as "gentlemen" with their British counterparts.

Many historians would have us believe that the American Whigs, in the end, fought a revolution to provide a new republicanism "by and for the people." Exemplifying this view, Wood (1998[1969]:20, 24) states that in

> the continuous contest among the estates of the society, a contest that since the seventeenth century had become more and more confined to one between Crown and Commons, the Whigs' loyalty was always with the people. Although the people were but a single estate in the realm it seemed self-evident to the Whigs that the promotion of the people's happiness was the sole purpose of government.

This kind of republican ideal represents the gold standard in American republican philosophy, a standard by which we can judge the history of American justice and the larger governmental system. As will be seen, the Whigs (i.e., the Founders and later the Federalists) may have made these kinds of lofty statements in such documents as the Declaration of Independence and in many public speeches during and after the Revolution, but the reality was much different. With the exception of a few like Thomas Jefferson, Patrick Henry, and Thomas Paine, the Whig Founders had no such notion of "good government," though most were still republicans. Indeed, invoking Hamilton in this democratic ideal is preposterous for, as we will see, Hamilton had an aristocratic disdain for "the people." As Wood (1998[1969]:67) finally acknowledges, "Many knew with Hamilton that when the people were 'loosened from their attachment to ancient establishments' they were apt 'to grow giddy' and 'more or less to run into anarchy.'"

This disdain for and fear of common Americans by the gentry is revealed in a letter from James Duane to Robert Livingston (the Lord of Livingston Manor in New York) in 1775 (in Lynd 2009[1967]:35):

> I am much pleased that young Mr. Livingston is raising a company [for the militia] in the Manor. I wish he may extend his View's further, in the only plan, which, independent of the grand Contest [Revolution], will render landed property Secure. We must think in

> Time of the means of assuring the Reins of Government when these Commotions shall subside. Licenciousness [*sic*] is the natural Object of a civil . . . discord and it can only be guarded against by placing the Command of the Troops in the hands of Men of property and Rank who, by that means, will preserve the same Authority over the Minds of the people which they enjoyed in the time of Tranquillity [*sic*].

Lynd (2009[1967]:35–36) continues with a discussion that demonstrates the suspicion the American gentry had of common Americans and the extreme measures they would take to ensure their safety. "The Whig leaders in Dutchess, wrote William Smith in 1776, had a 'general Suspicion of the lower Classes of the People' and not great confidence in the militia. . . . The chairman of the Dutchess Committee of Safety, writing eleven days after the Declaration of Independence, warned that the county's militia was untrustworthy and should not be called out."

At a level of particular individuals, Wood (2009:218–230) examines the animosity between gentry and commoners by appraising the histories of William Findley, Jedediah Peck, and Mathew Lyon. All were men of modest origins who rose to middling stature and became involved in post-Revolutionary politics. All three suffered the condescension and criticism of the gentry as they moved into community leadership roles and some into the Congress. Eighteenth-century thinking on rank had the gentry as men of leisure who could hold political positions with "disinterest." That is, they would be unbiased by economic need and, therefore, serve the country with only its best interests at heart. The middling sorts, on the other hand, were compromised by their lack of wealth and need to pursue their trade or profession. Likewise, many of the middle class were not well educated (Wood 2009:230–238). As a result of their experiences with such upper-class arrogance these three men became progressive and aggressive republicans.

In the end, the Constitution provided a reality very different from the radical republicanism so loudly proclaimed in Whig propaganda during the Revolution, a reality that minimized democratic representation and maximized executive power for the purpose of maintaining the elite's position. The American elite's attitudes and their frequently open disdain for common Americans cannot be simply dismissed or minimized when these same men were shaping a sense of justice through the creation of a new Constitution. Furthermore, it is not just the American gentry's attitudes about rank that are important. As the new history has revealed, these men were also quite ruthless in their pursuit of wealth and power, an American behavior that has been institutionalized in our value for and glorification of market competition. This kind of behavior, which ran the gambit from slave trading and piracy to fleecing the Continental government when selling war supplies, provoked social class antagonisms (Phillips 2002:3–15).

As noted, a common activity that reveals these gentlemen's hardened natures was in their ownership, treatment of, and trade in African slaves for the purpose of financial gain. Historically, American history has laid this indictment on the American South, but slavery was universal in the colonies. Even when slavery was outlawed in the northern states, slave owners freely brought their slaves with them when visiting northern states, as was notoriously demonstrated in the Dred Scott case (Irons 1999:157–159), and certainly northern traders continued their slave trafficking. Most northern Whigs were perfectly willing to support the Great Compromise in order to establish a government that served their needs. It is not the purpose here to recount in any detail the many horrors that American slavery contained. A casual reading of this history will make people recoil, even while they often ignore the nature of these men, their place in society, and the implementation of their attitudes in nation building.

In his review of pre-Revolutionary America, Phillips (2002) reveals more about the early American elite than most Americans are familiar with. In the opening citation of his first chapter, Phillips (2002:3) quotes not only a Founding Father and Patriot of the Revolution, but also one dear to American justice, John Jay, the first Chief Justice of the United States. Jay stated during the Constitutional Convention that, "The people who own the country ought to govern it." Phillips raises an old republican question, "How well can wealth and democracy coincide?" and then he develops a detailed argument demonstrating how, throughout American history, concentrated wealth has constantly subverted the democratic process. Phillips, a Republican and advisor in the Nixon administration, is not arguing that American society should have a flat income structure and an equal distribution of wealth. Rather, he argues that when too much of the nation's wealth is concentrated in the hands of a few, democracy is seriously threatened.

In pursuing his argument, Phillips examines the brutal nature and philosophy of these American men who wielded great wealth and power. It is not just their great wealth that is at issue but the fact that they are conscious of, and act upon, their interests with other men of similar character. Sociology has a history of studying this elite class, from Thorsten Veblen and C. Wright Mills to William Domhoff, and agrees that it is in the American elite's commonly erected institutions that they threaten democratic life. Because of their institutionalized and pitiless nature many of the early American families are still found in the American *Social Register*.

According to Phillips, the wealth of the nation originated from only a few sources— piracy and privateering, the slave trade, speculation in government securities, and war contracts. The latter have always been with us and are still controversial in the current wars in Iraq and Afghanistan. War and military contracts are lucrative and often tainted with corruption. Most Americans do not realize the scope of this source of wealth, but it includes not only weapons and munitions but shoes, belts, medications, toilet paper, food, and a broad range of other items. "This pattern began before the Revolution. . . . Estimates of the richest men in Massachusetts following King George's War (1744–48) fell on those who had managed, financed, and supplied the campaigns launched from New England against the French in Canada. . . . The French and Indian War (1754 to 1763) produced even greater profits" (Phillips 2002:10).

The Revolutionary War was no different and wealthy Americans got rich often at the expense of ordinary Americans.

> The common man personalized his grievances and blamed financial distress on the malevolence of speculators. Henry Luddington and others inveighed against the "wicked, mercenary intrigues of a number of ingrossing jockies [*sic*], who have drained this part of the State of the article of bread to that degree, that we have reason to fear there is not enough left for the support of the inhabitants." The "petition of the freeholders and inhabitants of Dutchess County" told the New York legislature that speculators were selling provisions to the enemy for specie and refusing to sell to Whigs for paper, and asked for action against "a vile set of Men whose God is their Gain." To many a perplexed householder, not only in New York but throughout all the struggling states, the revival of local committees seemed, ultimately, to be the way to check the monopolistic practices of merchants and the dishonesty of public officials (Lynd 2009[1967]:43–44).

One of the most well known of these wealthy offenders was Robert Morris, who had numerous financial dealings with the new nation and was a delegate from Pennsylvania to the Constitutional Convention. During the War, Morris had headed the Congress' procurement committee. In the first two years of the Revolution Morris awarded about one quarter of government contracts to his own firm of Willing and Morris. In addition, Morris got richer through privateering. "Although he is remembered as 'the financier of the Revolution,' one historian claims that the truth is 'the other way around—the Revolution financed Morris'" (Phillips 2002:12). In a similar vein, McDonald (1979[1965]:74) says of Robert Morris and his associates—who included some of the wealthiest and most influential men of the time—that "they were also the greediest, most ruthless, and most insistent in demanding political action in their behalf."

Other profiteers included William Duer, who was the primary supplier for the New York military, and Jeremiah Wadsworth, the chief commissary in Connecticut during the Revolution. Both men were involved in Morris' acquisition system and worked out of Morris' office continuing their joint enterprises after the war ended. "Timothy Pickering of Massachusetts, the Continental army's quartermaster general late in the war, insisted that corruption in the purchase of supplies and equipment . . . almost doubled what the new U.S. government owed in debt by 1783" (Phillips 2002:15). Not only did military and government suppliers commonly overcharge but much of what was supplied to the army was rotten, unusable, or it never arrived.

Piracy and privateering were common sources of wealth and helped build many American fortunes. As early as the seventeenth century, American merchants were financing pirate ships to sack various forms of wealth in the seas off of Madagascar, Arabia, and India and getting rich doing it. "In 1696, Edmund Randolph, surveyor-general of customs complained to London that 'pyrates' [*sic*] were welcome in most American ports, abetted by governors like Sir William Phipps in Massachusetts, William Makham in Pennsylvania, and Benjamin Fletcher in New York" (Phillips 2002:11).

The Revolutionary War was very profitable for wealthy Americans involved in privateering. "[P]rivateering seems to have been the single most lucrative enterprise. The seven years following the autumn of 1775 saw some two thousand vessels . . . sailed under letters of marque from the United States or one of the . . . states. Collectively they would capture three thousand British ships." (Phillips 2002:12–13).

Many American financiers were readily recognized in this activity, such as Robert Morris and his partners Willing and Bingham. Another was Asa Clapp, a privateer who became the wealthiest individual in Maine. A future US Senator, John Langdon, was the most successful privateer out of New Hampshire. "Providence boasted John Brown, privateer and slaver, whose family money gave Brown University its name" (Phillips 2002:13).

Massachusetts seems to have been the privateering leader, creating several wealthy families including the Cabots and John Hancock who was also a merchant and smuggler. Philadelphia's finest did a lion's share of privateering as well. As Brands (2000:639) states, agreeing with many historical sources, "Privateers were nothing better than pirates, and to allow—indeed encourage—their depredations was to foster disrespect for law and order." When the Declaration of Paris in 1856 abolished the Letters of Marque issued to privateers, the United States was one of the few modern nations not to ratify it. In Article One, Section 8, of the US Constitution, Letters of Marque are listed as one of the powers of Congress.

Probably the most controversial source of wealth occurred after the Revolutionary War ended. To finance the war, the Continental Congress, the state Assemblies of all the colonies, and the Continental Army all handed out debt instruments (securities) in great quantities to buy the necessary wartime resources. Sellers (farmers and small businesses) often had little choice but to comply or they were robbed and vilified. At war's end, with the new government broke and in debt, these governmental IOUs were essentially worthless. Included in this government debt were land warrants on the western frontier along with depreciated securities, both used to pay Revolutionary War soldiers.

Before the ink could dry on the Articles of Confederation there was, in 1786, a movement by the American Federalists to revise the Articles of Confederation to make them more conducive to interstate business and market activities. (See a fuller discussion in Chapter 3.) One of the first concerns of this group was the national, state, and foreign debts. With Hamilton leading the way, the Federalists strongly advocated that all US debt be paid at face value. Another conspicuous supporter of this policy was the Society of the Cincinnati whose Continental army officers had been paid with government debt notes and promises of Western lands. This debt payment policy would give financial credibility to the new nation and also ensure that money borrowed from wealthy Americans be paid in full.

Controversy occurred over Hamilton's plan because Federalists, usually through agents, had scoured the countryside buying up debt securities at bargain prices, sometimes as low as ten cents on the dollar. Although not everyone who sold their securities at a substantial discount were orphans and widows, many were Americans of modest means.

> "Assumption and funding," as Hamilton's debt redemption provisions were called, provided the nation's first cornucopia for financial speculators. From New Hampshire to South Carolina, cliques of wealthy Federalist supporters and officeholders, using traveling agents, had bought as many of the federal and state debt instruments as possible at cut-rate prices. Massachusetts seems to have had the largest bloc of holders, original and speculative, many from among the privateering, supply, and Continental loan elites (Phillips 2002:17).

A substantial political backlash helped congeal many Antifederalists into the Democratic-Republican Party headed by Thomas Jefferson and James Madison. But the battle to stop the implementation of the Constitution at this time by the Antifederalists was already lost and the American elite now had a Constitution that would be used (or ignored) to their advantage even to the present day. It is important to underscore the character of the people being discussed; they were commonly and willingly ruthless to the point of murder, enslavement, and depravity and morally corrupt in the pursuit of wealth. They would cheat their own countryman in times of war whether through the sale of wartime supplies, wartime financing, or speculation on wartime debt. In the end they would flaunt their plunder and hold the cheated in arrogant disdain. To add insult to injury, the war debt would eventually be paid by taxes on the backs of ordinary Americans.

As American society developed in the following centuries this elite upper crust of American society did not become less merciless. They continued to cheat Americans through wars, exploit the labor of emigrants and their children, do business with the Nazis (Matthews 2006: 116–133), and free themselves of taxes at the expense of everyone else. They commonly produce and market bad food, bad pharmaceuticals, bad cars, bad tires, bad tobacco, bad child car seats, and toys ad nauseaum. It is not what they will necessarily do, but that they will do what is necessary to achieve their ends.

The People

Americans found all of these displays of superiority of status particularly detestable, in fact "more odious than in any other country" (Wood 1998[1969]:74).

Most Americans in pre-Revolutionary America were of modest means, many either marginally or direly poor, and many disenfranchised. Numerous Americans were farmers and large numbers of these were working land that was exhausted and/or rented or they were squatting on someone's undeveloped estate[3]. Unable to raise enough crops to survive or pay their debts and rent, many farmers became little better than sharecroppers or, worse, ended up in debtors' prison. These circumstances also led "to a rise in the number of 'strolling poor' who wandered the countryside in search of work" (Raphael 2001:17). These wandering homeless people were not welcome in most communities so they often ended up in sea ports looking for odd jobs, committing petty crimes, and/or shipping out to sea. For many who worked as day laborers, or even had more permanent jobs, the pay was often meager. This resulted in living conditions that were filthy, infested with vermin, consisting of unhealthy diets, and manifesting much disease. For the more prosperous of common Americans who owned a small business or farm, life was better but often hand-to-mouth, suffering periods of distress when the economy was bad or crops failed.

A large estate in Dutchess County, New York, owned by the Beekman family, illustrates in terse terms the plight of many ordinary Americans.

> Historians . . . often assume that pre-Revolutionary society was . . . substantially democratic, but whatever may have been the case. . . . Dutchess County before the American Revolution was a harsh, hierarchical community of which one complainant said with much justice that there was "no law for poor Men." It was a society in which an heiress married "under a crimson canopy emblazoned with the family crest in gold—a demi-lion crowned," and, "as on rent day, the tenants gathered before the manor hall to feast and wish happiness to the bride while within a lavish banquet was spread for the Van Cortlands, Livingstons and other river families." It was a society, too, in which the leader of a tenant rebellion on the lands of this same heiress was sentenced to be hanged, drawn, and quartered for high treason (Lynd 2009[1967]:27–28).

This tenant life constituted the living standard and condition of many common Americans. The American middle class, referred to in early texts and historical accounts as "mechanics," "artisans," and "tradesmen," existed in only small numbers, a small percent of the overall population. As we will see in later discussions, the fledgling middle class was not well defined. Typically ambitious and hard working, they were more often literate and had a political ideology somewhat different from both the upper and lower classes.

Class frictions between elite and common Americans had a well-established history long before the American Revolution. As many historians have noted, the term "social class" was not commonly employed in early America. Alternatively, social divisions were referred to as ranks or "estates," and conceived to be much more solidified than social classes. Ranks were thought to reflect a more inherent nature, a group of characteristics with which a person was born. It was not precisely a caste system but portended many of the same traits. This rigidly ranked structure was a carryover from English culture, which, even today, is recognized as having a more stringent class structure than that found in contemporary America.

Because many common Americans were disenfranchised, their only voice was in town meetings or informal gatherings. Taverns were often favorite meeting places to discuss the issues of the day and to air grievances. When grievances mounted without relief, angry crowds appeared publically to demonstrate their displeasure. Because these demonstrations often originated in taverns, with a free flow of alcohol, angry demonstrations would at times turn into destructive and even murderous mobs.

In traditional American history, these demonstrations and riots are often either ignored or depicted as actions against British abuses. Consequently, the social class nature of these historical conflicts is regularly disregarded. Prior to the Revolution, most wealthy Americans considered themselves English citizens and loyal subjects of the Crown. Demonstrations and riots against British rule seldom included the active participation of the American elite, except as a myth in American history. Rather, the American gentry were often part of the very ruling structure that common Americans found objectionable.

This is not to imply that public disturbances were simply social class conflicts. Many factors came into play with these angry outbursts. As Wood (1998[1969]:75) observes, "The American Revolution was actually many revolutions at once, the product of a complicated culmination of many diverse personal grievances and social strains." But there is no doubt that a great animosity, quite conscious in the common American's mind, existed between the upper and common classes. This class tension had important political and economic implications at the time of the Founding and has continued throughout American history.

Antagonisms between the American gentry and common Americans, largely minimized in the traditional history of pre-Revolutionary America, actually existed long before considerations that the colonies might separate from Britain. One Constitutional thread reflecting the customary American tradition of expressing grievances in public forums is realized in the First Amendment of the Constitution, which allows the people free and peaceful assembly to petition the government for a redress of grievances. Indeed, the Declaration of Independence affords people the right to depose governments that do not serve their needs and protect their rights. As noted in Chapter One, the Federalists did not want the Bill of Rights, and there seems little doubt that the public assembly of common citizens was seen by the American elite as a serious threat. Unknown to most Americans is a rich history—both before and after the Revolution—of common Americans assembling to protest, sometimes in a violent manner.

Social class friction in the Revolutionary era involved many factors, but the essence seemed to be the sociopolitical favor shown men of wealth and influence, often received at the expense of common Americans. The British Crown and Parliament commonly dispensed lucrative business monopolies, land grants, and political positions to friends and allies. A noted example is the charter given by Charles II to William Penn and his heirs. Pennsylvania was probably the largest grant of land ever given to anyone outside of the monarchy. Even more important, the Penns "enjoyed sweeping powers subject only to the constraints of the common law" (Brands 2000:37).

Similar favoritism was also shown the American gentry by the colonial governing bodies they dominated with sanction by the British Crown and Parliament. All colonial governments had restricted voting privileges, which included laws that limited voting to those with substantial property. Similar property restrictions applied to those who desired colonial office, whether elected or appointed. These limits effectively removed common Americans from the governments that ruled them. Consequently, in the minds of ordinary Americans, the American gentry were accurately viewed as being in league with their British rulers.

In everyday life, the American gentry openly flaunted their wealth and privilege and showed open disdain for common Americans. As the Revolution neared, Gouverneur Morris, an important person in the powerful landed gentry, a member of the Continental Congress, and later the Constitutional Convention—credited for adding "We the People" to the preamble of the Constitution—noted, after witnessing a meeting that included mechanics in New York City, that:

> On my right hand were ranged all the people of property, with some few poor dependents, and on the other all the tradesmen, etc., who thought it worth their while to leave daily labour for the good of

> the country. These sheep, simple as they are, cannot be pulled as heretofore. In short, there is no ruling them; and now, to leave the metaphor, the heads of the mobility grow dangerous to the gentry; and how to keep them down is the question. . . . The mob begins to think and to reason. Poor reptiles: it is with them a vernal morning, they are struggling to cast off their winter's slough, they bask in the sunshine, and ere noon they will bite, depend on it. The gentry begin to fear this. . . . I see, and I see it with fear and trembling, that if the disputes with Great Britain continue, we shall be under the worst of all possible dominions; we shall be under the domination of a riotous mob (in Lynd 2009[1967]:89).

If Morris is too obscure a Framer then we can look to one of the many statements made about common Americans by James Madison, considered to be the Father of the Constitution and the Bill of Rights. When the Convention was considering the issue of suffrage, Madison expressed his fears about the growing numbers of industrial workers:

> Viewing the subject in its merits alone, the freeholders of the Country would be the safest depositories of Republican liberty. In future times a great majority of the people will not only be without landed [*sic*] but any other sort of property. These will either combine under the influence of their common situation; in which case, the rights of property and the public liberty will not be secure in their hands, or, which is more probable, they will become the tools of opulence and ambition; in which case there will be equal danger on another side (in Beard 1963[1913]:25).

Through all of the many pre-Revolutionary actions, it became clear that average Americans were unhappy with their situation and tired of the exploitation and abuse by their "betters." These average citizens had coalesced into groups and evolved to the point of articulating their grievances, demanding changes, and on occasion using violence. Common Americans did not make clear distinctions between British and American rulers because, in fact, such distinctions were not clear. So while most historians have left the impression that various actions by common Americans were anti-British, they were also, and often, in opposition to the American gentry. One has to read the details of these actions, including the angry words of common Americans to truly appreciate the climate of the times. When the Revolution concluded, these earlier class conflicts evolved into the clash between the Federalist elite and the Antifederalist commoner over the Constitution (Lynd 2009[1967]:109).

Violent Confrontations

If from the English perspective American law seemed more and more lawless, to Americans rioting came to seem more and more lawful. A classic medium of protest by society's voice-less (Keller 2007: 20).

Angry and violent outbursts by poor tenant farmers and other poor Americans, directed at landlords and local authorities, were common in early America. As Wood (2009:336) observes, "[M]obbing and rioting had been common in the eighteenth century. . . . [T]he mobs and gangs of the early Republic were composed of mostly unconnected and anonymous lowly people, full of class resentment, and thus all the more frightening." In fact, violent rebellions in the American colonies had a lengthy history beginning with Bacon's Rebellion in 1676 followed by Leisler's Rebellion in 1689, where Americans first expressed their distaste with British colonial rule (Keller 2007:15). Class hostilities of a violent nature were soon to follow.

> The antagonisms which rose to the surface of . . . politics as the [Revolution] went on were long-standing and familiar. Far from springing full-grown from the brow of revolution, these antagonisms centered on the old conflict between the ruling families of the landed aristocracy and the tenants and small freeholders of the county (Lynd 2009[1967]:57).

In New York and New Jersey rural unrest centered at times on conflicts between tenants and squatters, on the one hand, and tenants and landlords on the other. Numerous armed uprisings threatened social stability in various locations from the 1740s through the 1770s, with contested land claims generally at the heart of the disputes.

> When powerful New Jersey proprietors evicted small farmers from disputed land in 1746, the farmers, acting collectively, prevented anyone else from working the fields by ruining their crops and tearing down their fences. After some were jailed for their actions, others turned out in force "with clubs, Axes and Crow barrs"[*sic*] to free them. These ordinary people, fighting for their land and their livelihood, voiced great anger (Raphael 2001:31–32).

These outbursts could be more serious than the disturbances in the cities and towns because most farmers were armed, and this point was not missed when a Bill of Rights was demanded. Raphael (2001:34) cites Paul Gilje who found evidence of one hundred fifty riots in the colonies from 1765 through 1769. Gilje notes that such disturbances continued into the 1770s even as the Revolution approached. Although modern Americans have been led to believe that farmland was plentiful in colonial America and that most farmers owned their own land, this was often untrue. Many farmers were tenants on the large land holdings of the wealthy or were "squatters" farming on someone else's land without permission. Major disturbances occurred when angry farmers, faced with high rents or eviction, would not pay or leave having nowhere to go. Tenant farmers and squatters rebelled in the face of evictions, sometimes fighting with each other.

In some areas, such as Pennsylvania, farmers were angry with local officials and marched toward Philadelphia because they were not being protected from Indian attacks. Farmers in the South complained that authorities were not protecting them from bands of outlaws who burned, looted, and raped. They also expressed displeasure with corrupt local officials. Forming vigilante groups, referred to as "Regulators," small southern farmers took the law into their own hands, going after outlaws and officials alike. In a head-on clash, Regulators in North Carolina took on the colonial government but were defeated and six thousand Regulators were made to repudiate their actions and sign loyalty oaths to the Crown.

In 1766, on New York Manors, major disturbances broke out over rents. Some two hundred tenants threatened to destroy the Livingston Manor and kill the landlord if they did not receive better terms on their leases. As the uprising grew, seventeen hundred "Levellers," as they were called, with firearms had to be quelled by British troops as local authorities did not have the resources to stop them. "The New York tenant rebellion of 1766 is one of the most dramatic examples of internal social conflict during the era of the American Revolution, and the 'tine horns and calico' tenant riots 75 years later prove that class conflict in the Hudson Valley outlasted the struggle for national independence" (Lynd 2009[1967]:63).

In the same year, 1766, violence erupted on land owned by the Philipses that had until then been undeveloped. The squatters were Moravian missionaries who had sought cheap land and religious freedom. "In the 1750's the Philipse heirs had become more aggressive, ejecting tenants who would not accept onerous leases; and it was here that the formidable riots of 1766 had begun, when two thousand armed tenants refused to pay rents, rescued comrades from the Poughkeepsie jail, marched on New York City for the same purpose, and were finally dispersed only by redcoats with cannon" (Lynd 2009[1967]:31).

A year before the Revolution was to begin, in the summer of 1774, thousands of armed farmers, all over Massachusetts, took over government authority from the Crown by force. "Hats in hand, judges and members of the governor's council resigned their posts; muskets in tow, the farmers took over. This was the true beginning of the American Revolution; later battles at Lexington and Concord constituted a counterrevolution as the British tried to regain control of a countryside they had previously lost" (Raphael 2001:10).

One of the most open social class rebellions in pre-Revolutionary America happened in Pennsylvania. Although the political situation in Pennsylvania was more complex than will be explored presently, it is sufficient to say that the Pennsylvania Assembly, composed largely of Pennsylvania's most well-heeled Loyalist families, was unwilling to represent common American interests critical of British policy, unlike other colonial Assemblies. The Pennsylvania Assembly and its dominant groups were so far removed from the Revolutionary Movement that they adamantly resisted the idea of separating from Britain. As a result, middle class and working men came forward to fill the political vacuum and led a successful revolt against the Pennsylvania establishment.[4]

Loud criticisms against Tories and the Crown by Whigs, found commonly in the Pennsylvania press in 1776, were exceeded by class-driven protests from common citizens. "In fact, *to judge solely from the literature the Revolution in Pennsylvania had become a class war between the poor and the rich, between the common people and the privileged few*" (Wood 1998[1969]: 85. Emphasis added.). The radicals in Pennsylvania were demanding equality in the most pointed and social class terms. They charged that Pennsylvania was governed by a few wealthy men who had typically exploited common and middle-class persons. The sentiment was loudly expressed that wealth alone did not justify the right to rule.

> The Revolution against Britain was on behalf of the people. And who were the people . . . but the ordinary farmers and mechanics? . . . It must be made clear, the radicals argued, "that a freeman worth only fifty pounds is entitled by the laws of our province to 'all the privileges of the first Nabob in the country.'" . . . Was not one half the property in

> Philadelphia . . . owned by men who wore "LEATHER APRONS?"—the derisive term that well-to-do had used. And "does not the other half belong to men whose fathers or grandfathers wore LEATHER APRONS?" . . . Talk not, ye pretenders to rank and gentility, of your elevated stations.—They are derived from those very people who you treat with so much contempt (Wood 1998[1969]:86–87).

During the Revolutionary War another case of class conflict occurred as tenants rebelled again on the Livingston Manor in 1777. This revolt is one of the telling examples of class conflict in eighteenth-century America (Lynd 2009[1967]:63–77)[5]. This reoccurring unrest began as early as 1711 when Governor Hunter ordered troops into the area to put down a tenant uprising, and such rebellions happened periodically until 1841. Interestingly, the five hundred tenants involved took up arms to help the British in the hope that a victory would lead the British to give the tenants' title to their farms. Though this did not occur, the unrest did lead to the defeat of the conservative Whig party candidate for Governor, Philip Schuyler, to George Clinton because tenants withheld their votes for Schuyler (Lynd 2009[1967]:75–76). This defeat led the way to the destruction of aristocratic rule in the area. Writing to his son-in-law James Duane, Lord Robert Livingston, Jr. wrote about the tenants; "They are all a pack of Vagabonds who are fled from their Creditors & got together in the mountains & want my flat Lands to Settle on, but Chiefly to Sell & pay their debts, for they cannot live any longer in the mountains as they have nothing left to support on" (Lynd 2009[1967]:65).

These disputes over land and oppressive leases on the Livingston estate led many local ordinary Americans first into the Tory camp and, after the Revolution, into the Antifederalist camp. After the Revolution, in 1791, the Columbia County sheriff was shot in reprisal for attempted evictions. But those landlords, like the Livingstons, who declared themselves Whigs not only kept their lands but maintained their feudalistic land rental systems after the Revolution ended.

Bringing socioeconomic antagonists together was not an easy task and remained a challenge throughout the American Revolution. Symbols of wealth were constantly flaunted, keeping class communities separated geographically and emotionally.[6] "Committees" of ordinary citizens rose up where common people were exploited, deprived, and angered. As stated in a Poughkeepsie newspaper, "At length . . . is the virtuous part of the community alarmed, and the old and true friends to their country again step forth to remedy evils the laws cannot reach, by the exertion of Committees, the terror of all villains. . . . As soon as the authority of your Committee ended, knavery skewed its head, villains of every class came forth and practiced with impunity. . . . Let no time be lost then, my countrymen, in forming your Committees" (Lynd 2009[1967]:44).

In 1779, before the Revolution had ended, the Philadelphia Committees called for the formation of other committees "in every State and county," and they did become common (Lynd 2009[1967]:45). The existence of these citizens' committees not only enforced the law but helped push the Whig elite into providing effective local and state government. That is, government that did not enhance exploitation by the economic elite. These committees were likewise an effective method of fighting corruption at the government level. The corrupt and tyrannical activities of the elite also fed Antifederalist sentiment during and after the construction of the Constitution (Lynd 2009[1967]:46–49, 50).

The Tyranny of Taxation: The Social Class Glue

Americans who are knowledgeable about the American Revolution know that the problems with Britain started before 1775. Generally speaking these troubles were related to taxes levied after the French and Indian War. The concern raised by Americans was not just about the taxes themselves but how the taxes were imposed. The taxes were prescribed by the English Parliament with no American representation (Brands 2000:360–363). Parts of these taxes harshly affected Americans with little money, while other facets of the taxes harmed American commerce. The result was angry Americans at all social levels, an anger that did not necessarily unite them.

When Stamp Tax demonstrations and riots occurred, common Americans frequently found the property of wealthy Americans to be fair targets. Benjamin Franklin—by this time wealthy through business, investments, royal appointments, and marriage—was lobbying the British Parliament for Pennsylvania and became one of the targets of Philadelphia's Stamp Act rioters. John Hughes, who was named the stamp tax commissioner for Pennsylvania because of Franklin's influence, also became a target of Philadelphia's angry crowd.[7]

Stamp Act demonstrations occurred all over the colonies, involving Boston, Charleston, New London, Norwich, Lebanon, Windham, West Haven, Fairfield, Milford, Newport, and New York, among others, and were almost exclusively made up of common citizens. One such citizen from the working-class South End of Boston was

Ebenezer MacIntosh who led the Boston protests; "[MacIntosh was a] debt-ridden shoemaker . . . whose father, one of the strolling poor, had been warned out of Boston when Ebenezer was in his teens" (Raphael 2001:18). Under MacIntosh's leadership the working people in Boston retained some influence in public matters through violence or its threat, the only franchise open to them. On November 5, 1765, MacIntosh, combining North and South Boston, led the demonstration against the Stamp Act. This was unusual because the "North Enders" were prosperous and the "South Enders" were working people, and the two areas were at variance with one another.

Any credible attempt to dispute British rule necessitated large and impressive crowds. An unusual and shaky alliance under MacIntosh's leadership was negotiated between the two economic ends of Boston. With MacIntosh leading the protest, prosperous Bostonians could have their cake and eat it too. The North End Whigs openly denied responsibility and "issued official disclaimers to the destruction of property" while continuing to encourage MacIntosh's movement (Raphael 2001:19). It is not until the Tea Act of 1773, and the subsequent Boston Tea Party, that a fairly stable alliance between the haves and have-nots in Boston began to solidify. As Raphael (2001:21) explains, "Tea helped unite opposition to British policy, for the resistance to the tax on tea dovetailed nicely with lower-class resentments. . . . Some thought they were opposing taxation and protecting liberty and property; others (who paid no taxes [on tea] and had little property to protect) flailed against symbols of wealth and the intrusive military presence which kept the rich in power."

> The American Revolution was many revolutions at once. . . . [B]y freezing factional politics . . . around the issue of British authority, the controversy with the mother country . . . tended to obscure . . . quarrels Americans had among themselves. . . . For a moment in 1774–76 the imperial contest absorbed and polarized the various differing groups as never before in the eighteenth century and made the Americans a remarkably united people (Wood 1998[1969]:75,77).

This seems only a partial explanation for the unification of Americans of different social levels. Why would common Americans trade abuse and exploitation by the British for mistreatment by the American gentry? It seemed that Whig propaganda was beginning to work on common Americans and, in fact, seems to have had some substance. The Declaration of Independence was perhaps the most conspicuous artifact as Jefferson and the signers purported "that all men are created equal, that they are endowed by their Creator with certain unalienable Rights, that among these are Life, Liberty and the Pursuit of Happiness.—That to secure these rights, Governments are instituted among Men, deriving their just powers from the consent of the governed." Most common Americans had never experienced or been offered such a government. It seems likely that common Americans were beginning to see the possibility of an independence that would lead to a government of their making and concerned with their interests. In fact, serious acts of rebellion, not just angry riots, were being organized by common Americans in pursuit of the more radical republican ends proclaimed by the Declaration.

The Tea Act was different from the Stamp Act in that it affected mainly those who could afford this expensive beverage. Tea symbolized wealth. "Tea parties in genteel parlors required an elaborate material culture, including some, if not all, of the following items: teapots and their rests, teacups and saucers, tea canisters, teakettles or urns, teaspoons and spoon dishes, sugar bowls, sugar tongs, cream jugs, slop bowls, strainers, tea trays, and tea tables—plus plates and utensils for any good consumed with the tea" (in Raphael 2001: 20, 48–50). Gordon-Reed (2008: 515–516) makes the point that common Americans would often spend proportionately more money on their tea sets than their everyday dinnerware because it was a way of maximizing their status when guests were present in their homes.

Wealthy Americans opposed the Tea Act because it made their everyday luxury and status more expensive. This ultimately led to a tea boycott. This boycott was not difficult for lesser Americans as they seldom drank tea. But the wealthy, who had incorporated tea deeply, actively, and symbolically into their everyday culture, found that giving up tea was much more difficult, even though they, too, had called for a boycott. Patriotic leaders and newspapers carried on a campaign to dissuade the affluent from their tea habit by claiming that tea was unhealthy and then offered various substitutes.[8]

As history accurately reflects, tea became a powerful anti-British symbol for Americans across the socioeconomic spectrum. Best known is the Boston Tea Party on December 16, 1773, an act carried out by common Bostonians. As the *Dartmouth* and two other tea-loaded ships sat in Boston harbor because the watching crowd would not allow them to be unloaded, and the law would not allow the tea to be returned to England discussions went on among the people concerning what action was fitting. Meetings were held that allowed all people to attend including women, apprentices, African Americans, servants, and even a few wealthy Whigs. On December 16, a meeting of 5,000 citizens—the total population of Boston was about 16,000—met and made their plans. Young men, apprentices, and journeymen, dressed as Indians dumped some 342 chests of tea into the harbor while a large crowd quietly watched. This action was recorded in John Adam's diary with praise, though he generally deplored mob actions (McCullough 2001:70–71).

Violators of the tea boycott were dealt with harshly by working-class Bostonians. Enforcing the boycott, ordinary citizens asserted power over the well-heeled by seizing tea and creating fear and public embarrassment for the offenders. "When rumor spread that Isaac Jones . . . had been selling tea in his tavern, thirty common citizens disguised with war paint broke all his windows, smashed his bowls, mugs, and china, drank all his liquor, and then forced him to apologize for his crime" (Raphael 2001:21).

The alliance between common working people and the American upper-class Whigs, however, should not be overstated. Certainly, it was a union of convenience with each group needing the other. Common Americans needed the Whigs to give authority and credibility to their grievances and the Whigs needed the support of the common people to give numbers and strength to their complaints with the English Crown and Parliament. Neither were common Americans won over to the cause only because of Whig manipulations and propaganda. As the Revolution grew near, confrontations between ordinary Americans and British soldiers intensified. In 1768 there were some four thousand British troops in Boston, which had a population of sixteen thousand. The troops enforced a city curfew, took bribes, cheated and robbed people, and generally harassed working Americans. This behavior may have been worse at night but also occurred openly in the daytime. Robert Hewes, a shoemaker who was a member of the Boston Tea Party, reported seeing a British soldier rob a woman of her "bonnet, cardinal muff and tippet" (Raphael 2001:25). British troops also competed with working Americans for jobs as a supplement to their poor military pay.

On February 23, 1770, a confrontation between British troops and citizens, which did much to catapult America into the Revolution, resulted in the Boston Massacre. Eleven Bostonians were shot and five killed, including a ropewalk worker, two sailors, and two apprentices. The altercation seems to have begun when a large crowd of mostly school boys and young apprentices gathered outside of a shop whose owner was selling imported goods against the wishes of many Bostonians.

As the Revolution neared, common and upper class Americans came together in common cause and placed the disputes between them on simmer. From the Sugar Act of 1764, the Stamp Act of 1765, the Townshend Acts of 1767, and the Tea Act of 1773, American cohesion grew as Americans joined together to boycott British goods in protest over taxation and British actions that affected all Americans. The British Parliament responded with the Coercive Acts of 1774 that closed Massachusetts harbors, made all government officials accountable only to the Crown, and gave more authority to the occupying army. The colonial governments reacted by calling for a meeting of all colonies to respond collectively to British policy.

Whigs, as largely members of the upper class, publicly opposed the taxes of Parliament and the abuses of the British Army. Being influential men, they came to hold the most powerful positions in the growing resistance. On September 5, 1774 these men, representing the thirteen colonies, met to prescribe a common action to pressure the British to institute reforms that would give Americans greater voice in their affairs. In this atmosphere, the First Continental Congress met and concurred on a broad boycott of all British imports and American exports to England.

While the Whigs ultimately hoped to force the Crown and Parliament to give into their demands for greater independence, enforcement of the boycott fell largely to ordinary Americans. They adopted tarring and feathering as the "official" mode of punishment for those who violated the boycott. As common Americans became more engaged, their commitment and investment in the cause increased. Even though Whigs initially tried to quell the violence, they soon realized the futility of doing so. In this sense, it was not the Declaration of Independence and the Founding Fathers who started the Revolutionary War but the common American who had already been pushed to the point of violent revolt.

In this circumstance, the Whigs had little choice but to lead or get out of the way. As common Americans became more engaged in the resistance, so did their zeal for exercising power and creating a governmental system and society that reflected the needs of common people. They wanted freedom from the regulations, exploitations, and abuses of the upper class, whether British or American. And in the end, they wanted a government friendlier to their lives, a system in which they were actively engaged. Common Americans embraced a radical form of republicanism that had originally been introduced as propaganda to incite their support.

Ad hoc committees of citizens were organized to enforce the boycott initiated by the First Continental Congress. These committees of both Whigs and mechanics began to assume the everyday functions of the local governments that had been largely controlled by British and American Tories (Lynd 2009[1967]:92). Assuming these tasks the committees, as a shadow government, soon realized they could run their own affairs. As a result, various common citizens began to seek public offices through nomination by the committees set up to enforce the boycott. Being elected, they displaced the hated officials of the Crown, many in fact, who were upper class Americans. Through enforcement and self-rule, common Americans acquired the confidence to run and shape a government that served their communities' interests and thus began to advocate, if not demand, participation in representative government.

Similar takeovers were occurring in other places like Worcester, Great Barrington, Plymouth, Taunton, Concord, Springfield, and Philadelphia. Armed citizens took it upon themselves to alleviate Crown officials and judges of their duties (Raphael 2001:47–56). By the time of the Revolution, ordinary Americans had shaped a republican philosophy that included themselves as the primary foundation of self-government. Although the war would push the details of "government by the people" to the background, deep-seated differences in attitude still remained between Whigs and common Americans. As Lynd (2009[1967]:26–27) reminds us, these class divisions, though dampened by the Revolution, did not disappear and even threatened to break into a class war as the Revolution proceeded.[9]

With this view of common Americans, how can we not wonder about the thoughts and motivations later brought to the Constitutional Convention by the Framers? Would the attitudes of common Americans, as perceived by the elite, not strongly affect the government the Framers created? Perhaps it is fair to criticize Beard's thesis that it was individual interests that molded the Constitution. More accurately, perhaps, the Constitution was written to protect the interests, power, and way of life of the social class who wrote this founding document. Furthermore, why did the Framers resist the demand for a bill of rights, doctrine that was precedent in state constitutions and existed deep in

Western history? Certainly, it should come as no surprise that common Americans were suspicious of these upper class men and their motives. The opposition of common Americans would have probably killed the Constitution had they been allowed more involvement.

Notes

1. For a thorough review of the development of Anglo-American rights see Leonard W. Levy 1999.
2. Discussing the concept of "rank" in pre-Revolutionary America, Blumin (1989:17) relates: "On December 6, 1765, in the midst of the Stamp Act crisis, former Lieutenant-Governor Cadwallader Colden of New York undertook to explain to the British Secretary of State and to the Board of Trade how the crisis reflected basic divisions within the society of the province. 'The People of New York . . . are properly distinguished into different Ranks.' In the first rank Colden placed the 'The Proprietors of the Large Tracts of Land who include within their claims from 100,000 to above one million acres under one Grant.' Second were 'the Gentlemen of the Law,' while 'The Merchants make the third class.' In the fourth and 'last Rank,' Colden concluded, 'may be placed the Farmers & Mechanics. . . . This last Rank comprehends the bulk of the People and in them consists the strength of the Province. They are the most useful and the most moral, but alwise [*sic*] made the Dupes of the former, and often are ignorantly made their Tools for the worse purposes.' Colden's description is a peculiar one to the twentieth-century reader, who would not divide his own society into three sets of rich men followed by everyone else."
3. This is why many Americans would risk life, limb, and families to push illegally into Indian lands to claim property of their own to establish farms on rich soil (see Main 1961:2,4).
4. As Wood (1998[1969]:85) observes, "[N]ew men, led by James Cannon, Timothy Matlack, Robert Whitehill, George Bryan—all socially outside of the establishment (Matlack it was said, 'does not keep a chariot') . . . sought through the Revolutionary movement to pick up the pieces of political power. Through the use of the new Revolutionary organizations—committees, associations and militia—and through intimidation and coercion, and with the sanction of the Continental Congress, these political outsiders eventually circumvented the decaying authority of the much resented Assembly and in the summer of 1776 captured control of the convention [Pennsylvania state convention] that wrote the most radical constitution of the Revolution . . . with the most extreme Whig rhetoric expressed in the Revolution."
5. Lynd (2009[1967]) provides a thorough account of this uprising.
6. For example, "In Virginia the lower classes resented horse racing and gambling, customs of the plantation gentry. In New York theatrical productions were disrupted by 'disorderly persons (in a Riotous Manner).' A play in the Chapel Street Theater, according to newspaper accounts, was 'interrupted by the multitude who broke open the doors and entered with noise and tumult,' shouting 'Liberty, Liberty.' Patrons were driven into the street, 'their Caps, Hats, Wigs, Cardinals, and Cloaks . . . torn off (thro' Mistake)

in the Hurray.' The rioters 'immediately demolished the House, and carried the pieces to the Common, where they consumed them in a Bonfire.' Why was the theater so hated? Theatergoers dressed in high fashion, arrived in carriages, and spent their money on frivolities. A New Yorker writing under the name of 'Philander' complained that season tickets sold for as much as fifty pounds, while poor people starved. Another writer felt 'it highly improper that such Entertainments should be exhibited at this time of public distress, when great Numbers of poor people can scarcely find a means of subsistence'" (Raphael 2001:19–20).

7. "Franklin himself had reason to thank God, for the same mob that threatened Hughes made angry noises about him. The house he had begun building before leaving for England was essentially complete—and suggested . . . that its owner intended to fatten with his friend Hughes on the stamps the commissioner would sell to the oppressed Pennsylvania.

   Samuel Wharton, a Philadelphia merchant and political ally of Franklin, described the night of maximum danger in a letter to Franklin: 'In the evening, a large mob was collected at the coffee house and the party declared that your house, Mr. Hughes', Mr. Galloway's [a successful Philadelphia lawyer who remained loyal to the Crown] and mine should be leveled with the street, for that you had obtained the Stamp Act and we were warm advocates for the carrying it into execution'" (Brands 2000:367).

8. It was at this point that coffee gained popularity in America, increasing per capita consumption more than sevenfold between 1770 and the 1799. Although it, too, was imported, it did not carry the stigma that tea had with common Americans.

9. "Contemporaries had no doubt that the War for Independence was accompanied by a struggle over who should rule at home. Fear of just such an internal revolution made Robert R. Livingston hesitate long on the brink of independence. By the winter of 1777–1778, the historian William Smith observed that the New York Whigs were splitting into 'the Popular & the landed Interest' and wrote with some smugness of the latter: 'These People have had no Foresight of the natural Consequences of a republican Spirit in a poor Country, where Gentlemen of Fortune are but few. . . . They are losing their Significance every Day. They will be happy if they can save their Estates.' The financial crisis of 1779–1780, with its attendant clashes over price regulation and the confiscation of Loyalist lands, drew from Robert R. Livingston's mother a prayer for 'Peace and Independence and deliverance from the persecutions of the Lower Class who I forsee [*sic*] will be as despotic as any Prince (if not more so) in Europe.' As the war drew to a close, Thomas Tillotson of Dutchess wrote forebodingly that New York had 'a strong Democratic Spirit prevailing that will some day [*sic*] not far off give a stab to its happiness. . . . The people want nothing but to be a little more impoverished to prepare them for it. The first stroke would be at the Tenanted estates.' This conflict perceived by contemporaries was real. The egalitarian 'spirit' which Smith called republican and Tillotson democratic was not a figment of the Federalist imagination" (Lynd 2009[1967]:26–27).

3

The Making of the Constitution

In response to the passage of the Coercive Acts by the British Parliament in 1774, the American colonial Assemblies organized the First Continental Congress to formulate a unified response.[1] Although a few delegates at the Congress, like Patrick Henry, were ready to break completely with the British Crown, those who desired reconciliation prevailed. Joseph Galloway offered a "Plan of Union," which allowed the colonies their own legislative body with limited authority and whose consent was required before the implementation of imperial edicts.

Imprudently, perhaps, given the conciliatory sentiment behind the passage of the Plan of Union, the First Continental Congress also passed the Articles of Association implementing a boycott against British imports. Within a year, British imports dropped 97 percent, the boycott being largely enforced by crowds of common Americans. It seemed, however, that the time for reconciliation had already passed as ordinary Americans had already taken up arms against the British. The First Continental Congress acted to provide a second meeting in May of 1775. In addition to the American colonies, invitations to the Second Congress were extended to Quebec, Saint John's Island, and Nova Scotia, though none sent delegates. When the Second Continental Congress met in Philadelphia in 1775, the Revolutionary War was underway and individual states were seceding from Britain. At this point, the Continental Congress became the organizational body for managing the Revolutionary War, though it had little true authority. While the need for an umbrella authority was quickly realized, the first draft of the Articles of Confederation and Perpetual Union was not completed until the summer of 1777 and not adopted by the Second Congress until November 15, 1777 after a lengthy debate. Even though the Articles of Confederation were not approved by all the states until

March 1, 1781, the Second Congress used this document as their instrument of government for conducting the Revolutionary War.

The Federalists

The Revolutionary War had not officially ended before some members of the Second Continental Congress concluded that the Articles of Confederation were not sufficient for forming a single and well-functioning government (Brown 1993:171–175, 179–183). Americans have generally been taught that the Articles of Confederation and Perpetual Union were seriously flawed. Those flaws identified have often been related to economic issues. Rakove (1996:25–28) outlines these problems using a specific example involving the renowned Robert Morris. Morris had offered a federal revenue plan as an amendment to the Articles, arguing that the Congress needed a stream of income separate from states' approval. The new Congress had many financial obligations and debts but had a difficult time getting all of the states to agree on a plan of payment. Even when a states' agreement was reached, the US Congress had difficulty collecting what had been promised. To amend the Articles required unanimous support from the states and Morris was unable to assemble the needed endorsements.[2]

Many of those who advanced the Articles' failings began to privately urge the creation of a new constitution. They wanted a federal system that gave the central government more power and that did not depend on the consent and unanimity of the states. These advocates became known as Federalists. In the beginning, they were an informal group of like-minded men, mainly from the American gentry, who wanted property rights protected from the whims of state governments. Likewise, they wanted a centralized system that would enhance their economic activities and make business standards and regulations uniform across the states (Beard 1943[1915]:2–3). As would become clear later, the Federalists also wanted a central taxing authority that would spread taxes across the general population while also protecting and enhancing their wealth. This stratagem would soon enough play itself out in Shay's Rebellion (1786–87) and the Whiskey Rebellion (1794). After the new Constitution became law, the Federalists formed a political party of the same name to further advance their positions and philosophy.

The Federalists were largely composed of a distilled American gentry who fundamentally believed that "[t]he ideal harmonious society was one that recognized the 'necessity of subordination,' one in which everyone found his proper place and did not try to attain a rank for which he was unsuited. . . . If the Federalists were willing to be recognized as distinctive at all, they wanted to be thought of as the rightful rulers of the society, as disinterested leaders beset by hordes of Jacobinical sans-culottes who were out to destroy all harmony and order in the society" (Wood 2009:105–106; 214–215).[3,4]

The Federalists' concerns were mainly twofold—that the federal government be strong enough to protect private property interests from the economic vagaries of the various states and the masses of people and to command the authority of a collective entity with a distinct and legitimate identity that could wage war and collect revenue. Through a central military and foreign policy the government could more easily penetrate and protect the world market for American merchants.

Lynd (2009[1967]:110–111) states that the Federalists were "deeply public-spirited men" who were critical of those who put their self-interest before the country and its republican government, their own interests being given. Beard and others have a very different view. It is probably correct to say that the Federalists were publically minded individuals, but they had their own firm notion of what that meant. In other words, one could be a patriot and still hold strong negative attitudes about common citizens and strong conservative views concerning the nature of republicanism. This, essentially, is what Lynd (2009[1967]:111–113) ends up arguing. The two positions—public spirit and self-interest—are not mutually exclusive. In a letter from Hamilton to Robert Livingston, Jr., which Lynd (2009[1967]:112) cites, Hamilton wrote:

> [T]hat it is become a serious object of attention to those who are concerned for the *security of property* or the prosperity of government, to endeavour [*sic*] to put men in the Legislature whose principles are not of the *leveling kind* [italics in original]. . . . All men of respectability, in the city, of whatever party, who have been witnesses of the despotism and iniquity of the Legislature, are convinced, that the principal people in the community must for their own defence [*sic*], unite to overset the party I have alluded to. I wish you to be persuaded Sir, that I would not take the liberty to trouble you with these remarks with a view to serving any particular turn; but, from a thorough conviction, that the safety of all those who have anything to lose calls upon them to take care that the power of government is intrusted [*sic*] to proper hands [1785].

Herein lay the Federalists' dilemma—one that has faced the American elite throughout history. They wanted a strong central government that *they* controlled, for otherwise it might be a threat to them. It was one thing to dally in the affairs of average Americans, quite another to bother those of the elite. This concern was foremost on their minds while creating a new constitution and, certainly, they could not but help mold a constitution compatible with their interests. In the end, no matter how "publically minded" the Federalists might be, Lynd (2009[1967]:113) admits that "the political convictions on which they stood stemmed from a struggle for power between contending economic groups, and the power they sought meant economic security and dominion for their kind of people." Lynd tries to argue that this does not support Beard's critical observations of the Federalists, but his argument, in this regard, is very unpersuasive (see Miller 1988[1960]:112–121).

Another issue of contention among historians is whether mechanics and tradesmen (the "middling sort") supported the Constitution. Part of the problem occurs because historians cannot agree on how large the middle class was at the time. Lynd (2009[1967]:82) argues that they composed 50–75 percent of the American population. The more common consensus would seem to suggest that this social class was very small and not well delineated from the working classes or those who worked for wages. However, simply because the emerging middle class may or may not have supported the Constitution does not mean that their position or reasons were the same as the Federalist gentry. In the end, the inclusion of a bill of rights, which the Federalists generally opposed, swayed many middle-class members to support the Constitution.

Lynd (2009[1967]:124) is correct in describing the middle class' interests narrowly, as including "Federal power to regulate trade . . . and to reinforce . . . Non-Importation." These were everyday pragmatic concerns to American tradesmen and mechanics that owned small businesses and were subject to the vacillations of a market dominated by British merchants. The Federalists, though also concerned with British competition, had an economic concern in protecting large property interests from interference by the states, the state governments being entities more easily swayed by the general population. It seems clear, however, that the middle class' politics leaned strongly to progressive republicanism, which would have made them suspicious of Federalist intentions at the Philadelphia Convention. But with a bill of rights, and the pressures of everyday economic life, it should not be surprising that many in the middle class would support the Constitution's ratification. To conclude, however, that the middle class was "ideologically Federalist" is neither justified nor true. Not everyone could be placed neatly into the Federalist or Antifederalist categories. And, certainly, as with the inclusion of a bill of rights, the Federalists compromised their interests just enough to press the Constitution through ratification. "By thus fusing the old radical anti-British sentiment with the conservative interest in a stronger federal government, the merchants [Federalists] destroyed whatever hope there might have been for Antifederalism"(Lynd 2009[1967]:128).

The Antifederalists

Purported Antifederalists were not anti-federalist at all, but were various groups given this label by their Federalist opponents. Federalists employed the Antifederalist characterization for its derogatory inference—"anti" suggesting obstructionism. As Main (1961:xii–xv) discusses, the identity "Federalist" was actually fought over. Antifederalists asserted that they were the true Federalists because of their support for the Articles of Confederation and tried to re-usurp the label from the Federalists. Antifederalists sought to preserve a federal system as outlined in the Articles, a system that maintained a decentralized federal power.[5]

The Articles of Confederation and Perpetual Union is a brief document that is fundamentally an agreement for mutual defense, a coordination of foreign policy, and a document for resolving disputes that might arise among the various states. Many Antifederalists recognized a need to amend and improve the Articles and, for that reason, eventually supported the Convention in Philadelphia. This support was given with the understanding that the Convention would amend the Articles, not create a completely new constitution with strong federal powers. At the same time, there was considerable opposition to the Philadelphia Convention because of suspicions that the Federalists, for their own benefit, would try to form a more powerful centralized government. Many Americans, having suffered under the central powers of the British Crown and Parliament, were wary of Federalist intentions. As Amar (1998:10, 11) states,

> Probably the deepest Anti-Federalist objection to the Constitution was that the document took the skimming principle too far: Congress

> was too small, too rich, too 'refined' . . . Because the legislature was so small, the Antifederalists feared that only great men with reputations spanning wide geographic areas could secure election. Thus for Anti-Federalists the Constitution was at heart an aristocratic document.[6]

This diffusion of central power had been accomplished in the Articles of Confederation by giving each state a great deal of veto power over the proposed policies of the Congress. Maintaining a weak central government came in part from the philosophy of the agrarian landowners who valued liberty over authority. Antifederalists were composed of many middle-class small property holders and farmers, shopkeepers, traders, and mechanics[7] who, as part of the majority, believed that the system should be more democratic with greater participation from average citizens. "The Antifederalists . . . advanced much further toward democratic political ideas, so that the background of their thought is to be found in what might be called the left wing of Whiggism" (Main 1961:8).

We get a good sample of Antifederalist philosophy when examining two popular works being read at the time. One was *Cato's Letters* and the other *Political Disquisitions.* Both stressed the consuming evils of power. "Power renders men wanton, insolent to others and fond of themselves. . . . All history affords but few Instances of Men trusted with great Power without abusing it, when with Security they could" (from *Political Disquisitions* in Main 1961:9). The Federalist leadership fit this negative mold so well that it could only make the Antifederalist opposition more determined.

Understanding the source of Antifederalist thought helps us to appreciate their desire to maintain the Articles of Confederation and the reserve they felt in letting power leave the local community. "This mistrust of power was characteristic of American political thought during this period. Long before the doctrine was applied to the Constitution, it was frequently expressed by men who became Antifederalist" (Main 1961:9). In this atmosphere, the Federalists represented exactly the kind of arrogant and power hungry group that would make Antifederalists wary.

The Antifederalism of the western rural frontier is articulated well by Main (1961:1–2). "There was an embryonic class structure but it was potential only; property was, in comparison with other sections, equally distributed, and from the bottom to the top was but a short step. The men of the frontier wanted to keep it that way." The frontiersmen's central emphasis on equality of property arises from Cato and others who felt that government should "require a relatively equal division of property" (Main 1961:10, 11). This followed from the standard argument that vast differences in wealth leads to vast differences in power, thus destroying democracy. Similarly, the Antifederalists' vision of democracy included frequent popular elections, term limits, reduction of property qualifications in voting, expanding the franchise, foregoing a standing army, and giving greater power to the legislative body relative to the executive.

Whatever their status, small farmers were hard pressed to carry the burden of taxes for an entire nation. "The isolation of many farmers, their lack of formal education, and the limited horizons of their experience, also made them unwilling to surrender local advantages for the more general good" (Main 1961:7). These circumstances most often placed the small farmer in the Antifederalist camp.

The Articles of Confederation and Perpetual Union

When considering the Articles of Confederation the impression is often left that it was a ruling document hurriedly thrown together with little philosophical foundation. Likewise, the Philadelphia, or Constitutional, Convention, which ostensibly met to amend the Articles, is often depicted as an obvious and reasonable process where men of conscience met to peacefully work out a better republican government—a course traditional history suggests Americans deemed necessary. In this conventional version of Constitutional history, the members of the Convention were elevated to statesmen, reason prevailed over politics, and the results were brilliant (Keller 2007:34–41).

More accurately, the Articles articulated a federal government that was fiercely restrained because the authors of the Articles feared centralized authority leading to an antidemocratic establishment.[8] This was a very different vision of republicanism from that of the Federalists, and it makes clear why each group viewed the other with suspicion. In the beginning, those who would become Antifederalists created a government they were comfortable with and received the support of all the colonies/states, and certainly the Revolutionary War helped them reach this consensus. Only a short time after the Articles were ratified did the Federalists begin their scheming to end this form of government. The Articles had imperfections that were recognized by many in the Congress, but it is just as certain that they did not all agree on what those difficulties might be or how they should be rectified. Beard (1963[1913]:48) reminds us that "When it is remembered that most of our history has been written by Federalists, it will become apparent that great care should be taken in accepting, without reserve, the gloomy pictures of the social conditions prevailing under the Articles of Confederation."

There were expressed worries by the Federalists that the Articles of Confederation had placed no checks and balances on the government. This they feared would lead to an overly centralized and powerful Congress, which, being the closet branch of government to the people, might place the people's welfare above the interests of the merchant and commercial classes. To the contrary, there were several checks on the power of Congress and on centralized authority. Most notably in the latter case, there was no effective executive branch of government. The President of the Congress could only serve one year in any span of three years. Regarding the Congress, congressional delegates, chosen by state legislatures[9], had to answer to their sponsoring states and stand for election every year. A delegate could only hold office for three years in every six and could be recalled at any time. In a larger context, the power of Congress was checked by requiring consent of all the states on essential matters. Finally, the funding of the Congress could only occur through the consent of all the states.

A final check on the federal Congress as specified by the Articles of Confederation came during the Revolutionary period when twelve of the states altered the structure of their governments by writing new state constitutions that better incorporated average citizens. "The political ideas of the Revolution were incorporated into all twelve of the new constitutions, but they were most prominent in those drafted by conventions in which, as one critic complained, 'everyone who had the least pretensions to be a gentleman is borne down *per ignobile vulgus*' [by the common multitude]" (Main 1961:17, 19). Suffrage was broadly extended by eliminating or reducing property qualifications, thus expanding the influence of average citizens on both the state and federal levels. Under these circumstances, we can begin to understand the Federalists' concerns about constitutions, both state and federal, and the need to construct a different kind of constitution, especially at the federal level, that would restrict the legislative branch and the average citizens it represented.

The philosophy operating when state constitutions were being written "expressed clearly the doctrine that power should be concentrated in that branch which was most responsive to public opinion. Here, and above all among future Antifederalists, was to be seen a willingness to widen the franchise, to limit terms of office, to reject checks by a senate or the governor—in general, to extend popular control" (Main 1961:19). From this point of view (a largely middle class point of view [Wood 2009:31]), we can understand more clearly why Federalists conducted the Philadelphia Convention in secret and why the general population was furious when the new Constitution was unveiled, revealing strong counterpoints to popular sentiments.

Antifederalists had additional reasons to fear a strong centralized government other than what such a government might do with various economic policies, especially those regarding taxation. As Rakove (1996:37) notes, "Madison concluded that Congress needed 'coercive powers' to compel [the states] to do their duty. Thus, as soon as the Articles of Confederation took effect in March 1781, Madison drafted an amendment empowering Congress to use its armed forces 'to compel' delinquent states 'to fulfill their federal engagements.'" Similarly, Lynd (2009[1967]:121) observes, "Twice during the war the Federalist leaders had seriously considered strengthening Congress by dictatorial means. The first occasion was the [economic] crisis of 1780. In May, [General] Schuyler wrote to [James] Duane that it was necessary to 'lodge dictatorial powers' either in the Commander-in-Chief, or in him, together with a small committee."

Such proposals must have given pause to many who had just risked much to separate themselves from a power that had recently practiced the same dictatorial policies. Aside from the sectional tensions, to which traditional history has given much attention, this post-Revolutionary atmosphere included and continued a significant class tension (Main 1961:21). When the Constitution was finally ratified, it did not take long for the new Federalist government to use coercive power against its own citizens.

As Rakove (1996:30) continues his discussion on the problems with the Articles, we observe in his writing the typical strategy of traditional history: making the Framers' misgivings concerning the Articles those of the American public at large. Citing Madison, Rakove (1996:30) writes, "As Madison observed soon after the Convention, 'the evils issuing' from the states 'contributed more to that uneasiness which produced the Convention, and prepared the public mind for a general reform, than those which accrued to our national character and interest from the inadequacy of the Confederation to its immediate objects.'" Of course Madison would say this given the point of view emanating from his upper-class position and political-economic philosophy. We also know that "the public mind" did not refer to common Americans who were mostly Antifederalists (Lynd 2009[1967]:109–110). In one sentence, then, Rakove leads the reader to believe that Madison's appraisal of the Articles of Confederation was accurate and also captured the public's concern while correctly concluding that the Articles of Confederation were inadequate to national problems. "National problems," however, are relative to one's social class.

Persisting, Rakove (1996:30–31) tells the reader that state constitutions, due mainly to haste, were not well written and that they provided the Framers with a contrasting pool of experiments from which to write a better national constitution. Rakove (1996:30) gives us scattered examples of problems with state constitutions and specifically observes, "Some of these constitutions, notably Pennsylvania's, provoked controversy from the moment of their adoption." The reader is then to conclude that the Pennsylvania Constitution (along with others) was somehow inadequate.

It should be noted that Pennsylvania's Constitution was controversial mainly to those in elite economic positions because it threatened their wealth and political hegemony. In the end, Rakove (1996:31) assures the reader that the lessons learned from observing state constitutions informed the Framers "about such major theoretical issues as representation and the separation of powers." This seems undoubtedly true but not necessarily in the sense Rakove wants the readers to conclude. The Framers certainly used state constitutions as examples of something to avoid and as being contrary to their economic interests and political control. Indeed, Wood (2009:31) makes the point that the Federal Constitution was crafted to counter "problems" created by the "middling men" who wrote state constitutions.

The Framers' poor assessment of the common American's character also compelled them to write a new constitution with greater central power. Some of these attitudes were reviewed in previous chapters and displayed the arrogance of the American gentry toward common Americans. This attitude of the American elite went further than just concluding that they, the elite, were generally "more capable" and more "deserving" than common citizens. They also concluded that the Articles of Confederation had failed because of the poor character of the American people. With this excuse, the Framers concluded that republican government needed to be more powerful and less democratic.

> [T]he Framers established the Constitution because they believed that the Republic under the Articles of Confederation would not be sustained by an unvirtuous American people. The revolutionary generation assumed that public virtue, meaning a spirit of patriotic self-abnegation and disciplined austerity, was the requisite, all-important basis of a republic. By the time of the Constitutional Convention, the Framers had become convinced that communal self-abnegation and austerity were not part of the American character. Describing this conviction, Wood writes, "The American people apparently did not possess and were unwilling to acquire the moral and social character necessary to sustain republican governments—they were a Luxurious Voluptuous indolent expensive people without Economy or Industry" (Brown 1993:156).

In fact, it is the Framers who are revealed. It is not that common Americans could not govern themselves democratically and effectively; they just would not do it in the same manner that the American elite preferred—that is, to the elite's benefit. "I believe that the calls for industriousness and frugality should be read, at least in part, as class-specific responses to popular demands for tax relief and to the popular obstruction and resistance that greeted the governments' tax crackdown" (Brown 1993:157).

Pre-Convention Meetings

Many of the Federalists' economic and political interests were clearly revealed in the events leading up to the Constitutional Convention. An important instance of such concern—which eventually led to the Constitutional Convention—was demonstrated by a pre-war dispute among the four Potomac states (Maryland, Virginia, Pennsylvania, and Delaware) over fishing and navigation rights on the river's waterway system. A meeting at George Washington's Mount Vernon plantation was held in 1785 to try and settle the question. The gathering was unsuccessful but the representatives from the four states agreed that an assembly of representatives from all states should meet in Annapolis, Maryland, in September 1786. The Virginia legislature sent an invitation to all states asking for a convention to "take into consideration the trade of the states" and to write a "uniform system in their commercial regulations" (Irons 1999:20). The subsequent Annapolis Convention, however, failed to reach the necessary quorum (see Brown 1993:28–30).

In the third attempt to call a gathering of state representatives, the delegates at Annapolis encouraged James Madison, Alexander Hamilton, and John Dickinson to again invite the states to send delegates for the purpose of considering amendments to the Articles of Confederation. Such a convention, by law, could not amend the Articles but could only make proposals for state action. The Articles could only be amended by unanimous support of all state legislatures, a difficult task at best (Brown 1993:179). Knowing this, Madison and the Federalists had their work cut out for them and, thus, began early on devising ways to achieve their goal of recomposing the federal establishment.

From the time that the Annapolis meeting ended until the convention in Philadelphia began, the Federalist kept their plans to write and present a new constitution to themselves. Their furtiveness was so successful that Antifederalists were taken totally by surprise when, during the first week of the Convention, the plans for a total revision were revealed. "In the months before the convention, Federalists had quietly discussed among themselves how to make the government of the United States more effective. To avoid stirring controversy, they said little publically but confined themselves to private letter and face-to-face conversation. As surviving letters indicate, they agreed upon much" before the Convention convened (Brown 1993:179–180).

Irons (1999:18) notes, however, "Whatever their concerns about the deficiencies of the Confederation . . . few men of stature wanted to scrap the Articles entirely; most agreed with Benjamin Franklin, widely admired for his wit and wisdom, that 'we discover some errors in our general and particular constitutions; which it is no wonder they should have the time in which they were formed being considered.'" Most historians seem to agree that Antifederalist feelings were strong and in the majority. Whatever problems the Articles contained, they seemed of minor concern to most Americans.

To help secure a convention in 1787, Federalist advocates assured their less enthusiastic peers that they had no comprehensive agenda and wanted to consider only minor revisions to the Articles (Irons 1999:19). After many reassurances, and with the help of men with national esteem, such as George Washington—who could easily be manipulated(See McDonald 1979[1965]:262–263)—and Benjamin Franklin—who was well into his eighties and contributed little—a convention was set for May of 1787. It should be noted that many men of revolutionary influence did not choose to go. Patrick Henry of Virginia did not attend because, he said, "I smell a rat" (McDonald

1979[1965]:260). Others may have caught the smell as well. Rhode Island categorically declined to send any delegates; New Hampshire decided its Congressional representatives could go as Convention delegates but did not fund their travel. Maryland elected five Convention delegates but they all declined to serve, and, even though New York did send delegates, they departed the Convention, thereby leaving New York unrepresented, once discovering what the Federalists had planned.

The Twelve

McDonald's (1979[1965]:259–307) assessment of the Constitutional Convention and its members is especially critical when evaluating the social class foundation of justice in American society. Convention members were mainly Federalists selected because of their willingness to attend when others would not. When assessing the Convention circumstances and the men who had arrived for the opening session, McDonald (1979[1965]:270) remarks:

> Never mind that Washington was preoccupied with his image as father of the country. Never mind, either, that twenty-four of the thirty-three . . . voices were voices that few would have listened to anytime, anywhere. For nine voices (and three more soon to come) were voices of men possessed of an idea of a great nation, and possessed of the ruthlessness and the daring and skill that make ideas into reality.

These twelve men included Robert Morris, Gouverneur Morris, Benjamin Franklin, James Wilson, John Rutledge, William Paterson, James Madison, Alexander Hamilton, Rufus King, Roger Sherman, Oliver Ellsworth, and John Dickinson.

We will examine how Beard (1963[1913]:73–151) described these twelve men though he, unlike McDonald, does not single them out specifically from other Convention members. Indeed, not every historian would have the same list of the most influential Convention members, nor would they necessarily evaluate them the same. Nevertheless, we will use McDonald's list simply to give the reader a more individualistic view of how the Convention operated and the type and circumstances of the men involved.

A partial picture of Robert Morris was already provided above. McDonald's (1979[1965]) assessment is lengthier but not any more flattering. Though quite notable in his day, Robert Morris—referred to as "the Great Man" by friend and foe alike—has probably faded from standard American history because of his shady business dealings, both private and public. As suggested by Phillips (2002), Robert Morris was well-known and complexly connected in business and political circles and the friend and business associate of many influential men among the Convention members (McDonald 1979[1965]:74–75, 103–107). His self-interest and underhanded dealings put the very success of the new nation in danger.[10]

When reading through Beard's assessments of the economic interests of the Framers, Robert Morris' name continually comes up in various financial dealings with other Convention members. It is clear that Robert Morris was a powerful person who initiated events and influenced important people in financial circles, and many more people wanted to be associated with him.[11]

For all the criticism of Beard's work from the establishment of his day, Beard made it clear he was a great admirer of Robert Morris ("the Patriot Financier"), and thus at odds with Phillips (2002) and McDonald (1979[1965]). There is no doubt that Robert Morris had great influence at the socioeconomic and political top of early American society. Washington asked Morris, the President's most intimate friend, to be Secretary of the Treasury, which Morris declined fearing it would interfere with his other dealings. As a US Senator he supported the Bank of North America and helped establish protective tariffs, both of which undoubtedly helped his fortune and the fortunes of his friends.

Gouverneur Morris (no relation to Robert Morris), McDonald notes, was part of one of the wealthiest families in New York (Beard 1963[1913]:132–133) and had intermarried with those other families that made up the New York aristocracy. Through these marriage connections Gouverneur became intimate with Alexander Hamilton and Robert Morris. McDonald (1979[1965]:75) continues, "These interconnections had an import far greater than merely business; because transportation and communications were synonymous, and because information was normally carried as a subordinate cargo with goods, whoso controlled commerce also controlled, in large measure, the flow of ideas and information."

Gouverneur Morris' full character is perhaps best witnessed at the Convention when he and many of his closest associates (including Johnson, Hamilton, Madison, and King) were appointed to the Committee on Style, assigned to do the final editing of the approved Constitution. This was meant as an exercise in cleaning up grammar and organization. The Committee on Style promptly assigned the task to Gouverneur Morris because of his known literary talent.

> The document itself attests the excellence of Morris' performance. Less visible are the liberties he took with the text. In rendering the language graceful, he also rendered parts of it ambiguous (and therefore elastic, and therefore viable). Elsewhere, he used words that slanted the meaning of clauses, and in at least one instance he audaciously inserted a clause that had been explicitly rejected by the convention. This would, in the passage of time, prove to be one prohibiting the states from passing laws impairing the obligation of contracts . . . "(Morris tried another and even more audacious insertion: a change in punctuation that would have given Congress virtually unlimited powers. Roger Sherman caught that one, however, and the original punctuation was restored)" (McDonald 1979[1965]: 305–306).

McDonald (1979[1965]:43–44, 259, 261, 270; also see McDonald 1958:63) includes Benjamin Franklin in the twelve, probably because of his national and international prestige. McDonald (1979[1965]:261) notes that Franklin, over eighty and approaching senility, could offer little that was constructive to the proceedings. That characterization might be a little harsh but most often when Franklin is discussed by historians at the Convention, it is in reference to his wit and humor. Franklin is important because of the credibility and status he lent to the gathering itself. While economically Franklin was a rags-to-riches story, his character as revealed in history seems quite honorable except, perhaps, when it came to his "flirtations" with women, unmarried or not. As noted above, however, Franklin was not above using his public position for private gain.

James Wilson, whom McDonald (1979[1965]:261; also see McDonald 1958:57–63) describes unsympathetically as Robert Morris' "brilliant henchman" was a successful lawyer and acquaintance of John Dickinson before he ever met Morris. Beard (1963[1913]:147–148) says of Wilson that he became one of the directors of the Bank of North America and was an original stockholder of the Insurance Company of North America. "Wilson's largest interest seems to have been in public lands, for he was among the members of the Georgia Land Company, a highly speculative concern tainted with fraud, to put it mildly. . . . 'James Wilson, of the Supreme Court of the United States, held shares to the amount of at least one million acres.'"

John Rutledge studied law at Temple University and became a highly successful attorney and "accomplished scholar" (Beard

1963[1913]:141). Rutledge was the president of South Carolina under the first South Carolina constitution, but when the legislatures drew up a more democratic form of government Rutledge vetoed it explaining, "However unexceptionable democratic power may appear at first view its defects have been found arbitrary, severe, and destructive" (Beard 1963[1913]:142). Rutledge resigned his office rather than accept the new South Carolina constitution only to be elected governor when the new Constitution became law. Rutledge accepted the new position because it restricted office holders to persons of wealth.

When arriving in Philadelphia to attend the Convention, Rutledge moved in with James Wilson. "[I]n Wilson's home they began to lay plans for 'managing' the convention. . . . [Rutledge] had likewise conspired with Madison and with the two Morrises; and the elder [Robert] Morris had, in turn, planned to manage Washington, who was living in Philadelphia as Morris' house guest" (McDonald 1979[1965]:265–266). As McDonald (1979[1965]:289–292 continues,

> Almost every delegate participated . . . in private discussions in behalf of some interest or another. By far the most effective negotiator was John Rutledge . . . a man with great instinctive knowledge of who was important (as opposed to those who merely appeared important), and a comparable skill in winning their support for ends he sought. . . . [H]is most important single transaction took place during the evening. . . . [a]t a private dinner in his quarters. . .Rutledge entertained Roger Sherman of Connecticut . . . [who] a year before, through skilled negotiations that were in some respects scarcely distinguishable from blackmail, Sherman had won for Connecticut the huge tract west of Pennsylvania called the Western Reserve. . . . Rutledge and Sherman struck a deal: that South Carolina . . . would support Connecticut on the land matter, and Connecticut would support South Carolina on the matter of slave trade and exports.

William Paterson graduated from Princeton in law and became a prominent attorney, eventually becoming a justice on the Supreme Court nominated by Washington for his strong Federalist position. For a time, he also worked in the mercantile business with his father (Beard 1963[1913]:136). Paterson authored the "New Jersey Plan" (also called the "Paterson Plan" or "Small States Plan") that went further in giving sovereignty to the federal government and proposed a strong executive elected by the Congress.

James Madison, who is much admired in traditional American history as the "Father" of the Constitution and the Bill of Rights, is not described so admirably by McDonald (1979[1965]: 263) who sees Madison as someone manipulated by others. "[Madison's] knowledge of what to do in a convention was vast, and his talents for doing it matched his knowledge. . . . [I]t was easy, and in retrospect it became easier, to overrate his intellectual power. . . . [H]e could sound wise when actually he was only quoting somebody wise. . . . [A]nd because he had read the right books—notably the works of Harrington, Hume, and Montesquieu—he sounded for all the world like a man with a flexible brain, whereas at base he was a brittle, doctrinaire theorist."

Beard relates that Madison was a member of one of the old landed families of Virginia whose wealth was mainly land and slaves. Madison studied law at Princeton but devoted his life to politics. Madison found the financial drive and manipulations of his peers distasteful and wrote to Jefferson in 1791 that,

> [T]he subscriptions [to the Bank] are consequently a mere scramble for so much public plunder, which will be engrossed by those already loaded with the spoils of individuals. . . . It pretty clearly appears, also, in what proportions the public debt lies in the Country, what sort of hands hold it, and by whom the people of the United States are to be governed. Of all the shameful circumstances of this business, it is among the greatest to see the members of the legislature who were most active in pushing this job openly grasping its emoluments (1963[1913]:125–126).

Although Madison was instrumental in creating the situation he describes, he was evidently naive as to its outcome and, in the end, seems to be at least as critical as Beard or McDonald of the men who captured the national helm. For this reason alone, Madison probably helped Jefferson found the Democratic-Republican Party, which strongly opposed the Federalists and their namesake political party.

Alexander Hamilton, as a self-styled aristocrat, was not only aware of the elite-heavy and less democratic republican government being created but vigorously supported this effort. Early in the Convention, Hamilton made a famous speech where he "praised the British constitution in highly unrepublican terms, celebrating the House of Lords as 'a most noble institution' and the monarchy as the very 'model' of 'a good executive', all to the end of suggesting that the Senate and executive of a well-constructed republic would both serve on the tenure of 'good behavior'" (Rakove 1996:64). Likewise, Hamilton was hardly unaware or disapproving of the use of government influence and positions as platforms from which to enrich one's self. He did not view such activities as immoral or amoral but supported it as the right of those of "higher society."[12] Hamilton may not be the most arrogant of the Framers but he is certainly best known for this quality—he *was* "Mr. Federalist." As a member of the twelve, men who were self-characterized as "'the sensible part' of Congress, they believed, as Hamilton put it, that 'the safest reliance of every government' is not the goodness of the people, but 'men's interests'" (McDonald 1979[1965]:29).

Beard (1963[1913]:100–114) credits Hamilton with knowing which interest groups to enlist to bring the Constitution through the various state conventions to national passage. The first group and "most easily consolidated and timorous . . . was composed of . . . creditors . . . financiers, bankers, and money lenders. . . . The second group . . . was the merchants and manufacturers. . . . The third . . . was composed of land speculators and promoters and embraced all the leading men of the time—Washington, Franklin, Robert Morris, James Wilson, William Blount. . . . Without the conciliation and positive support of these powerful elements in American society, the new government could not have been founded or continued. With keen insight, Hamilton saw this. He made no attempt to conceal it; for whatever may have been his faults he did not add the crime of demagogy. It is true that in private he often expressed a contempt for popular rule."

Even though Hamilton seems to have had no problems with the questionable economic activities of his many influential and wealthy friends, he did not enrich himself and died broke. Hamilton, however, had no qualms about giving his friends "insider information" and it is difficult to imagine a greater offense, in this regard, than telling Robert Morris of his "plans for redemption of the public debt in full, previous to their publication in the first report to the House on public credit" (Beard 1963[1913]:108).

Rufus King is identified by McDonald (1979[1965]:270) as one of the twelve but McDonald curiously has very little to say about him. Beard (1963[1913]:118–120) mistakenly says that King came from wealth, though King's father seems to have been only moderately successful as a farmer and part-time shopkeeper. McDonald (1958:41) notes that King's inheritance was not sufficient to pay for King's education, requiring him to borrow from family friends. Having finished law school, King developed a successful law practice and eventually married into the wealthy mercantile Alsop family of New York. "King thus had extensive mercantile and other business interests which were largely managed for him by others, so that he was able to devote most of his time to politics" (Beard 1963[1913]:119). King seems to have been involved in the financial schemes of the Morrises in buying up government debt. He was also a director in the first United States Bank, which was openly used to enrich the American upper-class.

Roger Sherman is described by McDonald (1979[1965]:272) as "a gnarled old man whose speech was as grotesque as his appearance but perhaps the shrewdest backroom politician on the continent"—as we saw above in some of Sherman's dealings with Rutledge when he bargained support for a land deal for Connecticut in return for Sherman supporting South Carolina on slave trading. Beard's (1963[1913]:143) depiction of Sherman as a rags-to-riches story and as a man who had no qualms in using his political connections to make money on public securities may be overstated. As a young man, Sherman tried various ways of making a living—as a farmer, surveyor, shoemaker, and lawyer. When he had saved some money, Sherman bought a small store with his brother. He later moved to New Haven and bought another small store at which he had some success. Turning his business over to his son just before the Revolution, Sherman successfully pursued politics, becoming mayor of New Haven and eventually being selected as a delegate to the Constitutional Convention. "Sherman invested almost all his property in the revolutionary cause, and he was almost ruined by depreciation of his securities after the war" (McDonald 1958:48). That he may have acted in a self-serving manner was likely motivated by the constant financial burden placed on him by his family. McDonald (1958:48) observes that "[t]hroughout the 1780's he trembled on the brink of insolvency, but his local prestige and reputation for honesty kept him out of debtor's prison." His government securities paid off handsomely one year before his death.

Oliver Ellsworth is depicted by McDonald (1979[1965]:271) as "a shrewd, stingy, and extremely able and dedicated nationalist." The son of a farmer, who through a variety of means eventually accumulated a large estate, Ellsworth was able to attend both Yale and Princeton and become an attorney. Ellsworth married well and built his legal practice into one the most successful of his day. He diversified the investments of his wealth, including a substantial amount of public securities from which he profited with the establishment of the new government, certainly with his complicity.

The final member of the twelve was John Dickinson, who was born into a substantially prosperous farming family with enough wealth to send Dickinson to London for his education. He established a very successful law practice in Philadelphia and married into a wealthy merchant family. During the Revolution he became a political leader in Pennsylvania and was closely allied to Robert Morris. Dickinson "was outspoken" (Beard 1963[1913]:194) in his belief of a monarchy and for that reason he refused to sign the Declaration of Independence. Like many of the other Framers, he supported a property qualification for voters. "He considered [these restrictions] as the best guardians of liberty; And the restriction of the right to them as a necessary defense agst.[*sic*] the dangerous influence of those multitudes without property & without principle, with which our Country like all others, will in time abound" (Beard 1963[1913]:194–196). By 1785 he had become a semi-retired gentleman farmer. Like other members of the twelve, he did not subscribe to the Age of Reason, but believed that since men were evil (i.e., controlled by their passions and prejudices) they needed a strong central government controlled by those who had experienced success (McDonald 1979[1965]:27–29). Dickinson was one of three Annapolis attendees, along with Hamilton and Madison, to draft a resolution for a constitutional convention.

Since most of the men at the Philadelphia Convention were influential Federalists, it is difficult to come to a complete consensus on who were the most influential in shaping the new Constitution. Nonetheless, the twelve reviewed by McDonald are certainly representative of the kind of men who attended and the philosophy that was dominant amongst them. These were men who were self-conscious of rank, and the belief that their position qualified them to rule. Those of lower ranks, even the "middling sort," were generally suspect and perceived as being at least a potential "democratic mob" that would destroy property rights and free market enterprise if not ruled with a firm hand. On the background of these class interests the new Constitution was written.

Notes

1. It was the first only in name as the colonies had reacted with a similar gathering when the Stamp Act had been passed in 1765.
2. Even if the plan had the urgency that Rakove describes, and even if it was a good plan, it would not be surprising to find that many rejected the plan simply because Morris had offered it and, thus, suspected it was offered to enhance the interests of Morris and his friends.
3. "The Federalists . . . exemplify even more dramatically the two-sided, ambiguous nature of the Revolutionary movement. Their brilliant leaders—[Alexander] Hamilton, [Philip] Schuyler, Robert R. Livingston, Gouverneur Morris, [James] Duane and [John] Jay [also George Washington]—*were*

conservatives, and not merely in the revisionist sense that what they sought to conserve was liberal. They took it for granted that society was a hierarchy of ranks, with a wealthy and leisured elite at its head and 'the lower orders' and 'the peasants' under their rule. They were conservative also in the very modern sense of resisting fiercely government intrusions on free enterprise" (Lynd 2009[1967]:110; emphasis in text).

4. Also see Beard (1963[1913]:152–158), on the *Federalist Papers* as a reflection of its Federalists' authors.

5. "Originally, a 'Federalist' referred to anyone who supported the Articles of Confederation" (Main 1961:xi). "From the beginning, the name thrust upon them by their adversaries, 'Antifederalist,' associated them negatively with a principle that they cherished highly in their own political talk. That label inhibited their effective advocacy of federalism as they understood it and masked the transformation of the concept of federalism in the new governmental design offered by the Constitution of 1787. Yet within the dominant tradition of the American Revolution, it was the Antifederalists, paradoxically, who articulated the more familiar concept of federalism, not the Federalists with their modified theory. Antifederalists, therefore were very much positively committed to established federal norms and perspectives, just as the dynamic thrust of the Federalists reflected their deep-seated opposition to this original federal idea" (Hoffert 1992:145).

6. "([A]nyone claiming that the new Constitution vindicated rather than betrayed the Revolution had to address the subject of representation head on). Direct democracy, Madison argued, was impossible in any society more expansive than a small city-state . . . Rather than cause for alarm, representation was a great blessing in Madison's eyes. *A small, select group of representatives could 'refine' public opinion and produce more virtuous, wise, and stable decisions. The image here is akin to skimming a small amount of cream (the representatives) off the top of a bucket of milk"* (Amar 1998:10; emphasis added).

7. "Most significant was the middle class, from which the Antifederalists drew much strength. The majority of white Americans, and by far the largest number of voters, were farmers who owned their land and who lived at a subsistence level" (Main 1961:5–7). Adding to this description of the Antifederalists Wood (2009:35) states that "most of the opponents of the Constitution were ordinary middling men such as Melancton Smith, William Findley, and John Lamb—spokesmen for the market farmers, shopkeepers, traders, and paper money borrowers who represented the future dominant force of American society . . . they did not hesitate to lash out at the federalists for promoting a government in which, as the New York Anti-Federalist Smith put it, 'none but the great will be chosen.'"

8. "When the Articles of Confederation were being considered, fears of excessive concentration of authority were often expressed. The town of West Springfield, Massachusetts, reminded its representatives of the 'weakness of human nature and the growing thirst for power,' and continued: 'It is *freedom*, Gentlemen, it is *freedom*, & not a choice of the *forms of servitude* for which we contend, and we rely on your fidelity, that you will not consent to the present *plan* of Union, til [*sic*] after the most calm & dispassionate examination you are fully convinced it is well calculated to secure so great &

desirable an object.' The powers granted to Congress, the town feared, were too great, and 'the sovereignty and independence of particular states nearly annihilated. . . . We entertain no jealousy of the present Congress but who knows but in some future corrupt times there may be a Congress which will form a design upon the liberties of the People & will it be difficult to execute such a design when they have the absolute command of the navy, the army & the purse?' . . . It was in accordance with such principles that under the Articles most powers were reserved to the states and that Article II guaranteed the sovereignty and independence of the states. It was also in accord with this political tradition that there was no independent executive—executive functions were performed by Congress through committees or, later, by departments responsible to Congress. Similarly, there was no judiciary except Congress itself, and that body appointed all officers" (Main 1961:15–16).

9. This "drew scattered criticisms" as many wanted election by the people with broader suffrage (Main 1961:16).
10. As reflected in McDonald's (1979[1965]:43) observation: "Had they known in detail . . . what was going on in high political palaces, the army's loyalty would have been even more strained. Intrigue and factional strife in [the Continental] Congress were common, and men of all factions embezzled public funds, profiteered in procuring army supplies, and speculated on the basis of secret information. A host of minor scandals broke. One major scandal—the dispute between Silas Deane (and by implication Benjamin Franklin and Robert Morris) and the Lee family, each of whom accused the other, with considerable justice, of grossly misusing public funds—created so many enmities and so hardened old enmities that Congress was almost paralyzed."
11. "Of all the members of the Convention, Robert Morris . . . had the most widely diversified economic interests. . . . [H]e owned and directed ships . . . engaged in iron and several other branches of manufacturing, bought and sold thousands of acres of land . . . speculated in lots in Washington [D.C.] as soon as he learned of the establishment of the capital there. He was instrumental in organizing the Bank of North America. . . . Before and after the adoption of the Constitution, he was busy interesting his colleagues in every kind of enterprize [*sic*] that promised to be profitable. James Marshall, a brother of John Marshall, was his chief agent. . . . [Morris] held practically every kind of continental security, and that in the Convention and in the first Senate under the Constitution, of which he was a member, he was uniformly strenuous in his support of public credit. No man of his time had such wide-reaching interests or involved in his personal affairs so many eminent men, like Hamilton, John Marshall, Thomas Fitzsimons, Thomas Willing, Gouverneur Morris, John Langdon and Robert Clymer" (Beard 1963[1913]:133–135).
12. In fairness to Hamilton, his dire view of human nature—that all people acted out of passion, prejudice, and self-interest, not rationally as the Age of Reason suggested— was universal. The aristocrats, representing the best in the pursuit of self-interest, deserved their plunder whether from corruption or cleverness (Irons 1999:67; Wood 2009:102–107, 110).

4

The Constitutional Convention

I conceive, sir, that the present Constitution was dictated by commercial necessity more than any other cause (Fisher Ames, 1789, in the House of Representatives in Beard 1963[1913]:7).

He had often wondered, [James] Madison recorded [George] Mason as saying, "at the indifference of the superior classes of society" to those on the bottom. Mason admonished [Elbridge] Gerry and his supporters on this issue that their "selfish motive" of protecting their property would best be served by providing "no less carefully for the rights and happiness of the lowest than of the highest orders of citizens" (Irons 1999:25).

The advantage Federalists had when asking for a convention to amend the Articles of Confederation was that they were already well organized and of a similar mind. This small group was made more effective because their Antifederalist opposition was taken by surprise, was not well organized, and did not have the wealth and influence of their Federalist adversaries. As Brown (1993: 208) observes, "Numerous studies demonstrate that the Antifederalists' most consistent popular support came from the middling and poorer class of yeoman farmers and planters." This observation, made many times by historians, supports the hypothesis that there was social class tension underlying the passage of the Constitution and the formation of the new government.

When the invitation went out from Virginia asking each state to send delegates to the Philadelphia Convention, the Federalists were already well placed, encouraging men of like mind to step forward and be chosen for their respective states' delegations. This was not particularly difficult as most of those who sympathized with the Federalists were well known and, being men of stature and means, generally had little difficulty being appointed as delegates. Furthermore, Antifederalists were not expecting that major changes would be made in the Articles of Confederation and, thus, saw no urgent need to attend the convention, believing that they would have opportunities to address any amendments at the state level.

Traditional history has described the Constitutional Convention as a mix of divergent groups creating a "bundle of compromises" (Brown 1993:184). To the contrary, Levy (in Brown 1993:184) observes that, "consensus, rather than compromise, was the most significant feature of the convention, outweighing in importance the various compromises that occupied most of the time of the delegates.'... This consensus was demonstrated by the Convention's speedy agreement to most of the basic principles of the Virginia Plan."

On the second day of the Convention, Edmund Randolph offered the "Virginia Plan," which had actually been written by James Madison.[1] By the end of the second week most of this plan had been accepted. The Virginia Plan proposed a totally new centralized government with three branches, much as we find today. "These actions confirmed the delegates' nearly universal desire for a 'strong, independent national government that would operate directly on individuals without the involvement of the states.' That three other of the Constitution's most essential provisions—the tax power, the necessary and proper clause, and the supremacy clause—were, in Levy's words, 'casually and unanimously accepted without debate' is further evidence of consensus" (Brown 1993:184).

The new history often articulates disenfranchisement of the common man as the major advantage enjoyed by the Federalists in calling for and writing a constitution. The same property restrictions placed on voters and office holders also applied to Convention delegates. In all, the Convention was largely a Federalist gathering. Slaves, indentured servants, a large number of men who did not qualify under common property requirements, women, and native peoples could not vote or attend the Convention as delegates. What has long been known is that disenfranchised white men were largely Antifederalists, thus potentially adding even more to the Antifederalist majority. At the Convention, Madison warned the Framers, when responding to George Mason's argument that suffrage should be broader than the property requirements inherited from English tradition, that suffrage for Americans without property might jeopardize republican government (Farrand 1966[1911] Vol. II:203–204).

Another danger of which Madison warned was the growing American cities with their masses of industrial workers. Madison had no crystal ball through which to view the American future, but he did observe the industrial process as it was happening in England. Ironic, perhaps, that Madison feared the very thing that Marx later hoped for! Madison and Marx, in an important sense, were correct and, as we will later see, American industrial workers reached a critical mass in American life and demanded, sometimes with substantial violence, changes in the law.[2]

Madison reasoned, as did Hamilton, that if the Constitution were to be accepted by the various states, he would have to enlist the major groups of wealth in the country. In addition to wealthy landholders and those who held substantial amounts of government notes of debt—both state and Continental—, Beard (1963[1913]:40) identifies other groups, such as "manufacturing and shipping" interests that also included merchants among others in the commercial class. As reflected in the Potomac waterways dispute, these commercial interests wanted uniform regulations across state boundaries, tariff protections, tax relief, uniform currency, and a strong military to protect trade. In other words, Madison, with substantial help from Hamilton, had to organize and convince these wealthy groups that the Constitution would serve their economic interests. In so doing, Madison could use these groups' influence with their respective state conventions and legislatures to get the Constitution passed into law. As Beard (1963[1913]:45) observes,

> Immediately after the Revolution the local groups were being welded into a national interest by correspondence committees. Before the formation of the Constitution, Boston merchants were sending out appeals to other merchants in the several states to join in a national movement for protection; and before the new government went into effect, they were active in stirring up united action among the merchants and manufacturers of the whole country.

The *Federalist Papers* was also meant to serve the purpose of uniting various groups of wealth once the Constitution was drafted and sent out for ratification. This process was enhanced by the fact that the major press was either owned by Federalists or largely dependent on their advertising support. "A study of the newspapers of the period shows a large number of prominent advocates of the Constitution among the merchants and brokers advertising in the Federalist press" (Beard 1963[1913]:51).

Although the Federalists went to some lengths to paint a grave picture of the American economy under the Articles of Confederation to justify the Philadelphia Convention, we must remember that the Federalists also wrote this part of American history. Their gloomy picture was not shared by all; Benjamin Franklin, himself a businessman of considerable success, was among the notables outside of the Federalist group. Just before the Convention convened, Franklin "declared that the country was, on the whole, so prosperous that there was every reason for profound thanksgiving." He was not unaware of problems but noted that such problems were not unusual, and "it is always in the power of a small number to make a great clamour [*sic*]." Overall, and compared to Europe, Franklin observed that the country was quite prosperous (Beard 1963[1913]:48).

Property Rights, Social Inequality, and Justice

In the Introduction to his 1935 edition of *An Economic Interpretation of the Constitution of the United States* (1963[1913]:xliii), Beard observes,

> At the time I began my inquiries the generally prevailing view was that expressed recently by Professor Theodore Clarke Smith: "Former historians had described the struggle over the formation and adoption of the document [Constitution] as a contest between sections ending in a victory of straight-thinking national-minded men over narrower and more local opponents." How some men got to be "national-minded" and "straight-thinking," and others became narrow and local in their ideas did not disturb the thought of scholars who presided over historical writing at the turn of the nineteenth century. Nor were those scholars at much pains to explain whether the term, "section," which they freely used, meant a segment of physical geography or a set of social and economic arrangements within a geographic area, conditioned by physical circumstances.

"Local opponents" refers to those who supported state control and autonomy (Antifederalists) over national authority. Local opponents, though they supported state sovereignty through their support of the Articles, were largely common Americans who feared a strong centralized government dominated by the wealthy—a government that, through its power, would deprive them of the liberties they had fought for in the Revolution. It is also true that during this period of history, most Americans were "local," which does not necessarily translate as "rural." The immediate community was the common American's life and sociopolitical participation at the local level came naturally. The Articles guarded this way of life while still providing for a federal umbrella to supply a common defense and a method to deal with issues common to all states.

As Brown (1993:46) argues, "Some historians label these men 'agrarian-localists' and explain their politics by citing the narrow isolation of their rural lives and their alleged indifference to national affairs. In this view, their opposition to federal taxes, the proposed 5 percent federal impost, and the federal Constitution is explained as the natural outgrowth of a rural lifestyle and their circumscribed experience." But these characterizations of common Americans—there were also other references to localists such as "factious" and "turbulent" (Brown 1993:47—, although containing some truth, largely amounted to upper-class condescension.

This conflict, as Brown observes, was immediately over tax policy but was more generally a class conflict. "[T]he wealthier Federalist core group were merchant, professional, artisan-mechanic, and better-off rural communities, who backed the Constitution because it promised stronger government, sound money, and better times. . . . [M]ost middle- and lower-class agrarian communities opposed the Constitution because they saw no good reason to abandon the Confederation system, having previously benefited from the majoritarian flexibility of the state governments" (Brown 1993:5). John Adam's grandson, who as Beard (1943[1915]: 8) observed, "enjoyed the unrivalled advantage of having access to documents closed to all his contemporaries, represented the adoption of the fundamental law of the United States [the Constitution] as a triumph of property over the propertyless."

We must remember that only a few years previously, in the common Americans' memory, many of the Framers had been aligned with the British Crown and had paraded themselves openly and arrogantly as their "betters." So the locals' suspicions were not without substantial foundation. We must also remember that by the end of the Revolutionary War, ordinary Americans were taking radical republican philosophy, a philosophy that touted "a government for the people and by the people," very seriously. They opposed the Constitution because they feared that the resulting national government would deprive them of these republican benefits. Thus, the debate over the Constitution was in many respects a class conflict.

On the side of the "straight-thinking national minded," we find Federalists who shared a common economic interest. "Economic interest" is frequently taken too literally or interpreted too narrowly.

It refers not only to wealth but also, and just as importantly, to wealth that is connected to a lifestyle and worldview. This worldview justifies how a person or group behaves, including whether and how wealth is attained, used, and maintained. The justification component is not simply a rational or logical process. In fact, most of the time it is not a rational process. Rather, it is a philosophy that gives certainty to doing and believing in the "right things."[3]

The Framers have often been depicted as men of high ideals and values. And there seems little doubt that, to varying degrees, they acted out of sincerity on those beliefs. So, the purpose in this writing is not to convince readers that the Framers were only greedy and cynical men in sheep's clothing. Rather, it is acknowledged that all groups of people share this same general characteristic that people will act out of their worldview. Their interests will be determined by their circumstances, and the most important circumstance a group shares is their economic condition. Indeed, most of the Founders accepted this very principle of human nature, which had the effect of creating among them a fear of common Americans. The problem for average Americans was that the upper class could act cogently out of their worldview while common Americans had more obstacles, largely resulting from their powerlessness, larger numbers, and lack of resources. In other words, the socioeconomic and political playing fields were not level.

Whether the Framers were men of principle and ideals is not the only important point. These were largely men of means who did not believe as a matter of principle that their interests should be subject to local control (Rakove 1996:47). Madison reveals this clearly in a letter written to his friend Caleb Wallace just before the Convention. "Even more significant . . . was [Madison's] discussion of suffrage. Here he expressed his mounting fear that rights of property—or, rather, the rights of the classes holding the most property—might be imperiled by economic legislation enacted at the behest of the mass of the populations" (in Rakove 1996:41). Madison's solution was essentially to restrict, to some extent, suffrage to those with property, mainly to those with a similar republican philosophy.

This was the kind of concern that had specifically arisen over the rights to the Potomac waterways. By having a strong central government the issue could be resolved in favor of those with large (interstate) economic interests; that is, they would not be subject to the conflicting rules of four separate states. The Federalists developed a whole philosophy around this principle that is apparent in the

Federalist Papers. While many of their ideals and principles resonated with Americans, the devil was in the fine print and in the subtle distinctions in meaning.

> The diversity in the faculties of men, from which the rights of property originate, is not less an insuperable obstacle to a uniformity of interests. The protection of these faculties is the first object of government. From the protection of different and unequal faculties of acquiring property, the possession of different degrees and kinds of property immediately result; and from the influence of these on the sentiments and views of the respective proprietors, ensues a division of the society into different interests and parties. . . . The latent causes of faction are thus sown in the nature of man. . . . But the most common and durable source of factions has been the various and unequal distribution of property. *Those who hold and those who are without property have ever formed distinct interests in society. . . . The inference to which we are brought is, that the causes of faction cannot be removed, and that relief is only to be sought in the means of controlling its effect* (*Federalist Papers*, Number 10; emphasis added).

A more succinct statement of the American gentry's worldview would be difficult to find. Beard (1963[1913]:xliii) states, "[M]y masters taught me . . . to go behind the pages of history written by my contemporaries and read 'the sources.' I read the letters, papers, and documents pertaining to the Constitution written by the men who took part in framing and adopting it. And to my surprise I found that many Fathers of the Republic regarded the conflict over the Constitution as springing essentially out of conflicts of economic interests. . . . This discovery . . . gave me 'the shock of my life.'"

That this should "shock" Beard should also shock us all, for how could a philosophy so obvious be so hidden in history! What does all of this mean? First, Beard's critics were inexcusably partisan and in error. Beard claimed no more about the motives of the Framers than they did about themselves. Second, the Framers' argument is simple; individuals will have different "faculties" (abilities) that will naturally result in an unequal distribution of wealth. As a result, the "first object of government" should be to protect this naturally unequal outcome. Of course, the Framers had a rigid notion of the source of these "faculties;" that is, they believed that the gentry inherently had more "faculties" than common people. These traits, they felt, were likely to be passed to their descendants, and this privileged group should be protected from majority control or aggression as a fundamental right of property. Even if abilities are not passed through inheritance in particular cases, the privileges of property allow holders to pass these gains to their progeny, no matter how incapable.

As the Framers sat down to revise or replace the Articles of Confederation, could they forget the anger of the "mob" many of them had personally faced only a short time ago? Most of these mob actions concerned economic issues, the remedies of which might very well impair the economic interests of the Framers, their social class, and particular form of republicanism. Indeed, such remedies at the expense of the wealthy had been suggested not only by the Pennsylvania rebels but by Daniel Shay in Massachusetts.

In 1786, less than one year before the Convention opened in Philadelphia, thousands of farmers in Massachusetts lead by a former Continental Army officer, Daniel Shay, spread across the countryside closing down courthouses to prevent farm foreclosures. Many of these foreclosures were the result of taxes levied to pay the war debt largely held by wealthy speculators (Rakove 1996:33). As the rebel farmers were about to seize the federal armory in Springfield, a private army raised by the wealthy of Boston ended what has come to be known as Shay's Rebellion. The state militia had been called to put down the rebellion but these militia men would not fire on their neighbors whose cause they sympathized with.[4] These kinds of actions were a fundamental part of the "localism" Federalists feared.[5]

Surely the Founders had these conflicts on their minds as they gathered to create a new constitution. The Society of the Cincinnati, a group well organized and embittered in their condemnation of the popular movements like Shay's Rebellion and holding large amounts of debt securities and notes of payment for their military service in western lands, supported a strong central government for which many of them would become appointed officials (Rakove 1996:34; also see Wood 2009:108). As the Framers pondered the form of republican government, how much power would we expect them to place in the hands of average citizens? How many legal rights would the Framers want common Americans to have if control of wealth was going to be an issue? Indeed, what kind of justice could the common American expect from a group of wealthy Federalists writing a new constitution in Philadelphia? No sooner was the Constitution ratified then it was put to the test in the Whiskey Rebellion of 1794, an uprising examined later in this treatise.

Secrecy and Government

When the Constitutional Convention began its deliberations, the first rule of the proceedings was that all discussions in the Hall remain secret—that "nothing spoken in the House be printed, or otherwise published or communicated without leave" (see Irons 1999:22). This was not a new practice as the Continental Congress had also kept their deliberations closed, and when the new Constitutional government was operational, the Senate was also allowed to keep its deliberations confidential. Madison did keep copious notes of the Convention proceedings but they were published only after his death. The fact of secrecy in the Convention's deliberations is often noted in discussions and texts and is commonly justified by reasoning that the delegates could speak freely if the proceedings were closed. This would certainly seem to be true, but it is surprising that modern Americans accept this rationalization without pause since such practices are no longer acceptable. Behind this secrecy the Framers could discuss eliminating the Articles, which they had been sent to revise, and could openly discuss the codification and implementation of the conservative republicanism that was commonly accepted in the Hall but not outside in the streets.

The few Antifederalists who made it into these deliberations were not happy about the general tenor of the meeting. "New York's Antifederalist delegates Robert Yates and John Lansing left the convention once it became clear that a majority intended the central government's reconstitution and that they could not defeat it" (Brown 1993:179). Others stayed and argued against the Constitution and some refused to sign it. Others changed their minds later when it was promised that a bill of rights would be added to the Constitution after adoption by the states. It seems very unlikely that if common Americans outside the Hall had known what was transpiring—and they were already very suspicious, especially the common Pennsylvanians who were actually there—that the Convention would have ever succeeded. Addressing this issue, Beard (1963[1913]:40) observes that, "Moreover, they [Federalists] were consolidated by the popular hostility to them on account of their 'secret' and 'aristocratic character.'"

Today's Americans have expressed their disapproval of secret government by insisting on "sunshine" and open meeting laws directed at governmental agencies. In no small part, such laws are the result of organized citizens' groups of the 1960s and 1970s and their experience with the secret activities of governmental agencies. Secrecy is a long-established practice in American government and still occurs today, most recently with the Patriot Act. Other noted disclosures of secrecy in government have included the Pentagon Papers, Watergate, and Iran-Contra.

Domhoff (2010[1967]) has discussed and documented the legal secrecy in modern American government carried on through quasi-governmental advisory groups that are privately funded and legally subscribed as "non-profits" (e.g., policy-discussion groups such as The Council on Foreign Relations, The Committee for Economic Development, The Business Council, and The Business Roundtable; see Domhoff 2010[1967]:100–113). These advisory groups are populated with wealthy corporate Americans, most of who subscribe to the conservative republican philosophy of the Framers. Because these advisory groups are private, they have no obligation to keep or publish the minutes of their meetings and discussions where governmental policies are developed. The Bohemian Grove (see Domhoff 1975) is perhaps the best-known example of this kind of activity: private corporate wealth interacting with high government officials in private and closed meetings.

That secret government is alive and well was recently recognized by a two-year investigation by the *Washington Post* (Priest and Arkin) entitled "Top Secret America." Priest and Arkin documented an extensive network of governmental agencies (1,271) and persons (854,000) that comprise a sprawling secret organization "so large, so unwieldy and so secretive that no one knows how much money it costs, how many people it employs, how many programs exist within it." All of this secret activity grew after the attacks of 9/11 and does not necessarily encompass other facets of secret government.

The Economic Principles of the Constitution

In identifying the economic principles of the Constitution, Beard (1963[1913]:153) states that "the most illuminating . . . sources [are] the records of the debates in the Convention." Beard (1963[1913]:153) also points to the *Federalist Papers* as presenting

> in a relatively brief and systematic form an economic interpretation of the Constitution by the men best fitted, through an intimate knowledge of the ideals of the framers, to expound the political science of the new government. This wonderful piece of argumentation by Hamilton, Madison, and Jay is in fact the finest study in the

> economic interpretation of politics which exists in any language; and whoever would understand the Constitution as an economic document need hardly go beyond it.

Beard suggests that the authors of the *Federalist Papers* modified their tone to appeal to average Americans even though the Constitution was not ratified by popular vote but by state conventions that in large part were dominated by Federalists and their sympathizers.

Beard's economic analysis of the Constitution recognizes that the economic system of the new federal system "consisted of two fundamental parts—one positive and the other negative: [The first is a] government endowed with certain positive powers . . . so constructed as to break the force of majority rule and prevent invasions of the property rights of minorities" (Beard 1963[1913]:154). In this context the "majority" refers to the general populace and the "minority" to the small wealthy elite (Rakove 1996:42, 44–45). "Positive power" means the ability to act quickly in favor of the economic interests of the elite, interests often construed as part of the national welfare. These might be protective tariffs, various subsidies, railway land grants, improvements in water, road and airways, and military action to protect investments and resources. All of this can be, and usually is, guised as being in the "national good."

The North American Free Trade Agreement (NAFTA) is a good example because it was supported by the Executive and passed by Congress even though widely unpopular. Though there was much popular opposition to NAFTA at the grass roots, it was constantly portrayed as being a positive benefit for all Americans. In earlier history and against the general will, the new Congress passed tariffs to protect American manufacturing from cheaper English products. "[O]ne of the strongest arguments for the writing and ratification of the U.S. Constitution was that a stronger and more vigorous central government was needed to promote commercial development and success. In addition to promoting this intention, the 1787 document grants Congress the principles by which this purpose can be pursued and achieved—power over 'interstate commerce' coupled with a 'supremacy clause.'" (Hoffert 1992:183).

As Beard (1963[1913]:155) concludes, "When it is so analyzed, immediate and remote beneficiaries are discovered; and the former are usually found to have been the dynamic element in securing the legislation. Take for example, the economic interests of the advocates who appear in tariff hearings at Washington."

The Supremacy Clause and Necessary and Proper Clause

The second and "negative" part of the federal system identified by Beard (1963[1913]:154) is the ability of the federal government to restrict undesirable state laws. That is, "Restrictions on the state legislature which had been so vigorous in their attacks on capital." There is no doubt that the Framers were conscious of this need when they met in Philadelphia and thus explored various means of controlling and overriding state powers. Considered, and strongly advocated by Madison, was a Congressional veto on state legislation, or a "Council on Revision," which with the President's consent could reject state laws (Rakove 1996:81, 175; Brown 1993:198–199). In the final version, the power to review state laws for their "constitutionality" was not only given to federal courts but the Constitution obliged state courts to do likewise (Irons 1999:44). Irons (1999:45) observes, "From the perspective of political theory, it makes sense that an opponent of democratic 'excesses' made the strongest defense of judicial veto power over laws passed by democratically elected legislators. Not a single state at the time of the Philadelphia convention elected the judges of its highest court; most often, the men who received judicial appointments represented the social and financial elite whose interests they furthered."

The "supremacy" clause and "necessary and proper" clause were specifically designed to strike down state laws that might compromise the capital interests of the national financial elite. Under the supremacy clause of Article VI of the Constitution, state laws are subordinate to federal laws. "This Constitution, and the Laws of the United States which shall be made in Pursuance thereof; and all Treaties made, or which shall be made, under the Authority of the United States, shall be the *supreme Law of the Land;* and the Judges in every State shall be bound thereby, any Thing in the Constitution or Laws of any State to the Contrary notwithstanding" (*US Constitution*, Article VI, second clause; emphasis added). Similarly, Article I (*US Constitution*, Section 8, clause 18) of the Constitution states, "The Congress shall have Power—To make all Laws which shall be *necessary and proper* for carrying into Execution the foregoing Powers, and all other Powers vested by this Constitution in the Government of the United States, or in any Department or Officer thereof."

Not surprisingly, these clauses have often been used in enforcing the commerce clause (Article I, Section 8, clause 3), which states, "The

Congress shall have Power . . . To regulate Commerce with foreign Nations, and among the several States, and with the Indian Tribes." Early in the Republic's history, the Federalist-appointed and Federalist Chief Justice, John Marshall (1801–1835), made strong rulings in *McCulloch v. Maryland* (1819) and *Gibbons v. Ogden* (1824) that confirmed the federal government's power and ability to preempt state laws. In *McCulloch*, the state of Maryland supported its action by invoking the Tenth Amendment; "[P]owers not delegated to the United States by the Constitution . . . are reserved to the States." Marshall sidestepped this Amendment by invoking the supremacy clause. Since the supremacy clause makes federal law the supreme law of the land, "states' rights" are largely an illusion and the Tenth Amendment is an essentially toothless tiger, a pacifier that was meant to appease Antifederalists. States' rights exist only in the sense that state laws have efficacy when the national Congress does not act and/or the Supreme Court abides state laws.[6, 7] Needless to say, these clauses have been controversial and abused or ignored at the convenience of those in power. [8]

Judicial Review

The Framers were uneasy about giving the Court the power of constitutional review even though this power was meant to protect wealth from state and Congressional laws. For this reason, the Constitution was written so that justices have to run a narrow and conservative gauntlet to be appointed to the federal bench. Some Framers considered giving interpretive constitutional review to the federal legislature but concluded that it would be more dangerous than judicial review since part of the legislature was created by popular vote. Of course, review by the executive would have made an already strong executive a virtual dictatorship. It is difficult, perhaps, for us to imagine how worried the Framers were that the words and strictures of the Constitution might come back to bite them. We can still observe this worry from conservatives every time a Supreme Court justice is appointed and must pass through review by the Senate.

Only once in American history have neo-Federalists feared that their precautious mechanisms for selecting Supreme Court justices did not work, and that was with the Warren Court (1953–1969). Strong measures were later taken by conservatives to curb and "correct" the Warren Court's decisions, exceptions to the Exclusionary Rule being perhaps one of the most visible. In the end, fear of what the states might do to property rights moved the Framers to reticently allow federal judicial review. Madison (see Beard 1963[1913]:178) explained the need for judicial review in protecting private wealth in a letter to Jefferson as the Convention commenced. "The mutability of the laws of the States is found to be a serious evil. The injustice of them has been so frequent and so flagrant as to alarm the most steadfast friends of Republicanism." The power of final review was confirmed by the Federalist Supreme Court in *Marbury v. Madison* in 1803 led by the ardent Federalist Chief Justice John Marshall. Marshall's personal experiences had made him wary of localism and state laws that might hamper federal interests.[9]

Though we now take judicial review for granted, as something necessary and logical in our republic, this is only true in large part because Federalists in the early government were in power and, thus, in a position to write history. They placed judicial review into law and then wrote its justification through a media they largely controlled. What has been forgotten—or denied—is that there were strong voices against judicial review precisely because it denied local interests. Most notably, Thomas Jefferson, who earlier supported judicial review, came to be one of its strongest critics. Going against the grain, Jefferson became truly extreme in the eyes of the establishment, even to the modern authors who write on this subject (Rosen 2006: 48). But Jefferson's intellect should not be so easily dismissed. "Writing to Madison in 1821, when both were out of office, Jefferson seemed to deny the power of the Supreme Court to strike down unconstitutional laws, suggesting that constitutional change could come only through formal amendments. . . . Jefferson ended his life, therefore, as something close to a pure majoritarian, convinced that state legislatures, rather than independent judges, should be the ultimate arbiter of constitutional questions" (Rosen 2006:48).

Whether Jefferson was ultimately correct in his assessment of judicial review can never be definitively decided. If one knows the cronyism in the Court's history (Irons 1999) and its recurrent abysmal behavior, it quickly becomes clear why Jefferson found the Court's activities wanting. In its very first session in February of 1790 the Court could not even muster a quorum much to the disappointment of the crowded courtroom. When a quorum was present the next day there was no one seeking the Court's judgment. "The men Washington placed on the Court . . . were a thoroughly undistinguished lot. One spent time in debtors' prisons for defaulting on loans; one returned his commission after five days to serve in state office; one never attended a single Court session; one was impeached for political bias on the bench; one was insane; and another was senile. . . . One reason for Washington's sorry record was that he limited his selections to men whose common attributes was loyalty to the Federalist cause" (Irons 1999:86).

The cronyism of the Court became a tradition. If appointees were not personal friends of the President, then they were political allies being paid-off by an appointment to the Court. Almost every appointee to the Court has come from the President's own party. "Washington's first choice for the Supreme Court, and the first Chief Justice, was John Jay of New York. Jay was born into the American aristocracy of mercantile wealth, and he married into the landed wealth of the Livingston family, the richest in the country. His favorite maxim was that 'those who own the country ought to govern it,' and he advocated stringent property qualifications on voting" (Irons 1999:87).

When Jay resigned after two years on the Court to pursue other political passions, Washington appointed John Rutledge, a vehement defender of slavery. Like Jay before him, "Rutledge had little attachment to democratic principles" (Irons 1999:88). Rutledge's "political blunders" (Irons 1999:88) were so egregious that the Senate rejected his appointment, no small feat in a time when noxious behaviors were easily tolerated among the ruling elite.[10]

With such an inauspicious beginning, which was to repeat itself well into the twentieth century, one must reassess Jefferson's "extremism." Not only did the Court reflect mainstream Federalist philosophy, but it was largely remembered for its partisan, bumbling, or do-nothing associates. This Federalist partisanship was guaranteed with Adams' last minute appointment of John Marshall, who later in his tenure all but scuttled the Bill of Rights. As Irons (1999) readily demonstrates, the Court remained a political-economic and conservative body bent on protecting property rights, including slavery, while ignoring individual rights even in the face of the Bill of Rights and the Fourteenth Amendment.

The Contract Clause

Another important part of the Constitution that reflects the Framers' economic interests is Article I, Section 10 on contracts. This Section was considered essential for protecting property rights. It was the fear of commercial interests that state governments would continue to interfere in contracts motivated by voters' needs for debt relief.

In addition, it is no coincidence that in the same sentence with the contract clause the Constitution reserved to the federal government the monopoly to produce money. Commercial interests worried that if paper money were printed, it would cause inflation and contracts would be paid off in money of decreasing value. As such, they wanted debts paid in "species," or coinage made from precious metal.

> Article I, Section 10. No State shall . . . coin Money, emit Bills of Credit; make any Thing but gold and silver Coin a Tender in Payment of Debts; pass any Bill of Attainder, ex post facto Law, or Law impairing the Obligations of Contracts (US Constitution).

Beard (1963[1913]:179) specifically identifies the contract clause as written for those with "personal property," as opposed to those with "real property" or land. Personal property or "personalty," as Beard often refers to it, included loans, state and continental securities, stocks of goods, manufacturing plants, soldiers' scrip, and shipping.

> Two small clauses [of the Constitution] embody the chief demands of personalty. . . . [T]he emission of paper money is prohibited and the states are forbidden to impair the obligation of contract. The first of these means a return to a specie basis—when coupled with the requirement that the gold and silver coin of the United States shall be the legal tender. The Shays and their paper money legions, who assaulted the vested rights of personalty by the process of legislative depreciation, are now subdued forever, and money lenders and security holders may be sure of their operations. Contracts are to be safe, and whoever engages in a financial operation, public or private, may know that state legislatures cannot destroy overnight the rules by which the game is played (Beard 1963[1913]:178–179).

The Federalists and their constituency did not want worthless or deflating paper money being used to pay contracted debts. Likewise, they did not want contracts altered retroactively by states that might have different notions of fairness and thus provide temporary relief to its citizens in times of economic crisis. Under the Articles of Confederation debt relief had been a common practice in the states.

> Hamilton on several occasions laid great stress on the contract clause as one of the features of the Constitution which had warmly commended it to its supporters. In a communication to Washington . . . he wrote: "This, to the more enlightened part of the community, was not one of the least recommendations of that Constitution. The too

> frequent intermeddlings of the state legislatures in relation to private contracts were extensively felt and seriously lamented; and a Constitution which promised a preventative was, by those who felt and thought in that manner, eagerly embraced" (Beard 1963[1913]:180).

Contracts have been a focal and notorious point of conflict between Americans of the upper and lower classes. There was some expectation that with the election of Andrew Jackson, and his appointment of Roger Taney as Chief Justice replacing Marshall, that "the happiness and prosperity of the community" would become the Constitution's first principle, replacing property rights and the contract clause (Irons 1999:144). But as Irons (1999:112) continues, "Even the presidential victories of Andrew Jackson in 1828 and 1832, riding a populist wave of protest against bankers and businessmen, did not dislodge—or even threaten—those who controlled the economy and took the biggest share of the national wealth." Even during the Great Depression of the 1930s with the great financial despair among average Americans, the "contract clause" held sway over state laws that tried to provide general relief (Irons 1999:297–298).

Common Americans have historically complained about the legalese and fine print of contracts, and they lose billions of dollars each year because they cannot understand what they have agreed to in contracts. No law student finishes law school without compulsory courses on contracts, many attorneys specialize in contracts, and corporations and other agencies hire numerous contract lawyers and make no agreements without them. The courts are jammed with contract cases as each side argues the meaning that benefits their interests. Few would deny the theoretical importance of contracts but average Americans do not have the means to hire the expertise to make sure they are not cheated in contractual agreements.

War Powers

The Constitution, in Articles I and II, gives the federal government a monopoly on war.

> Article I, Section 9. To provide for calling forth the Militia to execute the Laws of the Union, suppress Insurrections and repel Invasions; To provide for organizing, arming, and disciplining, the Militia, and for governing such Part of them as may be employed in the Service of the United States, reserving to the States respectively, the Appointment of the Officers, and the Authority of training the Militia according to the discipline prescribed by Congress. . . .

> Article II, Section 2. The President shall be Commander in Chief of the Army and Navy of the United States, and of the Militia of the several States, when called into the actual Service of the United States (US Constitution).

In the minds of the Framers, war powers and the military were not simply a matter of defense but also a projection of economic self-interest. Wars, the threat of war, and the military are the "stick" of economic interests as demonstrated by the Revolution itself. Just as importantly, the war powers and the military act as a safeguard to protect property and economic interests. The latter was demonstrated early in the country's history by the military suppression of Shay's and the Whiskey Rebellions (see Wood 2009:111).

Common Americans have often been unenthusiastic about the wars they have been conscripted or recruited to fight. Drawn in by humanitarian values and the high ideals of patriotism, ordinary Americans regularly find they are fighting and dying to enrich wealthy interests through the extension or protection of markets and/or the expropriation of foreign resources. As we saw in the Revolution, wars always enrich the suppliers or the "military industrial complex," as President Eisenhower called it. Woefully, American history also has its share of military power being used to control its own citizens in less than righteous ways.

Although the Congress is given the power to declare and finance wars, this has all but become antiquated. Article I, Section 2 of the Constitution states that, "The President shall be Commander in Chief of the Army and Navy of the United States, and of the Militia of the several States." In the oath of office for the Presidency, he or she is sworn to protect and defend the United States. From these sparse phrases the United States presidency has become a formidable war-making office, and over time has been largely released from the balance of powers. If the property rights of wealthy Americans and corporations are threatened, the president can act swiftly.

Taxation

Article 1, Sections 7 and 8 of the Constitution give the federal Congress the power to levy taxes. As discussed above, one of the major concerns of the Congress when it operated under the Articles of Confederation was that it could not directly compel taxes in order to operate the federal government. Rather, all tax revenues had to come voluntarily from the states. As also noted, the Congress had considered a law that would compel states to pay taxes on threat of military intervention.

Whether the taxation system under the Articles of Confederation would have worked had the Articles been amended is now a matter of speculation, but certainly the Federalists did not think so. Subsequent history has accepted the Federalists' arguments on taxation as one of the fundamental reasons for writing a stronger federal constitution. As Brown (1993:3) argues, "[T]he key to the constitutional Revolution of 1787 is to be found in the Framers' experience with taxation by the state governments and in the Framers' perceptions of why their plans for taxation failed. Facing heavy state and federal financial obligations, state legislatures levied specie taxes on cash-poor farmers who could not pay. When the states attempted to force collection, they met protest and resistance," as seen with Shay's Rebellion.

The history of taxation in American society is a long, complex, and contentious subject (see Phillips 2002) that, though abbreviated here, underscores the point that taxation has been a social class issue. The burden of taxation has always fallen unequally and disproportionately on the shoulders of common Americans. The major justification for this unequal load is one that Americans are all too familiar with: that taxation on wealth, whether individual or corporate, harms the economy for all persons by burdening capital investment. This argument is largely a smoke screen to cover the fact that the wealthy do not want a tax tradition that looks to wealth and capital for societal revenues.

Though subtle, the Constitution allows taxation by a government that the Federalists designed to be dominated by those with wealth or those representing the interests of wealth. They, in turn, have used three basic strategies in American taxation: tax items before they reach the consumer, thus avoiding bringing taxation to mind; impose regressive taxes—sales taxes, gasoline taxes, cigarette and liquor taxes, and Social Security taxes so that the burden of taxation is greater on the poorest; or avoid progressive taxes or at least provide that they are greatly attenuated at the top income levels. Through regressive taxation, greatly attenuated progressive taxes, tax loopholes, and minimal taxation on investments, the American elite have greatly curtailed taxation on their wealth.

Direct federal taxation authority was used immediately after the Constitution was ratified in 1791. No person was a more obvious symbol of centralized taxation than the first Secretary of the Treasury, Alexander Hamilton, who proposed a tax on whiskey to help pay government debt. The resulting Whiskey Rebellion of 1794 enveloped a popular insurrection in the area around Washington and Pennsylvania in the Monongahela Valley and eventually spread to many other parts of the country (Wood 2009:134–139). Many traditional historians have dealt with the Whiskey Rebellion by largely ignoring it or otherwise making it seem to be of little significance. The fact that the tax placed a great burden on small farmers has often been historically left out of Hamilton's intentions (McCullough 2001:455; Brown 1993:239–240; Marshall 2000[1803–1807]:415–420). Although the Whiskey Rebellion may not represent the normal reaction of common Americans, this rebellion does exemplify the friction that existed between upper class and common Americans. Similar tax tensions have covered the entirety of American history (see Brown 1993).

John Marshall's (2000[1803–1807]:415–420) history of the Whiskey Rebellion is a nondescript account without much detail that portrays Washington as patiently and generously dealing with a few "malcontents."[11] Washington blamed this tax revolt on Republican "democratic societies" that were popular in America after the French Revolution. When tax resisters persisted, Washington personally led an army of states' militias to put down the challenge. Concluding, Marshall would have us believe that there were no grievances, just the actions of an irrational mob. "[W]ithout shedding a drop of blood, did the prudent vigor of the executive terminate an insurrection which, at one time, threatened to shake the government to its foundation. That so perverse a spirit should have been excited in the bosom of prosperity, without the pressure of a single grievance, is among those political phenomena which occur, not infrequently in the course of human affairs, and which the statesman can never safely disregard" (Marshall 2000[1803–1807]:420).

As noted, the whiskey tax originated with the Secretary of the Treasury, Alexander Hamilton, who in 1791 asked the largely Federalist Congress to impose an excise tax on distilled whisky. Deliberately avoiding whiskey merchants, who were his steadfast supporters, Hamilton selected to tax small western farmers to pay off the war debt.[12] These farmers raised a substantial amount of grain but, unable to easily transport their crop to coastal markets and being cut off from transport down the Mississippi River by Spain, western farmers made transport and preservation of their grain easier by distilling it into whiskey.[13]

In Hamiltonian style, the whiskey was taxed by the gallon for small distillers but taxed with a flat fee for those who produced whiskey in large volume. The tax on small producers was "oppressively high—about 25 per cent of the net price of a gallon of whiskey" (Miller 1988[1960]:156). The farmers' complaints were answered arrogantly by Hamilton telling them that if they did not like the tax to stop drinking whiskey that was not good for their health.

Hamilton's purpose was not just to raise revenue for the federal government but to deliberately incite a conflict for the purpose of establishing federal authority as envisioned by Federalist philosophy. In this way Hamilton hoped to also defeat the Republican-Democratic movement led by Jefferson and Madison (Wood 2009:196–198). Without broad-based revenue there could be no substantial military, societal infrastructure, or uniform law. While these things might be to the advantage of all Americans, Federalists knew that a large-scale economy with large-scale profits was not possible without these resources. They thus compelled common Americans to pay for it with the threat of federal authority.

To make the point clear, Washington personally commanded the militia for ending the insurrection. Hamilton, Washington's former aide-de-camp in the Revolutionary War, served at his side. Ellis (2004:225) depicts the confrontation as a resolution of the meaning of the Revolutionary War. Washington's decision to command the federal forces,

> provides the most graphic and dramatic illustration of the two competing versions of what the American Revolution had come to mean in the 1790s. On one side stood the rebels, a defiant collection of aggrieved farmers emboldened by their conviction that the excise tax levied by [the Federalist] Congress was every bit as illegitimate as the taxes levied by the British ministry. On the other side stood Washington and his federalized troops, an updated version of the Continental army, marching west to enforce the authority of the constitutionally elected government that claimed to represent all the American people. It was "the spirit of '76' against 'the spirit of '87'" (Ellis 2004:225).

The protest over the tax on whiskey started in western Pennsylvania and spread to Maryland, Virginia, North and South Carolina, and Georgia and was partially instigated by new excise taxes on snuff [tobacco] and loafsugar. These new taxes were imposed by a Federalist Congress in 1794 at the instigation of Hamilton. Although no accurate count of rebels is known, rumor swelled their numbers into the thousands. Tax collectors were being harassed, mail stolen, and federal judicial proceedings interrupted. At one point, General John Neville, the excise inspector for western Pennsylvania, and his small contingent of regular troops was forced to surrender to the rebels. Rumors then spread that a rebel army was going to attack Pittsburgh and Philadelphia.

The Pennsylvanians already had a defiant reputation. So, taking no chances, Washington raised an army of over twelve thousand states' militia and marched on Pennsylvania. There was never an actual confrontation and only a handful of arrests. The only death was a rebel who died while in jail, the others being released under a general amnesty granted by Washington. But the point had been made. "Hamilton declared that the government had gained 'reputation and strength' by demonstrating that it was capable of compelling obedience to the laws. The quick collapse of resistance in the West was made to appear as a vindication of Hamiltonian energy" (Miller 1988[1960]:159). Of course, no American army ever marched on merchants, manufacturers, and large landowners for the purpose of extracting taxes. Their tax evasion was done legally through the Federalist government they supported.

At this point in American history the tax question was impossible to separate from the paper money and specie dispute. Federalists opposed paper money because of their experience with inflated paper currency during the Revolutionary War, currency that was not backed by precious metal or an established government. The result was the devaluation of wealth through inflation. Those who held government or state securities did not want to be paid with inflated paper currency. As Brown (1993:41; also see Ferguson 1961) observes, "The patrons of hard money taxes were recognized elites of wealthy and accomplished merchants, bankers, lawyers, and planters who held office in the postwar state governments as legislators, executives, and judges. [They] believed that taxes could be paid [in specie] if the common people were frugal and industrious." The problem, as Ferguson (1961:4) makes clear, is that hard currency was rare, of foreign origin, and mainly used in trade. Common Americans had little access to specie, so often found it impossible to pay their taxes. The whole thing began to smell of a Federalist scheme to not only retrieve their wealth but to confiscate property in lieu of taxes from middle and modest Americans.

The wealthy, who had most of the specie, did not want their wealth taxed. Precious metals (silver and gold) held their value but made specie scarce because precious metals were not being mined and minted in the United States. As a result, debt and tax payments were very difficult for farmers, artisans, and other common Americans. When they could not make their payments in specie, their property was confiscated.

As Brown (1993:48) continues

> The persistence of the patrons of hard money taxes also resulted from their conviction that such taxes would spur the economy and thus make taxes easier to pay. By paying the annual interest on state debts in specie and enabling Congress to pay domestic creditors in the same medium, the state governments would signal a mistrustful commercial community that property rights under the new popular assemblies would be protected and that the inflated money of the Revolution would be stabilized. Thus reassured cautious merchants would extend credit and invest in commercial and manufacturing enterprises, and the entire economy including the farming sector would prosper—the trickle-down effect.
>
> In fact, members of this elite regarded taxes as a prosperity producing stimulant to lower-class industriousness and saving. Alexander Hamilton justified an early proposal for creating a permanent federal debt to be funded by permanent *state* revenues by arguing the taxes would "be a spur to industry" and thus instill a healthy "habit of labour in the people" (emphasis in text).

This self-serving and patronizing attitude is a fundamental part of the dominant economic philosophy that has persisted throughout American history. As a result of American prosperity over the past two hundred years, the attitude about paper money has changed but not the attitude about which part of the American population should be taxed. Those scholars who support this philosophy point to its success without really exploring the question "successful for whom?"

While Americans continue to complain about taxes, federal power in the form of tax collecting authority (such as the Internal Revenue Service; Social Security Administration; the Bureau of Alcohol, Tobacco, Firearms and Explosives; and other tax agencies too numerous to enumerate) is well established and effective. The aggressive collection of taxes also can be found with the Federalist Framers. "When sums of unpaid taxes accumulated, upper-class leaders blamed not depressed agricultural prices, frozen credit, or unprofitable markets, but the indolence and extravagance of individuals. . . . The antidote for the mounting arrearages of unpaid taxes was not tax relief, but firmer collection by the government" (Brown 1993:49).

The Structure of Representation: A Check on the People's House

For all the early Republic's commitment to representative government, voting and office holding did not substantially change from the colonial pattern until the 1820s. The Constitution prescribed a republican form of government, not a democratic one. Property, religious, tax, age, gender, and racial restrictions abounded. The president was chosen by an electoral college, not voters, and in most states until the late 1820s, electors were selected by the legislature. Congressmen were the only directly elected federal officeholders (Keller 2007: 71).

There was much discussion at the Constitutional Convention about representation in the Congress and how the number of representatives for each state would be determined. Southern states being principally agrarian and less densely populated were concerned that representation based on population would leave them less powerful. Geographically small states, also lacking population, had a similar concern. As Americans have been taught, the problem of representation was partially solved by increasing the count of persons in the south by including slaves as partial persons and, for both southern and small states, by giving each state two senators in the second house.

The Senate, however, was perceived as solving other problems. The Senate was viewed by Federalists as a crucial part of their protection against the "majority" since Senators were elected by state legislators once removed from the general population (Rakove 1996:41). Lobbying states legislators to appoint particular and "proper" men gave substantial assurance to the American upper class that their interests would be preserved. "The stronghold of this 'monarchical faction' was the Senate, a body that prided itself upon its aloofness from the people and dedicated itself to maintaining a 'steadying influence' upon the public councils. . . [T]he Senate, like the Continental Congress before it, preserved the rule of secrecy—and thereby incurred the charge of being a 'divan' of aristocrats who sneered, from the safety of their chambers, at the 'common herd'" (Miller 1988[1960]:6).[14]

The Senate, having the power to write its own rules of operation (US Constitution, Article 1, Section 5,), provided its support for the concerns of wealth and power by early on allowing a filibuster to thwart unwanted legislation and then later requiring a "super majority" for the passage of most legislation. Being small in number and running statewide for office ensured that Senators would draw the support of the largest and wealthiest interests. This small-bodied bottleneck in national legislation has been so important that campaign funds have commonly come from national sources.

The Senate must also approve all federal judges, prosecutors, and Supreme Court justices, thus having strong influence over justice, both conceptually and practically. These Senate powers provided the Federalists with assurance that the more popularly elected body, the House of Representatives, would not pass laws and legislation that might hurt the interests of wealth. Although not infallible, this system has served its purpose well throughout American history as a conservative buttress against change and a protector of established property interests.

Another structural obstacle to unwanted legislation designed by Madison and his Federalist compatriots was the power bestowed on the Executive. The authority of the Congress was an early concern to Madison and the Federalists. Should "unwanted" legislation pass the House and somehow survive the Senate, the president can still veto the legislation, thus requiring a two thirds super majority of the Congress for its passage. "But the most radical aspect of Madison's position was to extend the scope of this veto beyond avowedly national concerns so that it could also serve as a 'controul [*sic*] on the internal vicissitude of State policy; and the aggressions of interested majorities on the rights of minorities and of individuals'" (Rakove 1996:51). In this context Madison's reference to "minorities" and "individuals" could literately be read as wealthy groups.

If all else failed and unwanted legislation passed the House, Senate, and the Executive, there was always judicial review that allowed the Supreme Court to decide on the constitutionality of the law. Judicial review was unequivocally and unanimously established by the Federalist-appointed Supreme Court led by Chief Justice John Marshall in *Marbury v. Madison* (1803). This complicated gauntlet worked well to keep most American legislation moderate or conservative and in support of wealthy interests.

It seems clear that the Framers feared a parliamentary type system because it granted greater representation and power to common people.

> In monarchical regimes the chief danger arose from the excesses of the crown, but in a republic that distinction necessarily fell to the legislature. Not only did it enjoy the political advantages that flowed from direct popular election, *it could also exploit its formal rule-making authority to circumscribe the discretion of the other branches, override particular decisions to which it objected, or use its power of the purse to make the other departments bend to its will.* Nor was this concern merely speculative. [Madison states [e]xperience demonstrated that "[t]he legislative department is everywhere extending the sphere of its activity, and drawing all power into its impetuous vortex."
>
> Notwithstanding his hopes that Congress would be a more select body than its counterparts in the states, Madison thus recognized that legislative excess remained the crucial problem of republican constitutionalism. His proposed institutional remedies followed his 1785 letter to Wallace: the creation of a true senate, safely insulated from popular pressure, to check the lower house; and the establishment of a joint executive-judicial council of revision, armed with both a limited veto over national legislation and an advisory role in the negative on state laws (Rakove 1996:53; emphasis added).

Finally and perhaps less obvious to common Americans, is the culture of deferential politics that was both customary and disseminated in the American polity. In early America,

> Survivals of a more deferential political era abounded. In New York, The Council of Appointment designated mayors and other local officials. In some states the legislature chose the governor. Tennessee's new constitution in 1796 . . . provided that the state assembly appoint justices of the peace—key local officials—for life. The JPs in turn appointed county officers. In Virginia, deferential political ways lived on. Planter John Campbell wrote to his son David in 1811: "I have heard with much pain that you have not recovered your health yet. Would a session in the legislature be of benefit to you" (Keller 2007:71).

Although patronage in American politics has often been criticized, and many offices once appointed are now directly elected, appointments to powerful offices still abound, especially in the executive branch, which also has the power to appoint judges and prosecutors for the federal judiciary, a purportedly co-equal branch of government.

Much has been made in traditional American history of the "separation and balance of powers" and how this system safeguards our republic by keeping one branch of government from acquiring too much power. The above discussion strongly suggests that this is more cliché than a reality. The "separation and balance of powers," as devised in American government, were meant to control the legislative branch, especially the House of Representatives, and the desires of the common people; in other words, it was to construct a government that addressed the Federalist's fear of the "majority." Though Madison's proposal for controlling the legislative branch was not realized exactly in his terms, it was, nonetheless, realized in the Constitution. The House of Representatives, that body directly elected by the populous and most similar to a parliament, was checked in the Constitution by the appointed Senate and an Executive with veto power over legislation and the co-authority to appoint the federal judiciary.

District Voting: All or Nothing and the Two-Party System

Usually missing from the dialogue on congressional representation is a discussion of district voting (Domhoff 2010[1967]:136–139). The Constitution was composed to allow each state a number of representatives based on its population with each representative appearing on behalf of a district within a state. For Senators, the state itself is the district.

The problems with this district system are well known as partially demonstrated in the melee and corruption surrounding redistricting as each party tries to gerrymander their state. Indeed, gerrymandering was the method used in post-Revolutionary South Carolina to assure enough Federalists' votes to confirm the Constitution (Brown 1993:200). Scholars have been so focused on the discussion of district formation that a major question has been all but lost. Why did the Framers choose district elections in the first place?[15] Within the Framers' experience and knowledge there were certainly other solutions for structuring representation.

Claiming that political parties are too divisive, the Framers were disappointed when parties emerged soon after the Constitution was ratified. By and large, this attitude can be interpreted to mean that the Framers did not want a parliamentary system with multiple political parties and proportional representation by party vote. By design, parliamentary systems result in multiparty configurations where the various factions represent relatively constricted interests, often resulting in adversarial relationships. The principal party to emerge is often a left-of-center party most concerned with the average citizens' interests, a circumstance unacceptable to the Federalists and to wealthy interests today.

By setting up a district system of elections, the Framers created a winner-take-all structure. Such an arrangement has a number of critical consequences: first, large portions of the population will not be represented if their candidate loses even by a small margin; second, a two-party system of moderate parties is almost ensured because a vote for a third party is, in effect, a vote for a person's least favorite choice. This is why Ralph Nader's candidacy was blamed for electing George W. Bush in the 2000 presidential election.

This two-party system ensures that both parties will be large centrist parties because in order to win they must appeal to a large proportion of the population that includes a substantial number of independent moderates. If a party goes too far to the right or left it will lose the moderate votes necessary to win an election. Moderation itself is a safeguard to the interests of the status quo.

Another serious effect of district elections is that many citizens will not vote. Americans commonly hear, and believe, that to vote is to select between the lesser of two evils—between Tweeddle Dum and Tweeddle Dee" Such an outlook suggests that the candidates are not that different from one another and therefore cannot represent the diversity of voters' interests. The nature of the American electoral system makes those sentiments essentially true. So many citizens ask, why bother to vote? As a result, Americans have a very poor voter turnout, thus disenfranchising the very voters furthest from the political center and elite interests.[16]

Did the Founders know and anticipate this outcome? It is difficult to imagine that they did not. In proportional parliamentary systems, almost all voters receive some representation of their interests because parliamentary systems do not have winner-take-all elections. In some manner a party receives representation in proportion to the number of votes it receives. Many of these smaller parties are more politically distant from the society's elite, yet they may have some power in creating a majority government and thus influencing policy different from or even contrary to elite interests. By definition parliamentary systems are far more democratic, and voter turnout is much greater because most individuals will feel that their vote will count even if their party does not win a majority.

Simply because Madison believed "that legislative excess remained the crucial problem of republican constitutionalism" (Rakove 1996:53) does not necessarily mean that other Americans would come to this conclusion (Rakove 1996:53). History has built the Framers' status to such a point that Americans now assume that if the Framers supported a proposal or idea then it must have reflected the best interests of all the people. In examining the historical factors that influenced the creation of the Constitution, Rakove (1996:20) observes that the "[c]olonists naturally regarded their own legislative assemblies as miniatures of the mother Parliament, and the provincial elites who ruled there sought to acquire for these bodies the same rights and privileges that the House of Commons had struggled so long to acquire." Implicit in the above observation is the question, "Why did the Constitution not reconstruct a parliamentary system of governance, the system the Framers were intimately familiar with?" To the contrary, the executive prerogative won the day and a government that restricted the legislative and enhanced the executive was conceived.

Parliamentary systems do not readily produce and support a wealthy elite or an executive heavy government. In fact, the opposite is often the case. If we examine European parliamentary democracies, we find that the normal outcome has been governments representing common people; labor or center-left parties are the typical outcome. Even when conservative parties rule in parliamentary systems they are reluctant to eliminate programs and privileges granted under labor or social democratic rule and are, nonetheless, constantly checked by opposition from the left. Left-of-center governments closely regulate business activity and persistently tax wealth, whether individual or corporate. Through regulation and political party interests, these governments confine elite formation, in part, by restricting the government's executive office. In the end, their revenues are spent on establishing a welfare state that provides services for common people and thus a higher standard of living.[17]

Interestingly, when the US "nation-builds," as it is currently trying to do in Iraq and Afghanistan, it creates parliamentary systems. Parliamentary systems do not have strong executive governments that more readily might pose a threat to US interests. Prime ministers, who are subject to votes of no confidence and the collapse of their governments, must appear before an elected multiparty body and seek approval for executive activities. In examining the United States' greatest military rivals of the past century, we find that they were all executive-centered governments. Executive-heavy governments allow the leader to more easily use military and police powers and to veto any unwanted legislative actions. As we often find in the United States, the executive can effectively legislate through executive orders that have the authority of law. Certainly the Federalist-packed Convention of 1787 understood this fact. The Federalists were republican enough to provide highly constrained democratic institutions, but we are nowhere close to being "the most democratic society," as is often boasted. The result has been a US republican government that ensures the wealth and power of elite Americans. Any objective examination of wealth distribution over US history would be hard pressed to make a different argument (Noah 2010).

Americans are told that parliamentary systems are too divisive, making governmental operation arduous. Likewise, it is said, American society is too socially, geographically, and ethnically diverse for a parliamentary system to function well. Even if these criticisms are true, American society was not diverse at its founding but was a small homogenous society. At times, parliamentary democracy may be a more considered process exactly because it is more democratic and includes a greater diversity of interests. The United States is absent a parliamentary system because such systems are threatening to private capital and property groups.

Once the Federalist-dominated Constitutional Convention created and passed a Constitution, both federal and state legislatures concluded by electing Federalist majorities. These majorities then began revising state constitutions to fit the Federalist model. "[S]everal states, having passed under the control of Federalists, began to revise their constitutions along the lines laid down by the Federal Constitution. In 1790, Pennsylvania abolished its unicameral legislature, establishing in its stead a bicameral body. Equally important, the executive was empowered to check the activities of the legislators, and the judiciary was given tenure during good behavior" (Miller 1988[1960]:4).

As a final note, the practice has emerged in the American press and polity of referring to third party representatives as "independents" no matter their party affiliation. Most Americans would be surprised to know that the US Congress has Libertarian and Socialist members. If Madison (Rakove 1996:47–50) and his fellow travelers were so concerned about the failures of the Articles of Confederation, they could have just as easily resolved these problems with the introduction of a national parliamentary government, a governmental form very familiar to them. We are told in American histories that Madison spent considerable time reading about and studying various republican governments but parliamentary forms are never mentioned. Since neither Madison nor the other Framers considered this obvious republican form but went to the trouble of inventing a new one, it would suggest that they had another agenda—that of creating a republican form that served and protected their class interests.

Ratification of the Constitution

> *Every State shall abide by the determination of the United States in Congress assembled, on all questions which by this confederation are submitted to them. And the Articles of this Confederation shall be inviolably observed by every State, and the Union shall be perpetual;* nor shall any alteration at any time hereafter be made in any of them; unless such alteration be agreed to in a Congress of the United States, and be afterwards confirmed by the legislatures of every State *(Articles of Confederation and Perpetual Union, Article XIII; emphasis added).*

What would surprise most Americans is that the US Constitution was not a legally implemented document. It was illegally authorized and very questionable tactics were used in its ratification (Beard 1963[1913]:217–238). Article XIII of the Articles of Confederation, cited at the beginning of this section, prescribes the lawful way the Articles were to be amended. Instead, a Convention was called in Philadelphia under the auspices of amending the Articles when the greater majority of Federalist attendees had already drafted the outlines of a new constitution. As intended, this Federalist tactic caught Antifederalists completely off guard, leaving them little time to organize an opposition. Rather than submitting the new Constitution to the various state legislatures for approval, as required by law, the Federalists took it upon themselves to write their own ratification process, a totally arbitrary act meant to increase the possibility of approval. They called for each state to quickly call their own constitutional conventions with members being appointed by the legislatures. In many cases the Federalists already had men lined up to seek state delegation membership. The state conventions were instructed by the Philadelphia Convention to vote up or down on the Constitution without consideration of amendments. Furthermore, the Philadelphia Convention proclaimed that the new Constitution would be authorized when nine states had ratified it, not all thirteen as required by law. Following these extralegal procedures, the Federalists were able to quickly, though narrowly, pass the new Constitution into law.

The obvious question might be, "How could the Federalists rewrite the amendment process of the Articles without objection and forfeiting legitimacy?" The answer is complex, but many people and some states did object and did question the legitimacy of the process. Indeed, for a long time the Federalists feared that the opposition might successfully call a second constitutional convention. But through prearrangement and organization the Federalists were able to move quickly and persuade the Federalist-populated state conventions to swiftly ratify the new constitution. As the number of states supporting ratification increased, those abstaining began feeling their precarious situation. The Federalists were also able to engage the support of notable persons, especially George Washington. Through ownership or influence over the media, the Federalists were able to conduct a ratification campaign, which we now see reflected in the *Federalist Papers.* Finally, the Federalists were able to tip the scale for ratification by promising to add a bill of rights in the first Congress to meet after the Constitution was approved.

As Beard (1963[1913]:189; emphasis added) notes, "As intensely practical men they [the Framers] were concerned with tangible results, *not with the manner in which political scientists might view the details of their operations*." "[T]he discussion of ratification generally took a more pragmatic and political cast. Would it aid or impair the prospects for ratification to adopt some procedure other than that specified by the Articles?" (Rakove 1996:103–104). Once ratification was accomplished, this process became a precedent for those in power. "Pragmatism" was, and remains, the "common sense" excuse used by government and its officials to stretch or sidestep the law when it becomes convenient. In fact, the arguments given at the Convention to sidestep the Articles became a good template for future extralegal actions.

The extralegal process had Federalist justifications (Rakove 1996:101–103), which, through the looking glass of Federalist history, may sound reasonable today. But this process did not slip by unnoticed. There were Convention members like William Paterson and John Lansing who raised legitimacy issues, as did some members of state legislatures and members of the population at large. Those who opposed the Constitution and its method of ratification, became known as the Antifederalists. This label, which they opposed, wrongly suggested an opposition to a national identity and to federal governance.

> [T]he "unconstitutional" procedure of the Convention was attacked by the Anti-Federalists. "A system of consolidation," says another writer, "has been formed with the most profound secrecy and without the least authority: And has been suddenly and without any previous notice transmitted by the federal convention for ratification—Congress not disposed to give any opinion on the plan, have transmitted it to the legislatures—The legislatures have followed the example and sent it to the people. The people of this state, unassisted by Congress or their legislature, have referred to the newspapers for information, have been divided by contending writers, and under such circumstances have elected members for the state convention—and these members are to consider, with all its imperfections, and bind the people by a system of government, of the nature and principle of which they have not at present a clearer idea then they have of the Copernican system" (Beard 1963[1913]:224–225).

Madison had anticipated the ratification process even before the Convention was called (Rakove 1996:103). As Brown (1993:200) observes, "From the beginning, the Federalists realized that ratification of the Constitution would be an uphill struggle." At the Convention's conclusion, Federalists reasoned that if they moved quickly before the opposition could organize, they had their best chance of success. "In late August Gouverneur Morris had urged the Convention 'to hasten their deliberation to a conclusion' so that this session of the assembly could arrange the immediate election of a ratifying convention. Any delay was dangerous, Morris warned; the more 'the people have time to hear the variety of objections' the Constitution would evoke, the more 'doubtful' its fate would be" (Rakove 1996:94).

Antifederalists became aware of Federalist tactics. "[T]he 'Federalist Farmer' suspected that the unseemly haste with which the framers had returned to their states to 'precipitate measures for the adoption of a system of their own making' proved the need for caution" (Rakove 1996:114). Opposition to the Constitution began before it was even read in Congress because of those Convention delegates, like Mason and Randolph, who had opposed it. Other strong opponents, who also carried political clout, included Richard Henry Lee and Elbridge Gerry. Lee's and Patrick Henry's skepticism had run so deep that they had refused to serve as delegates to the Convention. Patrick Henry, the most radical republican of some renown, was greatly feared by the Federalists who worried that he would "poison and prejudice the lower orders of the people" (in Brown 1993:209).

But the Constitution, as the Federalists had planned, was quickly passed to state legislatures who were to call state conventions for ratification or rejection. In some cases ratification was quick, but in each case, until nine states had ratified, the Federalists were organized and on the spot adapting their strategies to the circumstances raised in each state. Antifederalists, caught off guard, were not as well organized and many in their ranks, being from western rural areas, did not even hear about the contest until it was over. Nonetheless, Antifederalists nearly stopped ratification of the Constitution (Rakove 1996:114–116).

Because much of the Antifederalist opposition was rural and travel onerous, many Antifederalists had a difficult time getting to their state legislatures to voice their opposition and stand for election to their states' conventions. These Antifederalists knew of the original Convention but were under the impression that the Convention had authorization to only offer amendments to the Articles, which then had to be unanimously approved by the state legislatures. Under these rules, Antifederalists had few worries that changes would occur, at least quickly.

Much of the Antifederalist opposition took one of two general forms: the radical Whig republicans argued that state legislatures and the people had the right to discuss and debate the proposed Constitution article by article and to offer amendments. Other Antifederalists commonly rejected the very idea of the Constitution because it represented a strong central government and the potential for abuse.

One Federalist tactic that worked well after the Constitutional Convention adjourned was to have state legislatures quickly call for the election of delegates to state conventions. In several states, eligible voters had but a few days to cast their ballots, and then the state conventions met quickly and ratified the Constitution. In other states, the Federalists took extreme measures to have the Constitution ratified. In Pennsylvania, when the state assembly gathered to elect delegates for a state convention, some members argued that the procedure was irregular. When the opposition lost the vote, the Pennsylvania legislature moved to call a convention but then adjourned and left the details of the state convention until the afternoon. The opposition decided to stay away from the afternoon session thus preventing a quorum and further planning.

> The Federalists in the legislature, now having secured the sanction of regularity, determined not to brook further delay, so they sent

> officers after some of the recalcitrant, who thought "filibustering" justifiable in view of the importance of securing more deliberation before acting. These officers, ably assisted by a Federalist mob "broke into their lodging, seized them, dragged them through the streets to the State house, and thrust them into the assembly room, with clothes torn and faces white with rage. The quorum was now complete." The legislature . . . fixed the election of delegates to the state convention at a date five weeks distant. . . . Thus the people of the state were given a little over a month to deliberate on this momentous issue before selecting their agents to voice their will (Beard 1963[1913]:231–232).

Although the Pennsylvania state convention promised to publish their minutes and deliberations, these were, instead, concealed and only an abbreviated accounting was eventually published. In addition, Federalists "withdrew their subscriptions from every publication that warmly supported the Antifederalist cause" (McMaster and Stone in Beard 1963[1913]:232–233). This did not stop vigorous dissension in Pennsylvania to the Constitution, which included riots and violence, ending with the Whiskey Rebellion during Washington's presidency (Beard 1963[1913]:232–234). Other states also resisted quick passage of the Constitution with Rhode Island being the last to confirm. As momentum built for passage, it became more difficult for those reluctant states to resist, largely out of fear of being economically, politically, and militarily isolated.

The Constitution was never submitted to the people for a popular vote of ratification. If it had, in spite of the post-Revolution restrictions on suffrage, the Constitution most likely would have failed to pass. As it was, even with the manipulation and scheming tactics of the Federalists, the passage of the Constitution nearly failed. Had all adult Americans been able to vote there seems to be little doubt that the Constitution would have overwhelmingly failed.

> [I]t was exceedingly doubtful whether, upon a fair canvass, a majority of the people, in several of the states which ratified the Constitution, actually favored its adoption; that in the powerful states of Massachusetts, New York, Pennsylvania, and Virginia, the majority in favor of the new frame of government was very uncertain, so uncertain, in fact, as to raise the question whether there had been any majority at all; and that everywhere the voters of the states were sharply divided into two well-marked political parties. . . . Only those publicists concerned with the instant need of political controversies have been bold enough to deny that the fundamental law of the land

> was itself the product of one of the sharpest partisan contests in the history of the country (Beard 1943[1915]: 2).

But for all of the issues in the debate over ratification, there can be no doubt that social class divisions were prominent. The Federalist elite supported ratification and the middle and lower classes, who comprised the vast numbers of Antifederalists, opposed it. These class divisions were deep and bitter before the Revolution and did not change after passage (Brown 1993:208–211). Apologists often deny class conflict by omission and by stating that in the end America needed a unifying constitution. As Rakove (1996:230; also see Brown 1993:222–233) reveals, "Whatever else might be said about the legality or illegality of this process, it produced a completely unambiguous result that ensured that the Constitution would attain immediate legitimacy." Rakove (1996:128–129) elaborates saying,

> The adoption of the Constitution has been described, with good reason, as the result of a series of acts that were illegal, even revolutionary, in character. Refusing to be bound by either the requirements of Article XIII, or the sanctioning resolution of the Continental Congress, or the formal credentials of their states, the framers seized the main chance and then developed procedural and conceptual innovations to give their revolutionary act as much legitimacy as they could muster. . . . Their stroke was not a coup d'état but a demarche—a sudden bold movement that shifted the country from a condition of political torpor and entropy into a feverish burst of activity. Yet in the end, as the legal scholar Bruce Ackerman has ably argued, the framers and many Federalists also knew they could never defend their decision to abandon the Articles of Confederation in strictly legal terms. Madison conceded as much in *Federalist* 40, when he observed that "in all great changes of established governments, forms ought to give way to substance, for a rigid adherence in such cases to the former, would render nominal and nugatory the transcendent and precious right of the people to abolish or alter their governments as to them shall seem most likely to effect [*sic*] their safety and happiness." . . . In the critical situation in which the framers were placed, they would have deserved far more blame had they "taken the cold and sullen resolution . . . of sacrificing substance to form," Madison concluded. Even if all the charges of subversion that Anti-Federalists leveled against the framers were true, "does it follow that the Constitution ought, for that reason alone, to be rejected."

So much for strict constructionism. Madison's sentiment is exactly what is meant when, over and over again, historians tell us that the Framers were pragmatists or realists. With regard to Madison, Rakove (1996:37) tells us that "his political intelligence was eminently pragmatic." "[S]ubstantial and successful upper-class rural property holders and commercial farmers favored the Constitution over the Confederation system because it promised a more energetic, stable, efficient central government that could protect their property interests and provide a hospitable environment for the market-oriented commerce in which they were already involved" (Brown 1993:211).[18]

But for Brown, and many others, this is not enough motivation to explain the American elites' support for the Constitution, even knowing the questionable and extralegal methods the Federalists used to achieve ratification. "Influential as these economic concerns were, the Framers' commitment to the revolutionary mission of building an enduring Republic was an equal if not more important motivation" (Brown 1993:222). Brown's final caveat returns the heroic mantle to the Framers' shoulders.

This kind of characterization of the Framers sounds benign and reasonable but the fact is that economic motives and the desire for republican government can be much the same thing, depending on the meaning of "republic." We must remember what most historians and other scholars are so willing to overlook—that the kind of people we are talking about were often a ruthless, high-minded, and greedy group. They had few qualms about making money on the backs of the common people through enslavement and slaughter or simply holding their noses and turning a blind eye to those who suffered. This suffering was often unimaginable. All the while these men condemned the victims (the "mob") so that a few could live in luxury.

These condemning words are themselves inadequate. What does it actually mean to be poor and be kept poor, enslaved, slaughtered, and publicly derided? Americans have learned to live with these conditions, leave them out of their history so they are forgotten, or convince themselves that some lesser people are deserving of such treatment or that their suffering was and is the exception or simply the conditions of the time. The historical record is filled with the misery perpetrated by the American upper class against their less economically substantial fellow citizens, many activities that are alive and well today. The Framers created a system that rewards the most ruthless and leaves those kinds of people with wealth and the reins of power.

That Americans have any kind of republican government can be credited mainly to common Americans, even if they were often not allowed in the halls of power. These Americans, like other common people in the Western world, were tiring of noble tyranny. The average American had advantages over their European counterpart in class struggle, one being that they were armed and another being that they were wealthier. That common Americans at times resorted to violence, or the threat of violence, was an important element in leveraging progressive republicanism into the Constitution, and it seems clear if they had had their way the new Constitution would have been friendlier to their lives. Apologists have argued that had the Constitution been more republican the wealthy class would have supported monarchy. While this may contain some truth, historically there were strong tensions between the merchant class and royal authority (see Gouldner 1970:61–78).

As we will see in the next chapter's discussion on the Bill of Rights, American social class tensions have never ended. It has at all times in American history resulted in violence, sometimes exceeding the violence of Shay's Rebellion. Throughout this text, we will be reminded in graphic terms just what this Constitution has wrought in the hands of the politico-economic elite. It runs the spectrum from unfairness to bloodshed. The extralegal reasoning that accomplished the US Constitution is not confined in American history to this particular moment, for, among other things, we can remember internment camps for Japanese Americans and, more recently, the Patriot Act and torture. America has a long list of such "pragmatic" and expedient acts that sidestep the law and almost exclusively favor the American elite and their wealth. Some of these pragmatic acts will surface as we continue to review the history of American justice.

Although we will not give a lot of ink to speculating on what would have happened had the Articles remained the governing document, the dire scenarios provided when such speculations do occur are suspect. No one ever seems to take note that all of Europe has, until recently, been a geographical area of totally independent states without even the benefit of an Articles-like union. And yet history has worked out at least as well for them as for us. The American states, unlike the Europeans, would have had the advantage of sharing the same language and culture and, for defense, the Atlantic Ocean. Beard (1963[1913]:188) concludes, "To carry the theory of the economic interpretation of the Constitution out into ultimate details would require a monumental commentary. . . . But enough has been said to show that the concept of the Constitution as a piece of abstract legislation reflecting no group interests and recognizing no economic antagonisms is entirely false. It was an economic document drawn with superb skill by men whose property interests were immediately at stake; and as such it appealed directly and unerringly to identical interests in the country at large."

Notes

1. The irony here is that Randolph was a staunch Antifederalist who was maneuvered by Madison's flattery to propose Madison's plan as the Randolph plan, getting Randolph to introduce the program that came to be known as the " Virginia Plan." Randolph did not sign the Constitution.
2. Interestingly, after Madison speaks, "Docr. Franklin" makes a strong argument for broader suffrage (again, not for everyone) invoking the expectations of common Americans who sacrificed in the Revolution and warning of the "great uneasiness" that would occur when citizens were excluded from voting (Farrand 1966[1911] vol. II:205).
3. "While the rights of property occupied a central place in Federalists' thinking, it was far from being the sum total of their philosophy. Their range of vision was more spacious: it embraced the Good Society in all its aspects, political, social, and economic. The Federalists' objective was to mold the United States in accord with their vision of an established order securely protected against demagogues and democratic majorities. This vision took the form of a highly aristocratic, class-conscious society in which gentlemen knew their privileges and the lower orders knew their place – the price, the Federalists insisted, of order, stability, and progress" (Miller 1988[1960]:117).
4. Rakove (1996:33–34) tells a different ending to Shay's Rebellion. He claims that "government forces easily prevailed" by which he meant the Massachusetts militia. Brown (1993:25) says that, "In October 1786 Congress voted to borrow $500,000 by selling 6 percent bonds to private subscribers and asked the states to pledge money for repayment by voting tax funds. These measures were to finance an emergency increase in the federal army. The money from the loan was to pay and equip 1,340 new troops requisitioned by Congress on the states to help put down rural disturbances in Massachusetts (Shay's Rebellion) and to guard the federal arsenal at Springfield from possible seizure by the rebelling farmers. But the loan and the requests for taxes proved a total failure."
5. "The popular discontent of the mid-1780s was not limited to western Massachusetts. Other New England farmers protested in Connecticut, New Hampshire, and Vermont. In Rhode Island the debtor movement actually gained control of the legislature and forced the state to issue paper money. [Paper money was one of the major disputes between Federalists and Antifederalists, with Federalists fearing that paper money, through inflation, would reduce the wealth they gained through lending (see Ferguson 1961:19).] Governmental leaders in New York, North Carolina, and Georgia debated whether to circulate paper money in their own states in order to escape the wrath of indebted farmers. In New Jersey debtors attacked the courts at several locations. . . . In York, Pennsylvania, 200 men armed with guns and clubs took back cattle that had been seized by the government in

lieu of taxes. In Maryland 'a tumultuous assemblage of the people' closed the Charles County court. Debtors stopped court proceedings in the Virginia counties of King William, Greenbrier, and Amelia; James Madison wrote that 'prisons and courthouses and clerk's offices' throughout the state were 'willfully burnt.' After the court was closed in Camden, South Carolina, Judge Aedanus Burke believed that not even '5,000 troops, the best in America or Europe, could enforce obedience to the Common Pleas.' The distress of the farmers, who still thought of themselves as 'the body of the people,' was real and widespread" (Raphael 2001:390–391).

6. A recent example of the Court choosing to ignore well-established federal precedent in favor of "states' rights" is the *Whitner v. North Carolina* case (1992) where an addict mother was imprisoned because her newborn showed traces of cocaine in blood samples. State and federal appellate courts, before and since, have thrown out such prosecutions based in large part on *Roe v. Wade* (1972), a federal ruling.
7. By the time Andrew Jackson (of the Democratic-Republican Party, the Party of Jefferson, or "Democrats") was elected as a "people's" President (1829), states' rights enjoyed somewhat of a political resurgence. Though the differences between the two political parties are commonly exaggerated in American history, the Democrats did expand the franchise to include all white males. This change in political atmosphere tipped the country toward Antifederalist sentiments (though Antifederalism as an anti-constitutional movement was, by then for all practical purposes, dead), which included a stronger emphasis on state autonomy. With Jackson's appointees to the Court, some minor concessions were made to state jurisdiction rationalized by reference to the Tenth Amendment. The slavery issue, best known, became associated with states' rights and was used in justifying the continuance and expansion of slavery and later Jim Crow. This sentiment towards states' rights continued after the Civil War when Andrew Johnson, a southerner, rose to the presidency with the assassination of Lincoln. Johnson used the presidency, under the guise of state prerogatives, to hinder Reconstruction and support Jim Crow laws. Even though the Tenth Amendment and states' rights issues continue to be raised even today, the general situation was decided in favor of federal supremacy when the Constitution was written.
8. Lash (2009) argues exhaustively that the Framers went to great lengths to preserve states' rights citing especially the Ninth and Tenth Amendments. While this may be true in a historical and constructionist sense it was never true in a political sense. It seems clear that Federalists talked a good game about states' rights when it came to getting the Constitution ratified by the various states but never had any intention philosophically of following through with their promises of strict construction.
9. "After returning from the war, Marshall's burgeoning nationalism was reinforced by his experiences in the Virginia legislature. He was especially disturbed by Virginia's effort to repudiate the war debts owed to American merchants and to British creditors before the Revolution. Marshall was also alarmed by Shay's Rebellion, the antitax uprising in Massachusetts that Jefferson had glorified, which struck Marshall as an another example of the dangers of unchecked local mobs. All of these excesses of localism,

Marshall confessed, helped him appreciate the parts of the newly proposed U.S. Constitution that made federal law supreme over state law, and persuaded him to participate as an elected delegate to Virginia's constitutional rarifying convention. As a delegate to the convention, he warned about the dangers of unchecked democracy and argued in favor of judicial review. By the end of the convention, Marshall had defended the constitutional doctrines that would define his tenure on the Supreme Court: the advantages of national power, the dangers of localism, the importance of judicial independence, the sanctity of property and contracts, and the centrality of fair judicial procedures" (Rosen 2006:42–43).

10. "The first six men who actually decided cases on the Supreme Court differed in background, experience, and personality, but they shared four attributes. All were staunch Federalists; all had participated in framing the Constitution or campaigned for its ratification; all belonged to or represented the creditor class with wealth in land or finance; and all believed that government's primary function was protecting property rights from the debtor class of workers and small farmers. In these respects, these justices shared little with 'the people' in whose name the Constitution was framed" (Irons 1999:90).
11. As Ellis (2004:7, 115) notes, John Marshall was Washington's first serious biographer and "wrote the definitive Washington's biography of his time and subsequently imposed, for all time, Washington's version of America's original intentions." A great admirer of Washington, Marshall had served as a lieutenant in the Revolutionary War with some distinction. Marshall was to carry the Federalist agenda forward through such writings but more so as Chief Justice, even after the Federalists were turned out of office in 1800.
12. As recounted in Chapter 2, the war debt was in no small part held by Hamilton's Federalist friends in the form of securities, many of which they obtained quite cheaply.
13. Unknown to most modern Americans, colonial Americans drank considerable amounts of alcohol. The reasons are several but prominently include the European tradition of avoiding water, which was often contaminated in European sources, and also as a preservation technique as we see with western farmers and their grain. Early colonial farmers usually had orchards and, since fruit is quickly perishable, they would ferment the fruit juice so that the alcohol would preserve their product. Hard cider was the early preferred drink at every meal, even for children. Because of the primitive state of medicine, alcohol was also frequently used as a painkiller. If the reader can imagine having none of the modern pain killers, including aspirin, ibuprofen, etc. for chronic pains and nothing (opiates come later) for serious pain, it is more comprehensible that Americans would use alcohol for this purpose. Alcohol as a painkiller was used by Americans well into the twentieth century for both physical and psychic pain. The author's grandmother had the common habit of keeping a bottle of whiskey "hidden" under the kitchen sink for "medicinal" purposes.
14. The Senate became so corrupt in cultivating the interests of the wealthy that in the same year that Beard published his book (1913) the public clamor for popular election of the Senate was finally realized in the passing of the

Seventeenth Amendment. In some modest way this event was seen as a victory for the interests of common Americans.

15. This is also called a "single-member-district plurality system."
16. As a general rule, Americans have had poor electorate turnout. In looking at examples of early nineteenth-century election turnouts, Keller (2007:72, 80) observes that "[t]he presidential election of 1820 brought out 568 Baltimore voters (of a population of 63,000). Richmond (population 12,000) produced 17 votes; 9 percent of potential voters for state and local elections were common in Virginia, Maryland, and Massachusetts. Two-thirds of Virginia's congressional seats in the early 1820s were uncontested." It was not until the Jackson election that about half of the eligible voters turned out to vote, a proportion that remains about the same in today's general elections.
17. Specifically, and for example, *Time* (October 29, 2007:72) reported that the US ranked 41 out of 171 countries for women who die from complications in pregnancy or childbirth. The US death rate—1 in 4,800 women—is far higher than the European average of 1 in 16,400. Likewise, European crime and imprisonment rates are far below the United States. Rich Lowry, in the *Time* (November 19, 2007:51) article "The World of Hillary Hatred," writes, "When she [Hillary Clinton] adopts a standard left-wing position, it is taken as confirmation of her plans to impose a Euro-socialism on America." This statement reflects precisely what the American elite have feared since the Founding.
18. Brown "argue[s] that the Framers anticipated various benefits from the Constitution, including economic benefits. Certainly, the strong, steady central government established by the Constitution would enhance property, and real estate. It would establish a stable climate necessary for a prosperous commerce which the fear of paper money had greatly inhibited. The possibility that the state governments would sooner or later repudiate their public and private debts would also be dispelled. Some Framers had investments in state or federal debts which now would be secured. Some had mercantile businesses and law practices that would stand to gain if stable currency and economic prosperity returned" (Brown 1993:222).

5

The Bill of Rights: Origins and Early Federalist Resistance

The Bill of Rights stands as the high temple of our constitutional order—America's Parthenon—and yet we lack a clear view of it (Amar 1998:xi).

In the first century of our nation's existence, the Bill of Rights played a surprisingly trivial role (Amar 1998:290).

Given the nature and composition of the men who drew up the Constitution, it should come as no surprise that a bill of rights was only briefly considered. George Mason and Elbridge Gerry raised the subject of a bill of rights in the last days of the Convention, asking that such a bill be placed in the Preface to the Constitution. But their proposal was dismissed by every state delegate still attending the Convention. As Wood (1998[1969]:536) observes, "Even what semblances there were in the Constitution of a bill of rights, such as the prohibition against *ex post facto* laws, had been opposed by some delegates as irrelevant and useless provisions that would only bring 'reflections on the Constitution.'" The Framers' opposition to a bill of rights confirmed Antifederalist fears that the Federalists intended to produce a strong centralized government unencumbered by protections for individual liberties and states' sovereignty (Wood 2009:66).

As Miller (1988[1960]:20) comments, the Federalists were concerned "that a Bill of Rights would prove to be an entering wedge for amendments to the Constitution that would cripple the Federal government," especially compromising property and contract rights, as had already happened in some states. Madison, in pondering these concerns,

> drew upon his experience in the Virginia assembly and his observation of the course of legislation in other states. His concern

> about the security of private rights was rooted in a palpable fear that economic legislation was jeopardizing fundamental rights of property. Paper-money laws, debtor-stay laws, and the specter of Shay's Rebellion, all alarmed him terribly. So did the grim prospect he sketched at the Federal Convention when he warned that even in the United States a factious majority might eventually form from "those who will labour under all the hardships of life, & secretly sigh for a more equal distribution of its blessings." The constitution writers of 1776 [Virginia Constitution] had erred in assuming that by protecting "the rights of persons" they would also protect "those of property." Now he understood "that in all populous countries the smaller part only can be interested in preserving the rights of property." Although other classes of rights still concerned Madison, his analysis of the dangers to property was paradigmatic for the program of reform he carried to Philadelphia in May 1787 (Rakove 1996:314).

In part, the Federalist strategy was to argue that the various states' bills of rights were more than sufficient to protect American liberties. Federalists argued that rights and liberties did not have to be reiterated in the US Constitution, even though they knew that the US Constitution had been created with supremacy and necessary and proper clauses that effectively trumped state laws. Thus, state constitutions and their bills of rights were no real threat to the patrons of federal power. This point was not lost on Antifederalists who knew that if the principles of liberty required governmental restraint there was no reason to exclude any particular governmental level.[1]

Redundancy with state constitutions was not the Federalists' only argument. They publicly reasoned that the American people should rely on the tradition of individual liberties that came down to them by custom from English history and law. To try to enumerate all rights, the argument continued, would be to limit them. Unless every right and liberty could be specified unambiguously, "it would be implying, in the strongest manner, that every right not included in the exception might be impaired by the government without usurpation" (Wood 1998[1969]:537). This argument, taken seriously by Antifederalists, provoked the Ninth Amendment and its attempt to make sure that by enumerating certain rights, other rights were not lost: "The enumeration in the Constitution of certain rights, shall not be construed to deny or disparage others retained by the people" (US Constitution, Ninth Amendment). Regardless, many Justices on the Court have argued that rights not explicit in the Constitution do not exist.

The Federalists persisted, arguing that a bill of rights was unnecessary because in America all power is "of people and by the people," even though the Federalists had gone to great lengths to make this assertion erroneous. Nonetheless, echoing the former sentiment in the *Federalist Papers (No. 84),* Hamilton said of a bill of rights that "according to their primitive signification . . [they] have no application to constitutions, professedly founded upon the power of the people, and executed by their immediate representatives and servants. Here, in strictness, the people surrender nothing; and as they retain everything they have no need of particular reservations." In other words, the Federalists were quite willing to use the rhetoric of radical republicanism to get the Constitution passed without a bill of rights. Antifederalists were not fooled as they understood the difference between a law passed by the legislature, which could be changed at the whim of that body, and a constitutionally established right that required great effort to alter (Rakove 199:304, 307–308).

If basic liberties and natural rights could not be protected reliably by the executive—a fact colonists discovered while subjects of King George—and the legislative process was fickle and limited—what the House might pass the Senate or President could veto—, then the only other governmental option for protecting citizens' rights, short of revolution, seemed to have been an independent judiciary. Even this protection is often more rhetorical than reality as the executive and Senate have a great deal to say about who will be appointed to preserve the people's rights. As we will see, the Supreme Court often did (and does) an abject job of protecting individual rights and liberties, being more concerned with the interests of their corporate and wealthy patrons. Thus noted, rights and liberties, in order to be maximally protected, must be instilled in the Constitution itself.

The deliberate avoidance of a bill of rights was a major misstep by the Federalists, given the deep historical treasure of individual rights and liberties that are second nature to anyone of Anglo-American heritage. Moreover, Americans had just fought a revolution against Britain because the Crown and Parliament did not protect or observe those rights. That the Constitutional Convention had abandoned a bill of rights was proof to Antifederalists of the Federalist intent to create a powerful central government that would serve the interests of the Federalist elite. Reflecting this concern, many states highlighted bills of rights when seceding from the rule of the British Crown and drawing up constitutions.

Richard Henry Lee, an Antifederalist and member of Congress when the Convention submitted the Constitution for distribution to the states, immediately appreciated the lack of individual rights in the Constitution and quickly offered amendments to correct it (Rakove 1996:109). Lee, more so than Madison, might very well be considered the Father of the Bill of Rights. "Lee avoided broad statements of natural rights and first principles. Instead he detailed the specific rights that needed explicit protection: freedom of religious conscience and the press; prohibitions on excessive bail, cruel and unusual punishment, and unreasonable searches and seizures; assurances of free elections, independent judges, and the right to petition; and restrictions on standing armies in peacetime" (Rakove 1996:318). Lee also proposed that "the declaration of rights . . . should affirm . . . the right to trial by jury in criminal and civil cases and other common law protections in criminal prosecutions 'shall be held sacred'" (Rakove 1996:318–319).

As noted, these rights are deeply entrenched in Anglo-American history and tradition, which did much to enhance the Antifederalists' position. "The language of rights came naturally to the colonists—it was, they thought, their native tongue. As eighteenth-century writers repeatedly argued, the original English settlers had carried all their rights with them, and passed these rights on to their descendants as a birthright and a patrimony" (Rakove 1996:290, 297; also see Keller 2007:13–16).

Thomas Jefferson, the credited author of the Declaration of Independence (Keller 2007: 32), and Patrick Henry lent their significant credibility and popularity to the Antifederalist demand for a bill of rights. "A bill of rights," said Jefferson, "is what the people are entitled to against every government on earth, general or particular, and what no just government should refuse, or rest on inference" (in Wood 1998[1969]:537). In drafting the Declaration of Independence, Jefferson and his co-authors "drew on the ideas and language of a century-long radical tradition: The English Declaration of Rights of 1689, the writings of John Locke, the deism of the Enlightenment" (Keller 2007: 32).

The Declaration of Independence

> was the tip of an iceberg of grievance welling up in the American colonies. About a hundred mini-declarations of independence appeared between April and July 1775, reflecting an old Anglo-American tradition of petitions and declarations. George Mason's preliminary version of the Virginia Declaration of Rights in 1774 had

> many of the most potent phrases of the Declaration's preamble. The fact that Congress heavily edited Jefferson's draft, eliminating about a quarter of the original text (including a condemnation of the slave trade and some of the more extravagant accusations of royal villainy) may have toned down the Declaration's revolutionary substance. But it certainly improved its political potency, and even its language, with changes such as "certain inalienable rights" for "inherent inalienable rights" (Keller 2007:33).

In the Declaration and its historical context, we view the adamancy and depth of rights and liberties in American ideology and thus understand the reaction to a Constitution with these liberties and rights missing. Interestingly, the Federalists predicted that such rights, in their opinion being frivolous, would be violated by the government, the law notwithstanding. This often turned out to be true but not against the property rights so important to the elite.

The Jury: The Cornerstone of Liberty

In American minds, individual rights were far more numerous than what are now found in the Constitution. Nevertheless, Antifederalists felt that the complexity and confusion of unenumerated rights could be dealt with, in part, by two preeminent rights. These included the right of the people to have elected representation in government and the right to an indictment and trial by a jury of peers when facing criminal charges. Throughout history both of these rights have been compromised, beginning when elected representation was limited by Constitutional design.

The right to a grand jury and trial by peers has been constrained by the historical institutionalization of the judicial system. Today, for example, because of the judicially directed silence of defense counsel, juries are largely unfamiliar with jury nullification, a jury's right and duty to step above the law, if necessary, in seeking justice for fellow citizens (see Conrad 1998). "Jefferson argued that ordinary citizen jurors, where they suspected self-dealing or other agency bias on the bench could constitute themselves as judges of both fact and law. . . . 'It is left therefore to the juries, if they think the permanent judges are under any biass [*sic*] whatever in any cause, to take upon themselves to judge the law as well as the fact'" (Amar 1998:130–131).

Developing the jury's responsibility further, Conrad (1998:46–47) argues that "[t]he Sixth Amendment itself implicitly recognizes the right of criminal trial jurors to judge the law." Citing *Jacob's*

Law Dictionary, a common authority in defining the jury, Conrad (1998:46–47) records,

> Juries are fineable, if they are unlawfully dealt with to give their verdict; but they are not fineable for giving their verdict contrary to the evidence, or against the direction of the court; for the law supposes the jury may have some other evidence than what is given in court, and they may not only find things of their own knowledge, but they go according to their conscience. . . . The right of jurors to judge "according to conscience," then, was implicit within the word "jury" as the drafters of the Bill of Rights understood it. . . . The contemporaneous definitions of the word 'jury' have largely been neglected by courts seeking to determine the powers intended for the jury by the authors of the Sixth Amendment.

A trial by a jury of one's peers was supposed to arrive only after the Constitutional right to a grand jury indictment—also by one's peers—had decided that the state had enough evidence to prosecute.[2] "[J]uries existed first and foremost to protect the people against the abuse of power by an arbitrary Crown" (Rakove 1996:294). The sanctity of the jury in Anglo-American heritage is reflected in the number of appearances it makes in the Bill of Rights. "Juries, guaranteed in no fewer than three amendments, were at the heart of the Bill of Rights. The Fifth Amendment safeguarded the role of the grand jury; the Sixth, the criminal petit jury; and the Seventh, the civil jury" (Amar 1998:83).[3]

Today it is not the abuse of the Crown that is of concern but the abuse of prosecutors harboring political ambitions and the predisposition of judges reflecting elite conservative ideology. To this day, even though guaranteed by the Constitution, not all US citizens are afforded the right to a grand jury indictment. "The 'strong and twofold barrier' of requiring indictment by one jury and trial by another, Blackstone told his readers, was the 'the sacred bulwark' erected between the 'the liberties of the people, and the prerogative of the crown'" (Rakove 1996:300–301). Even in states where grand jury indictments are required, it is a well-known fact that prosecutors normally get the indictments they want, often because jurors do not know the process, philosophy, or rights foundational to the juror's duties and obligations.

Perhaps the greatest blow to the sanctity of the jury in criminal cases is the plea bargain. Coupled to the fact that Americans are still not protected against excessive fines and bail, common Americans are often given the choice of remaining in jail for weeks or months or pleading guilty to a crime they did not commit. Given the importance of juries in Anglo-American history, it seems clear that if the government is going to charge a citizen with a crime then it must prepare and present evidence first to a grand jury and then a petit jury. Citizens should not be placed in coercive situations where they are compelled to waive the rights guaranteed in the Constitution. In upholding a prosecutor's right to threaten defendants with horrendous sentences if they do not accept pleas offered by the state, the Court has effectively nullified the Bill of Rights, the very rights meant to protect citizens from a coercive and abusive government.[4] "The issues of jury review and jury waiver exemplify the vast erosion of jury power along any number of doctrinal and practical dimensions. Juries stood at the center of the original Bill of Rights but sit on the periphery today" (Amar 1998: 108–109).

The Bill of Rights and Its Constitutional Status: *Barron v. Baltimore* (1833)

The fight over ratification of the Constitution was so close, even with Federalist duplicity, that Madison finally gave in and promised Edmund Randolph of the Virginia legislature that he would support a bill of rights if Randolph would support ratification of the Constitution (Irons 1999:65). This promise conveyed that the first meeting of the Congress under the new Constitution would provide a bill of rights. Madison took it upon himself to write this bill, describing it in a letter to Richard Peters as a "nauseous project of amendments" (Amar 1998:289; Levy 1999:12). "In all, 124 amendments were submitted by the states. In the first Congress, Madison introduced eight resolutions, only five of which were relevant to a bill of rights. The House of Representatives adopted seventeen proposals; the senate rejected two and consolidated the remainder to twelve, and these were accepted by the House and were submitted to the states, which ratified only ten" (Konvitz 2001:8). How the Bill of Rights might have differed had Richard Henry Lee, Patrick Henry, or Thomas Jefferson written them is subject only to speculation, but it seems likely that the enumerated rights would have been more numerous and strongly stated (Hoffert 1992:184–186).

Beyond a nebulous impression that the Constitution was passed and a Bill of Rights included, most Americans know little of Constitutional history, especially as it relates to the Bill of Rights. Since the passage of the first ten Amendments, some conservative critics have questioned whether these amendments are even part of the Constitution and, if they are, have questioned how much authority they carry (Rakove

1996:288). Madison, himself, was not particularly impressed with the Bill of Rights' authority and predicted that they would be easily violated. His prediction was correct but not because of the failures of human nature as Madison alleged, but because the powerful have often ignored these rights at their convenience.

It has been the common belief that the Bill of Rights, except for the Tenth Amendment[5], was a broad grant of individual rights to the American people, a guarantee that government could not infringe on those enumerated (First through the Eighth Amendments) and unenumerated (Ninth Amendment) personal liberties. With the unanimous ruling in *Barron v. Baltimore* (1833) the understanding was expressed by the Court and Chief Justice Marshall that the Bill of Rights constrained only federal powers, not the authority of the states. Since the *Barron* ruling, many historians have accepted Marshall's opinion as the obvious fact and have sometimes applied their understanding retroactively, suggesting that this had always been the historical perception. This interpretation is commonly supported by the wording found at the beginning of the First Amendment, which states that the "Congress shall make no law." Even if this phrase is taken literally to mean that only the federal government is restrained, the same literalism cannot extract this meaning from the other nine amendments.

More recently, Lash (2009) has argued at great length that the Bill of Rights was not a concession of individual rights but is more correctly understood as protecting states' rights and sovereignty. Lash (2009:30) contends that historically "it was . . . common to equate the 'retained rights of the people' with the retained rights of the people in their respective states." Lash's (2009:35) argument was that Antifederalists, concerned with preserving the sovereignty of the states, demanded a Bill of Rights that "bound only the federal government.' Specifically, Antifederalists demanded strict construction in the reading of the federal powers specified in the Constitution. As Lash (2009:100) continues, "The burden . . . is to explain the common understanding of the founders that delegated federal power was to be narrowly construed in order to preserve the retained rights of the people in the states." Federalists, according to this view, were trying to limit federal power by demanding the strict construction of federal powers on the one hand and preserving the rights of the people in the various states through a bill of rights on the other.

Lash's analysis is compelling as far as it goes. However, Antifederalists' first concern was not state sovereignty, per se, but protection from abusive centralized power, an example of which had just been defeated in the Revolution. Preserving states' rights or state sovereignty was a method whereby individual freedoms would be doubly preserved. First by restricting federal power by preserving state sovereignty through the strict construction demanded by the Tenth Amendment and secondly through a direct demand for rights both enumerated (the First through the Eighth Amendments) and unenumerated (the Ninth Amendment). These extreme measures to guard individual rights makes sense when understanding the threat of Federalists' centralism faced by common Americans, and given the historical experiences Anglo peoples had with centralized power in centuries past. It makes very little sense that Antifederalists would go to such lengths to protect their individual freedoms and then leave the backdoor open for state abuse.

Barron v. Baltimore (1833), then, is an historic instance of how an important legislative initiative (the Bill of Rights), representing the interests of common citizens, was obstructed by a constitution designed to facilitate elite interests. In a unanimous decision by a Federalist Court, in an opinion written by the Federalist Chief Justice John Marshall, the Court concluded that the rights and liberties guaranteed in the first Ten Amendments to the Constitution only applied in federal jurisdictions, that the Bill of Rights did not protect citizens from state encroachments on their liberties. Even though the Bill passed the House of Representatives and Senate and was approved by three-quarters of the states' legislatures, the Court effectively neutralized the Bill of Rights.

Though the Federalist Party began to lose power with the election of Thomas Jefferson in 1800, Irons (1999:100–101) remarks that "the Federalists did not lose everything.... During his single term in office, Adams had the opportunity to place three justices on the Supreme Court." In 1798, Adams appointed Bushrod Washington, President Washington's favorite nephew. Bushrod had studied and practiced law and was a Federalist only thirty-six years old when appointed to the Court where he served until his death in 1829. The second Adams appointment came in 1799 when he chose Alfred Moore, a prominent Federalist from North Carolina who served until 1804. The third and historically most important appointment by Adams, which occurred just before he left office in 1801, was of John Marshall, also an ardent Federalist. Marshall, who had no judicial experience, served as Chief Justice for thirty-four years and used the power of the Court to appreciably affect the body politic. In effect, Adams created a Federalist watchdog on a Federalist-constructed status quo at the crucial time when the new government was becoming established and institutionalized. This scrutiny by the high Court helped the Federalists to assert and maintain their basic polity even while being voted out of office.

Marshall, who had been an aide-de-camp to General Washington during the Revolutionary War, was a flamboyant and charismatic character in his youth (Ellis 2004:115) and a Federalist Secretary of State before being appointed to the Supreme Court. As Irons (1999:101) explains, "Marshall and the Court he commanded swept away every dam and levee that state lawmakers, the Congress, and five presidents constructed in his path." A dedicated Federalist, Marshall used his position to implement Federalist ideology even though his party had lost the presidency and legislative majority. The most poignant of these Federalist assertions came in the *Barron* case.

> Marshall, of course, had voted in the Virginia ratification convention against Antifederalist demands for a bill of rights. But with the Fifth Amendment before him for interpretation, he took the "safe and judicious" course of deciding that it "is not applicable to the legislation of the states." . . . The Court's unanimous decision in *Barron v. Baltimore* came near the end of Marshall's long tenure as Chief Justice. His opinion attracted little notice in 1833 and little discussion since then; one recent history of the Supreme Court relegated the *Barron* case to a footnote. Most constitutional scholars have simply assumed that Marshall reached the right conclusion in this case and that those who framed the Bill of Rights had not intended to protect the people against oppression by the states as they did from Congress. *But Marshall was a fervent nationalist and almost always gave an expansive reading to the Constitution. It would have been more in character for him to force the states into compliance with federal standards. However, he had little respect for the rights of 'the people' against the government—state or federal. Forced to choose between these countering principles, he did not find "much difficulty" in rejecting the argument based on individual rights* (Irons 1999:136; emphasis added).

The first Ten Amendments to the Constitution containing the Bill of Rights were made impotent for nearly one hundred years because of the Supreme Court ruling in *Barron*. As Irons suggests above, the decision was ideological in tenor and was meant to block an avenue through which constitutional initiatives of a substantial order could pass; that is, the Federalists did not want citizens making claims to rights in state jurisdictions that might compromise private property and contracts. From a Federalist point of view, the Constitution and the Court worked as designed and to their ends.

This history of the Constitution is curious and should be pondered before continuing (see Amar 1998). We must ask why governmental authorities of the early nineteenth century were so casual about the Constitution, evidently following some parts, ignoring others, and narrowing or broadening interpretations to suit the demands of the powerful. How is it that the first ten amendments can be treated as if they are not part of the Constitution or, if recognized, are seen as somehow being less restrictive regarding the states? It seems apparent that these were political and not judicial decisions, which set an important precedent for future Constitutional law and practice. The Marshall decision in *Barron* is one of the most damaging precedents imposed on ordinary American citizens (Irons 1999:134–136). As Irons noted above, Marshall was a nationalist who strongly believed in central power except when he did not like it, as in the case with the Bill of Rights. Even more unfortunate, Marshall's bald political maneuvering involved the most sacred clauses of the Constitution, which he manipulated for partisan reasons. Yet Marshall is heralded as a great American jurist. Regrettably, thirty-five years after *Barron* we can find similar maneuverings with the Fourteenth Amendment.

The Fourteenth Amendment and the Incorporation of the Bill of Rights

I try to show how the Reconstruction Amendment transformed the nature of the original Bill of Rights, leaving us with something much closer to the Bill as conventionally understood today (Amar, 1998: xiii).

For thirty-five years after the *Barron* decision, American jurisprudence existed in a kind of Constitutional confusion. Taking *Barron* to its strictest construction, much of the authority of the Constitution could have been confined to federal jurisdiction as the Antifederalists had demanded. In the *Barron* ruling Marshall stated that the Constitution was "established by the people of the United States for themselves, for their own government, and not for the government of the individual states" (in Irons 1999:135). This kind of constriction of the Constitution to federal jurisdiction was not always the case nor does it typically represent Marshall's philosophy. "The Framers had placed in the Constitution, in Section 10 of Article 1, several express limitations on state powers. One of them . . . barred states from passing laws 'impairing the obligation of contracts,' a provision Marshall had used to strike down many state laws' (Irons 1999:135). In a similar fashion it would have been consistent for Marshall to limit the states by applying the Bill of Rights to their powers.

The traditionally conservative court was maintained after *Barron* and property rights were preserved as the sacred first principle of the Constitution overshadowing states' and individual rights. The Court continued to pick and choose what it thought appropriate and ignored or narrowly defined what it did not like, a pattern that continues today. In a very real sense the US government has become a tyranny of five; five justices in the majority can effectively nullify Constitutional precedent, Constitutional Amendments, and democratically-created legislation and even overthrow elections.

House Representative John Bingham's motives in writing the Fourteenth Amendment were laudable and clear. His purpose was to protect and restore freed slaves to full citizenship by overthrowing *Barron* and restoring the Bill of Rights as part of the supreme law. "In a speech in January 1867, while the Fourteenth Amendment was pending in the states, Bingham again reminded his audience that his Amendment would overrule Barron" (Amar 1998:183; also see 203).

Before extolling its virtues, however, it is important to remember that the Fourteenth Amendment is, in part, a reiteration of the original Constitution. The "supremacy clause" of Article VI states, "This Constitution, and Laws of the United States which shall be made in Pursuance thereof; and all Treaties made, or which shall be made, under the Authority of the United States, *shall be the supreme Law of the Land*; and *the Judges in every State shall be bound thereby, any Thing in the Constitution or Laws of any State to the Contrary notwithstanding*" (emphasis added). Correspondingly, the Fourteenth Amendment affirms, "*No state shall make or enforce any law which shall abridge the privileges or immunities of citizens*" (emphasis added). In other words, the first Ten Amendments were already the "supreme Law of the Land . . . [the] Laws of any State to the Contrary notwithstanding." Given the clear statement of Article VI, it would seem apparent that the Bill of Rights did not need incorporation.

Through various strained contortions, historians have tried to follow the Court's decisions in this matter and give it some kind of intelligence and reason. Like the *Barron* ruling, which ignored the supremacy clause and minimized the Bill of Rights, the Fourteenth

Amendment, meant by its author to reinstate the Bill of Rights, was restricted by the Court's ruling in the *Slaughter-House* cases (1873). In a maneuver reminiscent of *Barron,* the *Slaughter-House* decisions "interpreted" the Fourteenth Amendment and the "privileges or immunities clause" so narrowly as to again leave the Bill of Rights impotent against state authority.

It is practically impossible to come to any other conclusion than that the Court was deliberately voiding the Bill of Rights yet again. In *Slaughter-House* the Court held that the "privileges or immunities clause" only created a distinction between rights associated with state citizenship and rights associated with federal citizenship. "It concluded that the Fourteenth Amendment prohibited states from passing laws abridging the rights of US citizenship—which it implied were few in number—but had no authority over laws abridging the rights of state citizenship. The effect of this ruling was to put much state legislation beyond the review of the Supreme Court" (www.legal-dictionary-thefreedictionary.com/Incorporation+Doctrine) thus again minimizing the Bill of Rights.

Such maneuverings make little sense except in the context of Court and class politics. In this regard, Court politics have rendered the Constitution a malleable tool for the powers that be. It is clear that, from the beginning, the American elite did not want a Bill of Rights and when a Bill was used as leverage to get the Constitution passed, their Federalist President, with the approval of their Federalist Senate, appointed a Federalist Chief Justice who, along with other Federalist judges, effectively nullified those same Rights. Even with another Constitutional Amendment meant to reinstate these Rights, the Court simply ignored the clear direction of the Fourteenth Amendment.

The Constitution, which by 1791 included the Bill of Rights, was to be the first, final, and supreme law of the land. As such, American citizens should have always had the protections, liberties, and privileges proscribed by the Bill of Rights. Other rulings before *Barron* seem to support this conclusion.

> In the fifteen years before *Barron,* a considerable number of lawyers implied in passing or stated explicitly that various provisions in the Bill did limit the states' powers. Writing for the Court in 1819, Justice William Johnson obliquely suggested that the Seventh Amendment's guarantee of civil juries applied to states; and the following year he stated even more explicitly in a separate concurrence that the double-jeopardy clause "operates equally upon both [state and

> federal] governments." . . . That same year . . . the New York Supreme Court stated in dictum that the double-jeopardy clause "operates upon state courts" even where both prosecutions were for state-law crime, and in 1823 the Mississippi Supreme Court appeared to agree. In 1824, this view of the double-jeopardy clause was pressed in the Massachusetts Supreme Court, yet neither the government's attorney nor the judges appeared to challenge it (Amar 1998: 145–146).

Evidently, such cases did not set a precedent to be followed by Marshall. Often, the argument has been made in defense of Marshall's decision that the literal wording of the Bill of Rights references only the Congress regarding its application. If this literal interpretation is to be applied, then it only pertains to the First Amendment, not to the other nine. In the context of Anglo-history, however, such a literal interpretation makes little sense. Antifederalists demanded a bill of rights to protect their natural and inalienable liberties and privileges from all abusive governmental authority, not just the federal government. When constructing the Bill of Rights, Madison originally included an amendment that explicitly prohibited the states from violating those rights. Since the Federalist Congress ignored this depth and clarity we are again reminded that the constitutional quintessence is political and hence malleable to power, not simply a reflection of the idealism ordinary Americans assume.[6] Nonetheless, by 1868 this literalist argument should have been moot.

The Fourteenth Amendment, which is not ambiguous, is a remarkable text that best reflects the kind of sociopolitical republican system desired by the ordinary American. Passed into law on July 9, 1868, the Fourteenth Amendment has never come into full effect. Excluding those sections of the Amendment that deal with the rebellion (Civil War), war debt, and the enforcement of the Amendment (Sections 3 through5), the Fourteenth Amendment reads in Section 1:

> All persons born or naturalized in the United States, and subject to the jurisdiction thereof, are citizens of the United States wherein they reside. No state shall make or enforce any law which shall abridge the privileges or immunities of citizens of the United States; nor shall any State deprive any person of life, liberty, or property, without due process of law; nor deny to any person within its jurisdiction the equal protection of the laws (US Constitution).[7]

The third sentence of Section 1 ("No state shall . . .") essentially reaffirms the Supremacy clause and clearly includes the Bill of Rights.

Contrary to the Congress' intent, however, the Fourteenth Amendment did not incorporate the Bill of Rights for many decades to come.[8] The courts would simply ignore what the Congress mandated in the Fourteenth Amendment (Amar 1998:213) and continue to ignore it well into the twentieth century. It is likely that the Supreme Court, composed of and representing society's elite, still feared rights as wedges that might compromise property and contract interests.

As Domhoff (2010[1967]:109–111) discloses, the American upper class has a great deal of control over the federal judiciary. It is true that because of lifetime tenure, federal judges are independent but Domhoff demonstrates elite influence through three major avenues. In the first instance, the American elite have a great deal of influence on who is nominated and elected president of the United States. They do not have to contend with a multiparty system but can focus their considerable wealth and influence on two broadly middle-of-the-road political parties and thus strongly encourage the election of candidates that support the status quo. This influence goes a long way in narrowing who will be nominated to sit on the Court.

Second, the American elite have considerable control on who sits on the Committee of the Federal Judiciary of the American Bar Association. This committee has substantial influence in evaluating at a very early stage the search for candidates who might sit on the federal courts. Members of this committee are appointed by the president of the American Bar Association. This exclusive funnel assures that only persons with "proper" credentials will ever be in the line for nomination.

Finally, John Schmidhauser's study of the ninety-two Supreme Court justices between 1789 and 1959 reveals that the justices came "from socially advantaged families. . . . In the earlier history of the Court, he [a Justice] was very likely was born in the aristocratic gentry class, although later he tended to come from the professionalized upper-middle class. . . . It seems reasonable to assume that very few sons of families outside the upper, or upper middle, social and economic classes have been able to acquire the particular type of education and the subsequent professional, and especially political, associations which appear to be unwritten prerequisites for appointment to the nation's highest tribunal" (from Domhoff 2010[1967]:110–111). As a result, the Court resisted incorporation of the Bill of Rights even in the face of glaring law and Congressional pronouncements to do so. Indeed, this is exactly how the Framers would have the system work, to discourage legislation and judicial actions that might threaten their interests.

The major reversal in Constitutional philosophy that began with the Fourteenth Amendment occurred as a result of the disruptive circumstances of the American Civil War. It is during major social upheavals that ordinary Americans often make sociopolitical and economic gains that may run contrary to elite interests. After the Civil War came the Progressive Era and the Great Depression, both of which increasingly pushed Constitutional philosophy toward individual and human rights at the expense of property rights (Irons 1999:233–330). Correlated, and contributing to this history, was the rise of the American middle class (examined in Chapter Six). With the growing numbers of educated and informed persons in the population who also had considerable collective wealth, the interests of the elite were more successfully challenged.

The Espionage Act of 1917 is recognized in American history as the major impetus that initiated the Court to move toward incorporation of the Bill of Rights[9], commencing specifically with the First Amendment (Irons 1999:267–288)[10]. The Espionage Act was passed because World War I was very unpopular and resulted in loud opposition. It was this resistance that the Espionage Act was meant to stifle. "The Espionage Act was not directed against spying for the enemy, but imposed maximum terms of twenty years in prison for anyone 'who shall willfully cause or attempt to cause insubordination, disloyalty, mutiny, or refusal of duty in the military or naval forces of the United States, or shall willfully obstruct the recruiting or enlistment service of the United States.' The law's sponsors—and government prosecutors—argued that any criticism of the government's wartime policies might induce draft-age men to refuse military service" (Irons 1999:267). In 1918, in response to a federal judge's favorable ruling in a Montana case for a defendant charged under the Espionage Act, the Congress amended the Act by adding a "sedition" clause. It outlawed "any disloyal . . . scurrilous or abusive language about the form of government of the United States . . . or any language intended to bring the form of government of the United States . . . into contempt, scorn, contumely, or disrepute" (Irons 1999:268).

The war had scarcely ended before the first challenges to the Espionage Act arrived at the Supreme Court. In cases like *Schenck v. United States* (1919), *Debs v. United States* (1919), *Abrams v. United States* (1919), and others, First Amendment protections had been invoked by defendants. Decisions in these cases went against the defendants' First Amendment rights but nevertheless forced the Court to confront these issues and narrow the reasons under which the government's interest outweighed the individual's First Amendment right to free speech and press. In *Gitlow v. New York* (1925) the Court forwarded the opinion that the First Amendment right to free speech and press had been incorporated by the Fourteenth Amendment. Following in a piecemeal fashion, the Court in subsequent rulings came to protect other First Amendment rights against state authority.

Although average Americans commonly believe that the Bill of Rights protects them from all levels of government intrusion, some elements have yet to be incorporated. In fact, none of the Bill of Rights has been incorporated in any absolute way. Moreover, some protections in the Bill have not been incorporated at all (e.g., the right to a grand jury indictment and the right to bail and fair fines). Today, the Court continues to hear Bill of Rights cases and, in some instances, to restrict liberties and privileges. In fact, arguments over the meaning of the Bill persist.[11]

Notes

1. For a good review of state constitutions and their bills of rights see Levy 1999:9–10.
2. See Rakove's (1996) account of the Penn case in 1670 and discussion on page 300.
3. "What's more, trial by jury in all federal criminal cases had earlier been mandated by the clear words of Article III: 'The Trial of all Crimes, except in Cases of Impeachment, shall be by Jury.' Indeed, the entire debate at the Philadelphia convention over whether to add a Bill of Rights was triggered when George Mason picked up on a casual comment from another delegate that 'no provision was yet made for juries in civil cases.' Between the close of the Philadelphia convention and the opening of the First Congress, five of the six state ratifying conventions that advanced amendments put forth two or more jury-related proposals. State constitutions further confirmed the centrality of the jury. According to Leonard Levy's tally, the only right secured in all state constitutions penned between 1776 and 1787 was the right of jury trial in criminal cases. We should also note the emphatic words of the Declaration of Independence, condemning George III and Parliament '[f]or depriving us, in many cases, of the benefits of trial by jury.' . . . Spanning both civil and criminal proceedings, the jury played a leading role in protecting ordinary individuals against governmental overreaching. Jurors would be drawn from the community; like the militia they were ordinary citizens, not permanent government officials on the government payroll. Just as the militia could check a paid professional standing army, *the jury could thwart overreaching by powerful and ambitious prosecutors and judges. In the words of one Anti-Federalist pamphlet, 'Judges, unencumbered*

by juries, have been ever found much better friends to government than to the people'" (Amar 1998:83–84; emphasis added).

4. See the PBS Frontline video, *The Plea* (2005).
5. The Tenth Amendment reserves all powers not specially given to the federal government to the various states.
6. Amar (1998:140–145) makes this traditional argument defending Marshall's opinion in *Barron* that the Bill of Rights was not written as a constraint on state powers.
7. Interestingly, Bingham uses gender neutral language in the first section, which by itself gave women—not just former slaves—full rights of citizenship, which would include voting and military service. In Section 2 Bingham inadvertently, perhaps, allows states to take the vote away from women but not other rights. That it took another hundred years for women and minorities to feel the effects of the Fourteenth Amendment says much about the political nature of our legal system.
8. "Over and over in the years between 1868 and 1873, various members of Congress, both Democrats and Republicans, suggested that the Bill of Rights defined paradigmatic privileges and immunities of Americans that no state could abridge and the Congress could protect by legislation under Section 5 of the Fourteenth Amendment. This was no idle chatter, for Congress in fact legislated on the basis of this understanding. . . . In light of this reigning ideology, consider the now familiar words of Section 1983 of Title 42, first adopted as Section 1 of the act [*sic*] of April 20, 1871, known as 'An Act to Enforce the Provisions of the Fourteenth Amendment to the Constitution of the United States, and for other Purposes.' The clear words of this Section prohibited state officers from depriving persons of 'any rights, privileges, or immunities secured by the Constitution.' Given declaratory theory, this Enforcement Act section plainly obliged states to honor rights proclaimed in the federal Bill" (Amar 1998:208).
9. Technically, incorporation of the Bill of Rights began with *Chicago, Burlington, and Quincy Railroad v. City of Chicago* (1897)
10. Amar (1998:227–230) gives a more thorough history of the First Amendment, tracing its movement toward incorporation back to *Spies v. Illinois* (1887).
11. "Two centuries later the framers' oversight [of providing a bill of rights in the original text] appears even more striking because disputes over the interpretation of the Bill of Rights pervade constitutional law and theory. These disputes are part of a broader debate about Americans' marked propensity to assert their claims in a language not merely of legitimate interest or net public good but of absolute entitlements. 'Rights-talk,' as it is called, has its adversaries and advocates. To such critics as Mary Ann Glendon, rights-talk impoverishes 'our political discourse' through 'its starkness and simplicity, its prodigality in bestowing the rights label, its legalistic character, its exaggerated absoluteness, its hyperindividualism, its insularity, and its silence with respect to personal, civic, and collective responsibilities.' To its advocates, like Ronald Dworkin, the belief that rights are 'trump' provides a principled basis for assessing the claims that individuals and groups make in both public and private realms of life" (Rakove 1996: 288–289).

6

The Rise of the Middle Class

Only those could be trusted who earned their living by "honest industry" and who were men "in middling circumstances" (Main 1961:10).

The most valuable class in any community is the middle class, the men of moderate means. (Walt Whitman 1858 in Main 1961:1).

As noted previously, Revolutionary America was largely a bifurcated society with a large population of people of modest means and a small class of wealthy gentry. There was also a small and developing middle class referred to as "mechanics" largely composed of artisans, tradesmen, small shop owners, some farmers, and lower level professionals (Main 1961:2–4). Although dire poverty was not uncommon in this era, most common Americans lived plain and simple lives. Their existence was largely unassuming and humble and they were disfranchised in the broadest sense. Often, the common American could not vote and had little influence on the direction of the society. They lived in an everyday state of concern, often walking a fine line between grumbling and demonstrating in a fashion that sometimes turned violent.

By the time of the Revolutionary era, the American gentry had become socially delineated. They were a well-educated, high income or wealthy aggregate with a lifestyle that segregated them psychologically and materially from ordinary American life. They were plantation owners, merchants, traders, bankers, and some successful professional people. Significantly included in this group were privateers, smugglers, slave traders, and rentiers. Their peers ruled at the local and colonial levels, largely as a means of safeguarding their property and economic interests.

Still in its infancy during the Revolutionary period was the American middle class—the "middling sort" or "mechanics." During this time the term "middle class" seldom appeared on the printed page and probably was not often uttered in either the city or the country. Rather, a variety of less precise and usually plural phrases expressed the idea of social intermediacy—"people of middling ranks," the "middling sorts," "the middle condition of mankind," and occasionally the "middle (or middling) classes" (Blumin 1989:1; also Bledstein 2001:3–11). From a modern perspective this group is now referred to as the "old middle class" and roughly coincides with the American antebellum period.

These middle-class people were largely comprised of skilled tradesmen or artisans, some with their own enterprises, and included farmers of some commercial success (Main 1961:4, 5; Mills 2002[1951]:5). As Bridenbaugh (1950:155) affirms, "Contemporary Englishmen defined the mechanic arts 'as such Arts wherein the Hand and Body are more concerned than the Mind.'" While the poor artisan worked for wages, the successful artisan owned his own shop and might have hired a few employees (Lynd 2009[1967]:83; Mills 2002[1951]:7). On the lower end of the "old middle-class" were the "trades"—skilled laborers commonly involved in manufacturing a product. This would include such people as printers, shoemakers, and candlestick makers who worked for a shop owner and earned wages. They worked with their hands and lived a working class lifestyle. While in demand, the tradesman's manufactured products provided him with a secure living as compared to the poor—perhaps his own home, more furnishings and conveniences, and some education for his children. Mechanics who owned their own shop or business still worked side by side with their employees and, but for a higher standard of living, these employers would feel quite comfortable in the company of those workers to whom they paid wages (Ryerson 1978:203). In some cases, the mechanic could vote but this varied with his wealth and the definition of suffrage in his colony. As the Revolution approached, the mechanics' demand for the vote grew and their interests were more aggressively expressed.

The tradesmen and artisans, who owned their own businesses and made a comfortable living, as well as some successful farmers, might well pass into the upper middle class. The lines between the middle and upper middle classes are not particularly distinct because the lifestyles were blurred and varied with economic conditions. But the general body of the middle class was distinct enough in their way of life so as to be discussed with little ambiguity. As Blumin (1989: 3) concludes, "The all-encompassing American bourgeoisie . . . may well have been a class after all—the power of its values serving to reinforce rather than to destroy social class boundaries."

Some have defined the old middle-class so broadly as to make this class a majority of the population. Rather than defining mechanics as those between the gentry and the common people, some scholars have lumped mechanics with laborers and all farmers, thus greatly inflating their numbers (Lynd 2009[1967]:82). Mills (2002[1951]:7) counts every person as middle class who owned property but he is looking 50 to 60 years past the Revolution. Even then, property ownership cannot be the entire criterion of middle class membership. Certainly it is difficult to provide a clear and well-defined demarcation between the common American of the Revolutionary era and the old middle class, though it is easier to delineate between the old middle class and the American gentry. One can always provide specific examples of persons who stretch the common understanding, but this does not reasonably lead to the conclusion that mechanics, as a social class, composed 50 to 75 percent of the population as some suggest (Lynd 2009[1967]:82; Mills 2002[1951]:7–9).

Mills (2002[1951]:9) does strike an important note with the old middle class when he observes, "Within it no central authority allocated materials and ordered men to specific tasks, and the course of its history was the unintended consequence of many scattered wills each acting freely." The early middle classes, for all their burdens and uncertainties, were beholden to no person, especially no rich person. This resulted in a great deal of economic and political independence and allowed middle class people to assert their own interests. Some of the most dramatic examples were Shay's Rebellion, the Whiskey Rebellion, and Fries' Rebellion, all of which were composed of many middle-class farmers.

Mills (2002[1951]:10) goes on to remark that, "In the building of his new world, the enterprising [middle-class] individual had also to build a government that would guard him from centralized authority." As we have seen, this protection was initially achieved by adopting the Articles of Confederation, an action that was promptly challenged by wealthy Federalists who called for a constitutional convention and new constitution that created a strong central authority. The local control that ordinary Americans had won in the Revolution was quickly being eroded. Thus, a class conflict that was well established before the Revolution continued afterward but with the growing influence of a middle class. This class conflict has played out in American history with landmark events such as the ratification of the Constitution and Bill of Rights, the defeat of the Federalists in 1800, the election of Jackson in 1829, the *Barron v. Baltimore* ruling in 1833, the passage of the Fourteenth Amendment in 1868, the violent conflicts of the Progressive Era, the Constitutional Revolution of 1937, and the Due Process Revolution of the 1960s. This class struggle, which has always been a subtext in American society, often became a battle and continues today.

The middle class, then, was gradually being pulled and developed from the common aggregate of society. "An older tradition associated [the middle class] with very modest levels of social and economic aspiration, closer to the bottom of society than to the top" (Blumin 1989:1). Historians, who are not usually students of social strata, often struggle when trying to define the middle class. Regularly, humanists speak of a "middle-class culture" by identifying values and behaviors rather than more quantifiable characteristics like income, occupation, and education as found in the tradition of sociology. These latter quantifiable measures of the middle class, while providing some precision, have often ignored or minimized middle-class culture, values, and beliefs, which include a progressive republicanism. Beginning with the Declaration of Independence, the Constitution, and the Bill of Rights, the middle class also assumed the values of Temperance, abolition, the unionism of the Civil War, suffrage, Progressive Era reform, racial integration, and the Due Process Revolution at the mid-twentieth century. As the middle class grew, it could support progressive republican values by voting, engaging in social reform, volunteering for campaign activities, and providing campaign funds. Most significant in the twentieth century was the middle classes' support for the incorporation of the Bill of Rights. This significantly helped turn the country back in a progressive republican direction, developing a concern for human and individual rights.

The top end of the old middle class was blurred by the "professions," much as it is today. Only the most successful climbed into the upper classes where success was not simply a matter of wealth: one had to also "live right": not just a big house but with proper taste not just recreate in certain ways but in the right clubs and company, and not just highly educated but from the correct schools and universities. Central was a proper attitude about property, one that made wealth and a laissez-faire philosophy supreme to all else. This attitude about wealth is an important dividing point between the middle and upper classes. As Wolfe (1998:246) notes, "Very few middle-class Americans say . . . that [they] want to be rich. . . . [T]oo much wealth is like too much of anything else: a bad thing. People with too much money violate a deeply held middle-class belief in proportionality."

The Revolution and the Old Middle Class

The old middle class was maligned by the American gentry in a manner similar to the upper classes' stated distaste for the common American.[1] This animosity from the elite came in part from their commitment to the tradition of ranks. "Ranks were determined by birth (well-born), education (learned), manners (code of conduct), and to a less visible degree wealth (land ownership and/or mercantile enterprise). Different ranks, at least conceptually, were neither in competition nor in conflict, representing the essence of structure, order, and place—a fit calling—unlike the more mobile and open system of class designations a century later" (Bledstein 2001:5).[2]

This kind of categorical stratifying language did much to incite the situation. From their earliest beginnings, the middle class resented their genteel betters not only for their social arrogance but also, and in no small part, because the elite dismissed early middle-class organizations from political participation (Blumin 1989:17–18; see Ryerson 1978; Lynd 2009[1967]:31). As Wood (2009:29) observes, "[A]ll these tradesmen and other middling persons tended to be united in a common antagonism to the would-be aristocracy above them."

In major cities such as Boston, New York and Philadelphia, organizations or "committees" of mechanics were drawn into the politics of the pre-Revolutionary era by Whigs (or "radicals," as Ryerson (1978) refers to them) because mechanics' politics were also radical (Keller 2007:29–30). Lynd (2009[1967]:94–97), for example, states that the mechanics of New York found a kindred spirit in Thomas Paine, who was a former staymaker, because they agreed with Paine's expressed revolutionary philosophy (*Common Sense*) that advocated a more progressive republicanism. Paine explicitly stated that the franchise should be extended to the "people at large" (in Lynd 2009[1967]: 94) in selecting delegates to the Continental Congress, a proposal echoed by the mechanics' committees. Paine also advocated annual elections, rotation of office, equal apportionment, the secret ballot, popular election of all local officials, complete religious tolerance, and the abolition of slavery.

Lynd (2009[1967]:108) continues, "Becker was right, then, in his contention that mechanic radicalism began before the War for Independence and continued after it. Economically disadvantaged, socially excluded, only partially enfranchised, the mechanics sought by a variety of methods to influence the making of political and economic policy; by the mid-1780's, they were insisting on the election of men of their own 'class.'"

> In June 1774, a radical commentator wrote from Boston: "Those worthy members of society, the tradesmen [mechanics], we depend on, under God, to form the resolution of the other ranks of citizens, in Philadelphia and New York. They are certainly carrying all before them here. . . . This will insure a non-importation in this province, whether messieurs les marchands, will be graciously pleased to come into it or not"[3] (in Lynd 2009[1967]:90).

The American Whigs were composed of younger merchants of the gentry class who felt British restrictions on commerce more forcefully than their older, more established, and conservative peers. Mechanics felt the pinch of British restrictions and taxes even more than their young Whig counterparts because their business enterprises were smaller and more easily impaired. Because official political bodies were dominated by the wealthy and older conservative elite, Whigs and mechanics found it expedient to form unofficial committees to express their grievances (Ryerson 1978:25, 27).[4]

Ryerson (1978:31) observes that those who profited from importing British goods were eager to end the boycott and their efforts to do so only served to provoke a significant reaction from the middle class. "The importers' attempt to end the boycott united the community's many craftsmen and local manufacturers into one 'mechanical interest' for the first time in the city's history. Deeply concerned that a heavy importation of British manufactures would ruin the fragile prosperity they had built up during the boycott, the city's craftsmen eagerly responded."[5]

The crisis situation created by pre-Revolutionary activities opened the door for middle-class participation (Lynd 2009[1967]:58-59, 60–61, 92–108), an involvement allowed by necessity and because of the enthusiastic support mechanics gave to radicals of the merchant class. Philadelphia's major importers were simply outmaneuvered by radical organizers and overwhelmed by zealous mechanics. "The mechanics were ever-ready to back up their good advice with direct action" (Lynd 2009[1967]:94).

As observed with the recruitment of common Americans to the cause, the middle class was recruited by the elite to give population weight and, hence, credibility to their movement. Likewise, the middle class provided skilled persons to fill the needs of the growing political bureaucracy (Ryerson 1978:203–204).

> Charles Thomson observed that "the Committee . . . which was elected [in 1775] . . . was, for the purpose of giving them more weight and influence." Numbers did provide the basic muscle of Revolutionary politics, impress and persuade the public, and offer a broad range of expertise, but they gave the Revolution another dimension as well. A committee of one hundred men, organized into subcommittees based in the several wards in which their members lived and worked, could represent a city of twenty-five thousand in a way that no board of [elite] twenty could (Ryerson 1978:204).

With the leverage of necessity, the middle class became actively involved in Revolutionary committees as members and as leaders. This participation allowed mechanics to successfully run for elective office and thus to have significant influence on the kind of republican philosophy that emerged. "Greatly facilitating their control was the growing coherence of the mechanics. In August 1772, the artisans had formed their own political organization, the Patriotic Society, to promote candidates who would protect their rights and privileges against assault '*on [either] side of the Atlantic*,' and in October they placed artisans in six of the city's ten elected offices" (Ryerson 1978:34; emphasis added).

Even though the middle-class radicals joined the Whigs, they still understood that they had to look after their own interests against enemies both foreign and domestic. Part of this wariness led the mechanics to run their own ticket of candidates in elections. They organized themselves politically and independently early in pre-Revolutionary Philadelphia and forced the elite merchant class to take their middle-class members into what had been exclusively elite ranks (Ryerson 1978:204–205).[6]

While this transformation had its counterparts in New York and Boston, the influence of the middle class seems to have been greater in Philadelphia (Lynd 2009[1967]:88). Their radical republicanism is more recognizable to us as progressive republicanism, which as Ryerson notes, involved egalitarianism, individual rights, and a broader democratic franchise. It would be these "middling sorts," in league with some of their radical Whig allies, who would lay the foundation for Antifederalism (Lynd 2009[1967]:32). It would be this middle-class group who would be suspicious of the Constitution and who would demand a bill of rights. Though this radical mechanic group would lose ground after the Revolution through the creation of the federal Constitution, they did not lay dormant historically, but appeared over and over again to support Jefferson, Jackson, and the Progressives of the late nineteenth century and beyond. For the middle class there was not enough democracy (Wood 2009:31) and historically they have been a critical force behind progressive republicanism. In addition, ordinary Americans felt freer to make individual decisions in all kinds of social situations no longer bound by the traditions of the old colonial society.[7]

With the land boom after the war, by 1798 nearly half of free white men owned property, though the top 10 percent controlled almost half of all wealth (Appleby 2001:34), and more Americans experienced social mobility that supported their new egalitarian ideals. With increasing industrialization and urbanization, "[n]ew livelihoods carried an invitation to the sons and daughters of rural America to join the sprawling middle class of teachers, clerks, preachers, proprietors, lawyers, and physicians" (Appleby 2001:33).

Regardless of the disaffection of the Federalists, the body politic was changing, led less by the violence of the poor and disfranchised than by the participation of middle-class Americans who were upwardly mobile. Dissatisfaction and anger was being successfully channeled into institutionalized politics that allowed common men to participate. Notably this included a growing middle class that on one hand was motivated by progressive republican ideals but vested enough in the society to use peaceful means.

Post-Revolutionary America: The Federalists and Class Conflict

As noted previously, the American Revolution heightened the feelings of progressive republicanism among ordinary Americans. Appleby (2001:31) emphasizes that, "the Revolution had introduced a political philosophy subversive to distinctions based upon birth," thus setting the stage for post-Revolutionary class conflict. "The social struggle that took place during the three or four decades following the Revolution, especially in the Northern states of America, was essentially between these middling people and the American gentry who claimed to be 'exalted above the rest'" (Wood 2009:29).

The acceptance of progressive republican ideas and values not only set the stage for a new egalitarianism but extended radical change deep into the social structure. "[G]rowing numbers of ordinary folk used the popular and egalitarian rhetoric of the Revolution to challenge their so-called gentlemanly superiors" (Wood 2009:27). Common and middle-class Americans believed that the Revolution brought a republican emphasis on merit, which gave them as much right to govern as the aristocratic Federalists (Wood 2009:217). This greatly upset the more staid members of the socioeconomic elite and their Federalist political party. The Federalists' reaction to, or rejection of, not only progressive interpretations of republicanism, but social change in general, had the effect of stirring up ordinary Americans who came to be represented by the Jeffersonians, or the Democratic-Republican Party. Class conflict, defined here as friction (both ideological and behavioral) between those with substantial wealth and those without such wealth, became institutionalized—although without exactness—in American society in the two-party system.[8]

It has often been noted in American history texts that the Framers of the Constitution viewed the appearance of political parties as "a sinister turn of events. . . they regarded them as a source of weakness and division. . . . Had the ideals of the Framers been realized, the United States would have been a one-party state" (Miller 1988[1960]:99; also Keller 2007:48–49). As is the case in Miller, this notion of "the perfect union" is relayed to us as the high ideals of the Framers. "'If we mean to support the Liberty and Independence which it has cost us so much blood and treasure to establish,' Washington said in 1790, 'we must drive far away the daemon of party spirit and local reproach.' The objective of the men who assembled in Philadelphia in 1787 was to create a Union so perfect that the people would be united in furthering the national welfare" (Miller 1988[1960]:99).

While the Federalist ideal of a one-party state is undoubtedly accurate, and a powerful idea given Washington's support, to the Jeffersonian eye it was a formula for a dictatorship by the Federalist gentry (see Wood 2009:107–110). Miller's nationalistic interpretation does not change this fact, and certainly the Federalists, who had experienced colonial, state, and English governments, knew that parties were a natural outcome that often took on class overtones (Keller 2007:18–19). "In general, the Federalist spokesmen were the national-minded, conservative, well-to-do members of the community who believed that the cure for the 'excess of democracy' was a strong national government. If the aphorism 'those who own the country ought to run it [cited by John Jay]' had been realized, the Federalists were the kind of people who would have been installed in the seats of power" (Miller 1988[1960]:100).

Although sometimes hidden behind Federalist patriotic rhetoric, more frankly many of the Framers and supporters of a strong central government were also those holding "state and continental debt amounting to more than all the rest of the fluid capital in the United States. No less an important person than Washington assigned the satisfaction of the claims of the public creditors as the chief reason for the adoption of the Constitution" (Beard 1943[1915]:4–5). Without the support of those holding public debt, Washington, Hamilton, and other Federalists felt that the old Confederation would stand and the Constitution fail to pass. That many of these same men held substantial public debt has often been overlooked.

Given their suspicions of democracy, the Federalists were most wary of the Congress, especially the House of Representatives, which was that organization of government most closely embodying the common man and the growing middle class authority. The Senate, elected by state legislative bodies, thus focusing elite influence, was much less a worry and the Federalists were able to dominate and control these state legislative organizations. But it was the Executive branch that the Federalists perceived as their bulwark against democratic excesses, John Adams being one of the strongest advocates for a "strong executive" (Wood 2009:215–216).[9]

The fatal flaw in the Federalist Party was the coalition of northern merchants with southern planters. Hamilton's economic programs favored northern businessmen's speculations in government securities. "Hamilton himself admitted that his differences of opinion with Madison over discrimination between original holders and purchasers of government securities had 'laid the foundation of the great schism which has since prevailed.' Madison traced the quarrel to the same source: by encouraging the spirit of speculation, he said, Hamilton had 'wantonly multiplied' enemies to the Federal government and 'disgusted the best friends of the Union,' compelling them to choose 'between the loss of union, and the loss of what the union was meant to secure" (Miller 1988[1960]:101).[10]

Elite Federalists were a group too small to form a party of any substance so they were required to enlist non-elite Americans, much as they had during the Revolution. They tended to attract those elements of the old middle class who were most successful and nearer to the cities and large towns. This would include large commercial farmers, the artisan-businessmen, professional men, and small businessmen who had acquired some success. These persons would be most often the upwardly mobile and ambitious men who aspired to the ranks of the gentry.[11]

Only those more common men who aspired to such heights and abided such philosophy could withstand such snobbery and serve the Federalists loyally. The rank and file of the Federalist Party were also often attached by local politics or special issues like the abolition of slavery. Some were devoted to "high" Protestantism that correlated with nativism and a low opinion of human nature, an opinion that was especially attached to the poor and immigrant. "[T]he Federalists' principal sources of strength were that they had saved the country from 'chaos' in 1787–88; that they represented the forces of law and order against democratic 'levelism'; that they were the guardians of the rights of property and the upholders of the dignity and honor of the United States abroad. But the most precious asset of the Federalists was President Washington" (Miller 1988[1960]:122). Noting all of this, however, the Federalists began alienating their middle-class support by the end of the eighteenth century when, ignoring their more modest partners interests, they began taxing middle-class goods and products (Wood 2009:170–171).

"In the democratic state, as the Federalists viewed it, no one feared either God or government; instead, popular majorities ruled without let or hindrance and the sovereign people gave free rein to every whim and desire, however transitory and injurious to the public welfare. Federalists prided themselves upon being Fighters against Democracy: in their eyes, none were more worthy of honor than those who did battle against egalitarians and demagogues" (Miller 1988[1960]:111). John Adams may best represent this view or, at least, be the best known person who represented this view, which he expressed in social class terms. "Nothing," he told Jefferson in 1787, "but Force, and Power and Strength can restrain [common people]" (in Wood 2009:214; 215). Anticipating Social Darwinism, Adams believed that all men pursued selfish ends with little restraint, which resulted in a layering of society that reflected the success of such rancorous competition and conflict between commoners and gentry. Those at the top were naturally chosen to rule society.

Many of the middle class had shown themselves worthy of "temperate liberty" by accumulating some property and wealth, at least enough to get a tryout in the Federalist ranks. Because the Federalists feared "the mobbish workingmen of the cities, [they also] looked to farmers.... Like Jefferson, they regarded farmers as 'cautious and reflecting men' whose passions were moderated by the fact that they had a substantial stake in the country" (Miller 1988[1960]:120). The Federalist Party not only embodied a conservative concern for property rights and a fear of the "democratic mob," but also encompassed a dour outlook on human nature (Wood 2009:104), a general pessimism that moved them even further to the right and must have certainly turned many away from their party.[12]

If this sounds all too familiar, it is because this bitter, pessimistic, anti-democratic, heavy-handed authoritarianism exerted mainly through the executive and backed by the Court has reinvented itself repeatedly throughout American history in wealthy and conservative quarters.

> The Federalists never experienced the exhilarating sensation of riding the wave of the future; instead, they feared that they were about to be engulfed by that wave and to perish "miserably on the shoals of democracy"—the graveyard of republics. Seldom . . . was a Federalist politician a happy or optimistic man. Even in moments of victory, the leaders of the party were oppressed by forebodings of future disasters: they might win battles but they seemed certain to lose the war. Their work appeared to be built upon sand; in the United States, everything changed and, Federalists feared, for the worst. Keeping down the democrats in a country teeming with "faction and revolution" was to be an endless task much beyond the strength of a little band of gentlemen, however devoted to the cause of upholding reason and good order. George Cabot expressed a mood common among Federalists when he wrote in 1797: "Our friends have hope & even expect that things will all go well, but . . . I always expect the contrary." . . . Dismal as was the present, the Federalists feared that the future had even worse in store (Miller 1988[1960]:118–119).

By the end of the eighteenth century as Washington's second term was winding down, the split between Federalists and Democratic-Republicans had become so great that many feared armed conflict between the states. "As the Federalist and the Republican parties furiously attacked each other as enemies of the Constitution, party loyalties became more intense and began to override personal ties, as every aspect of American life became politicized. People who had known one another their whole lives now crossed streets to avoid confrontations. Personal differences easily spilled into violence, and fighting erupted in the state legislatures and even in the federal Congress" (Wood 2009:209). This animosity was not purely class conflict, but class conflict was certainly a major underlying factor. As seen, the Federalists wanted to maintain an elitist and wealth-dominated polity whereas the Democratic-Republicans, especially the northern Republicans, wanted a "citizens'" republic with liberty, equality, and justice broadly extended.

The Democratic-Republican Party: Jeffersonian and Madisonian Democracy

As political parties began to form in 1791, Jefferson and Madison seemed unlikely figures as the first choice to lead common, middle-class, and Antifederalist Americans who were wary of the Federalist gentry and their aristocratic airs. Once the Constitution was passed other issues came to the fore and "by early 1791 the press boiled with talk of the dangers of monarchy and monocrats—talk that resonated well beyond the world of the Southern planters concerned with slavery: many Northern middling sorts were also anxious about the dangers of monarchy and the kind of aristocratic society that accompanied it" (Wood 2009:146). This made for strange bedfellows but both southern plantation owners and the northern middle class were concerned about the appearance of a strong centralized government represented by the Federalists, though for different reasons. Southern growers worried that Federalism threatened the southern agricultural economy and the institution of slavery, whereas common and middle-class northern Americans worried that Federalism threatened democracy, which they felt was synonymous with local rule. With Hamilton's proposed national bank, opposition to Federalism, and the strong centralized government it represented "assumed a more strident and ideological character. . . . Everywhere there was a sense that the Bank represented a new and frightening step toward centralizing national authority and Anglicizing America's government" (Wood 2009:144).

The Federalist/Democratic-Republican division did not always fall neatly along Federalist, Antifederalist, or class lines. In fact, while various kinds of factionalism occurred during Washington's two terms, he avoided the formation of parties through his imposing stature, drawing the nation's attention toward making a success of the new government. "It was not until the administration of John Adams . . . that a real political party began to come into existence, and it was the alien and sedition laws that afforded Jefferson the opportunity to create a genuine political organization" (Beard 1943[1915]:13–14).

The Jeffersonian Democratic-Republicans were often depicted as the "champions of minimal government" (Miller 1988[1960]:72), but this seems in part true largely in contrast to the aristocratic Federalism of Adams and Alexander Hamilton, where the federal government was a tool for enhancing the wealth and power of the gentry/merchant class. Jefferson's opposition to the alien and sedition laws went a long way in demonstrating his progressive republican values, and hence his consideration of common people. Likewise, as the credited author of the Declaration of Independence and a supporter of the Bill of Rights, Jefferson was clearly contrasted with the heavy-handed and conservative republican values demonstrated by the Federalists. The Democratic-Republican Party, then, appealed to common Americans, perhaps most especially to the landowning farmers of the middle class.

For land-hungry Americans, Jefferson offered expanded Democratic-Republican rule with the promise of land ownership and an avenue into the middle class. Such agrarian romanticism, of course, overlooked the fact that Jefferson was hardly this kind of farmer himself. Indeed, his slave ownership makes duplicitous his claims to progressive republicanism and the democratic ideals that often cloaked him. But many other slave-owning southern planters supported Jefferson's party because of its emphasis on local democratic government.

Jefferson's agrarian idealism did not dispose him to look favorably upon the coming industrialization or the working people attached to it. This attitude he shared with Madison and the Federalists. Nevertheless, unlike his Federalist foes, Jefferson's democratic ideals and pragmatism allowed him to step aside if industrialism was the majority will of the people. "When victory depended upon the support of the 'degraded,' 'debauched,' and 'mobbish' workingmen of the eastern cities, Jefferson welcomed them as allies. He even permitted bankers to squeeze through the needle's eye and to wear the raiment of 'true republicans'" (Miller 1988[1960]:75).

Most telling when noting Jefferson's championship of minimal government was his devotion to Adam Smith's *Wealth of Nations*. According to Miller (1988[1960]:72), Jefferson believed that Smith's book was the best ever written on economics. Jefferson "eagerly embraced the philosophy of laissez faire, [and] he contended that government could best contribute to the public prosperity by letting individuals, businessmen included, manage for themselves." Jefferson also favored the adoption of the Constitution and in 1788 "pronounced *The Federalist*

Papers to be one of the greatest treatises on government ever written" (Miller 1988[1960]:70). As Miller (1988[1960]:71) continues, Jefferson "was of the opinion that the 'tyranny of the legislature' was more to be feared than the ambition and lust for power of the executive." That such a philosophy would unleash Hamilton's cohort seems to have been missed by Jefferson. If one did not conclude that Jefferson was a moderate Federalist, he would certainly seem to be eclectic or eccentric and maybe even naïve, unable inevitably to escape his class origins.

Madison, the other founder of the Democratic-Republican Party, was more "Federalist" than even Jefferson, though he may have had some progressive tinge as the assumed author of the Bill of Rights. As the credited author of the Constitution, Madison's nationalistic-centralist credentials were well intact. The difference between Federalist centralism and Democratic-Republican centralism was a matter of degree. The Democratic-Republicans gained a reputation for opposing "a strong, overbearing central government," as proposed by the Federalists, not opposing centralism per se. While Jefferson led the Party and received the glory and spotlight, Madison was the workhorse, defining the party's philosophy and crafting its tactics in Congress (Miller 1988[1960]:102–103). If both parties were "federalist," their differences were partially republican; the Federalists being conservative and the Democratic-Republicans more progressive or democratic in their philosophy, though Jefferson was much more "democratic" than Madison. More importantly, these parties represented different elite economic interests that also happened to be largely regional: the northeast merchants and growing industrialist Federalists vs. the planters and farmers of the south and west Democratic-Republicans.

The Democratic-Republican Party is often suggested as the party of the common Americans (Beard 1943[1915]:15), but this was largely true because of the many laborers and smaller farmers who gave their support. One could also argue that the Democratic-Republicans had a more sympathetic philosophy or progressive republicanism, even while supporting slavery.[13] "When Republicans declaimed against expensive government, they touched a deep cord in the American people; and when they defended local rights and privileges against the Federal government they were hailed as 'heroes of liberty'" (Miller 1988[1960]:104). However, the differences between these two parties were much more in degree rather than in kind. Both parties hailed the Constitution and lent their support to its veneration. The real difference seems to be between the economies of town and country.

But even this distinction was often nebulous as seen in the 1800 election when the Democratic-Republicans won power. In this election many former Federalist supporters voted Democratic-Republican because of Adams' and the Federalist Party's assault on the rights of citizens (Beard 1943[1915]:17).

Madison, unlike his Federalist counterpart, believed that factionalism was inevitable–"liberty is to faction what air is to fire"—and set about discovering how to use it (Keller 2007:25). Although the differences between Federalists and Democratic-Republicans were not ostensibly of class, class tensions were certainly implicitly apparent when the Republicans attacked the Federalists as touting aristocracy and monarchy. Of the Federalists, Madison publically wrote that they "are more partial to the opulent than to the other classes of society; and having debauched themselves into a persuasion that mankind are incapable of governing themselves, it follows with them, of course, that government can be carried on only by the pageantry of rank, the influence of money and emoluments and the terror of military force" (in Wood 2009:161).

In Philadelphia a Democratic-Republican Society was organized and encouraged the formation of other similar societies in the surrounding countryside. These societies demanded a general justice that would permeate the everyday culture of the new country and were decidedly oriented to the common social classes. "They were often composed of self-made entrepreneurs, mechanics and manufacturers, small-time merchants, farmers, and other middling people, angry at the aristocratic pretensions of many of the Federalist gentry" (Wood 2009:163). As Wood (2009:163) continues,

> These societies were more radical and outspoken than elite leaders like Jefferson and Madison, who tended to keep well clear of them. They represented a democratic future that few American leaders could yet accept or even envision. They challenged the older world of deferential political leadership and called for the people's participation in the affairs of government beyond merely periodically casting their votes. They told the people to shed their habitual awe of their so-called betters and to think and act for themselves. They adopted the French Revolutionary address of "Citizens" and resolved no longer to address their correspondents as "Sir" or use the phrase "Your humble servant" to close their letters. They took the notion of the sovereignty of the people literally and believed that the people had a continual right to organize and protest against even the actions of their own elected representatives.

Much of the radical republican fervor at this time in America was stirred by the French Revolution (Wood 2009:174–208), which helped formulate and define the Republican-Democratic movement. Federalists, on the other hand, were quite horrified, fearing that the French Revolution was a preview of what might happen in the United States. Jefferson aggravated the situation by openly supporting the French Revolution and had no issue with Louis XVI's trial and execution, symbolizing the death of monarchy.[14]

After the American Revolution radical republicanism was perhaps most overtly conveyed in what came to be the Republican press. There are few historians who would not agree that political publication in the post-Revolutionary era, on both sides, was particularly slanderous, defamatory, and malicious. It was often aimed at particular individuals, not just policy and ideology. For their part, the Federalists not only took such attacks as personal and offensive to their honor, but believed that such public criticism would undermine orderly government. As a result, they passed the Sedition Act to put a stop to such attacks. "The government arrested twenty-five persons and brought seventeen indictments of seditious libel against Republican journalists and editors (fourteen under the Sedition Act itself), of which ten resulted in conviction and punishment" (Wood 2009:260). These moves played right into the hands of Democratic-Republicans, greatly aiding Jefferson's election to the Presidency in 1800 and defeating many Federalists in the Congress. Likewise, the Republican press was not intimidated but actually increased its activities.

Though ostensibly political and often personal in nature, this press was frequently a thinly guised attack on social class. The Democratic-Republicans attacked Federalists as "monarchists" with "aristocratic" airs, the latter depiction considered especially derogatory. The Federalists for their part attacked the Democratic-Republicans as "democrats," which was akin to an accusation of mob rule. The Federalists also assailed immigrants and Catholics, people who were almost all poor and Democratic-Republicans, with the Alien Friends Act. It must be remembered that all of this post-Revolutionary turmoil was accented with three major armed rebellions: Shay's Rebellion in 1787, the Whiskey Rebellion in 1796, and Fries' Rebellion in 1799. All of these rebellions are typically depicted as tax rebellions, yet they also had a significant underlying element of class rebellion since the taxes opposed fell heavily on the middle and common classes.

Post Revolution, the middle class and other common Americans were not totally aligned with either of the existing parties, although most were Democratic-Republicans. This division is noted by Wood (2009:216) in describing Adams' contention that the American society was "divided between the few and the many. In fact, that was how many Americans in the 1790s had come to describe their society, as a contest between 'democrats and aristocrats,' which were the derogatory terms that the two emerging parties of Federalists and Republicans commonly used to label one another." Had the Democratic-Republican Party not included southern planters, this party conflict would certainly have been viewed as a class conflict.

Nonetheless, middle-class voters, while leaning heavily toward progressive republicanism and decentralized federal government, often voted by issue or region. This is not surprising since they were a small and a relatively politically weak group in a diverse party representing many groups (Wood 2009:167–168). However, the middle class was also growing and while the leaders of both parties were anticipating with trepidation the growth of the working class, they failed to foresee that industrialization would also grow a middle class that was in many ways unique and influential. This middle class would develop a culture of its own and, along with its growing wealth and increasing educational attainment, would become a political force to be reckoned with, though this would take more than a century and a half to come to full fruition. As Wood (2009:30) notes, "These middling sorts launched the momentous social struggle that eventually turned them into the dominant 'middle class' of the nineteenth century."

The Jeffersonian Revolution of 1800 and the Turn toward Popular Democracy[15]

With their constitutional victory in 1789 and their subsequent domination of the highest federal offices including the Presidency, the Congress, and the Supreme Court, the Federalists felt they had a mandate to impose their conservative brand of republicanism on the American society. Such deportment speaks volumes about Federalist arrogance. The democratic fever unleashed by the Revolution among common and middle-class Americans did not subside after the Revolution but was fanned into greater heat and flame by the Federalist efforts to suppress it. "Indeed, [the Federalists] were so out of touch with the developing popular realities of American life, and their monarchical program was so counter to the libertarian impulses of America's republican ideology, that they provoked a second revolutionary movement that threatened to tear the Republic apart" (Wood 2009:276).

Jefferson's election in 1800 unleashed a fervent optimism in most progressive republican groups. This encompassed a hope for a ground-level democracy geared to common people's needs and brought down to a local level. Consistent with his republican philosophy, Jefferson immediately dismantled the "royal" trappings of the presidency that Washington and Adams had acquired. Likewise, federalism was drawn back and a philosophy reflecting a "union of states" was to take its place. From the Federalist bureaucracy to the Federalist officer corps, Jefferson took steps to reduce and "Republicanize" them. Of great joy for common Americans, Jefferson eliminated "all the internal excise taxes the Federalists had designed to make the people feel the energy of the national government" (Wood 2009:293). He also stopped or greatly reduced patronage, which Jefferson viewed as Federalist corruption, and created a federal bureaucracy where men were hired or appointed for long tenure.

The relative decentralization of power and the minimization of government under the Democratic-Republicans met with broad public enthusiasm and increased participation. "Popular voting took on a significance that it had never quite had before, and the increased numbers of contested elections for both federal and state officials sent the turnout of voters skyrocketing" (Wood 2009:302). This was accompanied by an extension of the franchise in many states by eliminating property qualifications. Very disturbing to Federalists were not just the political and structural changes wrought by a Democratic-Republican victory but the cultural changes and the destruction of hierarchy and respect for traditional authority. "Vulgarity seemed to be spreading everywhere, and in their minds upstarts and demagogues and Jacobins had taken over the reins of government. 'We are sliding down into the mire of a democracy, which pollutes the morals of the citizens before it swallows up their liberties,' wrote a deeply pessimistic Fisher Ames" (Wood 2009:303).

The Federalists had always feared the democratic mob, a fear that was both political and cultural. As neo-Puritans, the American Federalist elite believed The Great Chain of Order gave them both ruling and cultural authority. They felt that common Americans lacked the natural or acquired abilities to rule and lived uncouth lives that drove a selfish self-interest that would lead to the chaos and anarchy exemplified by the French Revolution. This lower-class rabble would ultimately destroy the Revolution and republic that was guided by enlightened and (Protestant) God-fearing men. "They could not understand how so many uneducated and illiterate men were gaining elective office at the expense of men of talent and education. . . . What was most socially alarming about the new style of popular campaigning, said Webster, was that it could make a 'SOMEBODY' out of a 'MR. NOBODY.'" (Wood 2009:303, 304).

The Democratic-Republican revolution of 1800, as it is often called, was so forceful that many Federalists believed that they had lost power for good. Indeed, the Democratic-Republicans were to dominate the government until the election of the Whig William Henry Harrison in 1836. John Quincy Adams and others were so convinced of the demise of the Federalists that they changed parties. Some retired from office while more pragmatic Federalists held their noses and decided that they must engage in party politics and electioneering as their perceived lesser brethren in the Democratic-Republican Party had done. This latter group of Federalists had their way and the Federalists became established as a "practicing" political party.

In succeeding elections the Federalists continued to lose ground so that by 1820 they could not even nominate a candidate to run for president. As the Federalist Party fell apart there was room for a great social leveling of American society. Without doubt the common citizen's interests were heard and acted upon.

Common Americans benefited not only because of their political victories but also because of their growth by high birth rates and continuing immigration. The country was growing and moving rapidly westward and Westerners were not only largely of the common classes but generally had a strong ideology of individual freedom and egalitarianism that rejected the genteel culture of the Federalists. As western lands were opened up by the defeat of Native Americans, prosperity followed for average Americans. Fewer and fewer common Americans had to rely on lands rented from the wealthy and the economy became less elite-dominated, providing expanding enterprise opportunities for middle-class business persons and farmers alike, all of which they took to with great enthusiasm.[16]

Until the Civil War period, as we will see later, average Americans would hold their own politically, economically, and socially against their elite class counterparts, though there were often tensions and sometimes violence (see Wood 2009:333–334; 337–339). With the Civil War and rapid industrialization, this social balance would quickly be lost as the new industrial elite would amass vast amounts of wealth, and with that wealth they would dominate the American economy and polity. Likewise, the defeat of the South in the Civil War did much to handicap the Democratic Party that had represented Southern interests of decentralized government and slavery.

The Industrial Revolution and the Rise of the New Middle Class

Blumin (1989:11) identifies five characteristics that he describes as "areas of personal and social experience" from which he defines a mature middle class. These include "work, consumption, residential location, formal and informal voluntary association, and family organization and strategy—that would seem to encompass nearly all relevant aspects of an emerging middle-class 'way of life.'" It is not until the middle of the nineteenth century, argues Blumin (1989:12) that the American middle class solidifies as a social class. "Americans . . . of middling economic and social position were formed and formed themselves into a relatively coherent and ascending middle class during the middle decades of the nineteenth century."

Blumin (1989:13) divides the middle class into pre- and post-Civil War periods. "[A] middle class was not fully formed before the war, and that developments of the postwar period—most notably, widening differences between the worlds of non-manual and manual work, the expansion of middle-class suburbanization, and the resumption and expansion of social and economic conflict that was phrased in class terms—contribute to the further articulation of the American middle class." A similar way of dividing the "old" from the "new" middle class is by gauging its evolution against the development of American industrialization. Prior to the Civil War, and especially in the latter eighteenth century, the "middling sort" was mainly men of independent enterprise, shop owners, and landowning farmers raising commercial crops. As industrialization occurred, the middle class lost their economic independence and became "white-collar" employees of large capital enterprises that eventually evolve into corporations.

This distinction between the "old" and "new" middle classes is important for a number of reasons. Essential for the "new" middle class' social standing is the society's recognition of the separation of manual from non-manual labor. Because of industrialization, urban and suburban environments grew, bringing the middle class together in an increasingly standardized lifestyle. They came to live in the same neighborhoods, shop in the same stores, and go to the same churches and schools. "[T]he American middle class embraced a wide range of cultural forms—education, religion, moral reform, and child rearing among them—that created a distinct physical body associated with economic and social position" (Volpe 2001:160).

In addition, and of great consequence, middle class numbers began to grow rapidly making them the largest—and perhaps the majority—social class by the mid-twentieth century. The developing middle class became increasingly literate and educated, broadening their general awareness. At its foundation, education was pragmatically motivated because it led to higher occupational position and social status. Greater literacy and education opened large markets for books, newspapers, other reading materials, and for information in general, which, in turn, provided its own impetus for exploring history, religion, and philosophical thought. In churches, voluntary organizations, schools, workplaces, and the parlors of middle-class homes, the middle classes over time forged a culture of their own. Its morality was fashioned by religion but with liberal doses of scientific and secular thought growing out of the needs of the industrial complex, a combination that motivated learning and discussion in multiple directions (see Bledstein and Johnston 2001).

The American middle class, whether old or new, has frequently been characterized as conservative and reserved, characteristics that would be difficult to deny. The middle class has historically valued individualism, self-reliance, pragmatism, and cautious change. These values and attitudes were packaged in a reserved material and behavioral package that reflected Protestant-Puritan modesty. This pretense was more of the "new" middle class than the "old." As noted, the "old" middle class was often active in the politics of the Revolution, but the "new" middle class has hardly manned the barricades. It would be incorrect, however, to conclude that the new middle class has been uninterested in sociopolitical and economic issues of a progressive nature. Rather, they commonly choose to support these interests through the institutions of the status quo including voluntary organizations, religious institutions, and mainstream political organizations and processes.

With the industrial revolution of the early nineteenth century, the "middling-sort" began changing rather dramatically, becoming after the Civil War the middle class that would more readily be recognized today. With industrialization came white-collar jobs, and the middle class changed from the small, independent, and successful group of entrepreneurs who owned a small shop or farm, to middle-level employees of a larger business or company. A middle-class culture developed rather quickly and became increasingly uniform as communication and transportation developed. The middle class was removed from manual labor by shifting their location from shop floors to offices. Wages became salaries, which came to represent people who worked with their heads rather than their hands (Blumin 1989:1, 112–121). Salaries also meant a better income and lifestyle.

With greater income came a higher standard of living reflected most obviously in nicer, bigger, and more modern houses that were suitably furnished and occupied by properly dressed people with expendable income that could be spent on a variety of goods, services, and activities. The market responded with household appliances and furnishings ranging from furniture to china. Middle-class persons, being largely urban or suburban, began taking vacations that often removed them from cities to country resorts near water, especially in the summer when the cities became intolerably hot and rife with reoccurring diseases.

Voluntary organizations appeared that became significant in bringing middle-class people together and enhancing like-mindedness and manner. These kinds of civic and social organizations can directly and indirectly enhance political solidarity and cultural homogeneity, as was seen during the Revolution with committees. These organizations would include reform groups involved with the Temperance Movement, the abolition of slavery, prison reform, suffrage, and the improvement of public education and working conditions for blue-collar workers. Likewise, there were social lodges like the Masons, Elks, and Lions clubs involved in civic activities. By the end of the nineteenth century and the Progressive Era, the middle class had grown in size and wealth to the point where it was gaining substantial political influence.

Of great importance, the middle class of the latter nineteenth century was not only increasing its formal education in response to the demands of the industries that employed them, but they pursued education as a thing in and of itself. Education became highly valued for pragmatic reasons (i.e., "for getting ahead") but also for broadening a person's perspective and for appreciating the world in which they lived. The novel, travel logs, popular science, and other literature became increasingly fashionable pastimes, as did attending the lectures of traveling speakers and the joining of reading groups. "Bettering oneself" was largely seen as an educational process and was pursued throughout life.

With an increasing number of formal and informal forms of education came a mounting awareness of the American polity and its ideological foundations and a greater transparency of how all social systems function. Though never a radical social class, its moderation and conservative postures camouflaged the impact the middle class' growing size and wealth was having on the society. The middle class may have seldom marched or rioted but its mass at the polling place, its wealth, and civic activities did have a glacial effect on the body politic. This mass, both in population and wealth, is the entity proposed as the agent that came to effectively oppose elite notions of governance and cultural hegemony.

From the time of the Founding, the American elite have mainly viewed government as an agent for protecting its economic interests from foreign and domestic enemies and for maintaining a free market. The military and police were to maintain order so that market forces could operate unimpeded. The middle class largely accepted this position but added the belief that government could reform and improve the society for all persons. Reform was acceptable to the middle class in the manner suggested above: in Temperance, abolition, suffrage, and other incremental social reform movements. Societal improvement could also come in terms of better infrastructure, including public education that improves everyone's life and creates greater opportunity for the average citizen. For the middle class, "opportunity" was not welfare, except in a temporary sense. Things like better roads, bridges, sewers, electrification, and educational structures were meant to give individuals opportunities in fulfilling their aspirations. The middle class felt that if people did not use these tools to their benefit then they were avoiding their individual obligations and deserved little additional aid from government or society. Exceptions were made only for the elderly, children, and permanently disadvantaged.

The progressive republican rhetoric used often by the Democratic-Republicans (later the Democrats) to typify the society has been taken seriously by the middle class. Middle-class individualism translates easily into individual rights and liberties reinforced by a progressive reading of the Founding documents; middle-class citizens familiar with the Declaration, the Constitution, the Bill of Rights, and the Fourteenth Amendment believe their values are applicable all-inclusively within the United States and the world at large. This progressive reading of the Founding documents is found commonly at all levels of formal education and in public celebrations like the 4th of July. Where not explicit in the documents, rights and liberties are frequently construed by the middle class from the "spirit" of the republicanism they idealize, such as a right to privacy.

The middle class has only recently begun to understand the circuitous history and legal manipulations that have compromised treasured rights as seen in the case of the Bill of Rights and its qualification by the *Barron* ruling. The middle class knows little about *Barron* or "incorporation" and is often surprised when these things are revealed, leaving them wondering why such subjects were not included in their basic education.

A recent example of how the law and legal system operates contrary to the middleclass' sense and understanding of justice is the *Ledbetter v. Goodyear Tire & Rubber Co.* (2007) case. *Ledbetter* demonstrates the historical habit of the Court to protect property rights over the rights of individuals. Ironically, in *Ledbetter* the Court agreed that Lilly Ledbetter had been discriminated against by Goodyear but interpreted Title VII of the Civil Rights Act of 1964—specifically passed to protect individuals from the discriminatory practices of employers—to protect the interests of Goodyear Tire & Rubber Company.

Lilly Ledbetter was the only woman among sixteen men at the same management level working for the Goodyear Tire plant in Gadsden, Alabama. After twenty years of employment, Ms. Ledbetter discovered that she was being paid substantially less than the lowest paid man as well as being paid a smaller salary than those with less seniority. A federal jury awarded Ms. Ledbetter back salary and damages but, as is all too common, the jury's award was reduced from $3 million to $360,000. The jury's decision was further compromised when the appellate courts, though recognizing the discrimination, reversed the decision reasoning that Ms. Ledbetter's lawsuit fell outside of the 180-day statute of limitation. Likewise, the Supreme Court majority interpreted Title VII as requiring Ms. Ledbetter to file her lawsuit within 180 days of the "discrete act" of discrimination rather than following past precedent that recognized "the continuing effects of past violations." It mattered not to the Court that Ms. Ledbetter was unaware of the discrimination until some years later or that in similar cases employers commonly hid such discrepancies from employees. The damage to individual rights was not limited to the *Ledbetter* decision but has had a ripple effect on subsequent cases involving age, race, housing, and sex discrimination (www.nytimes.com/2009/01/ 05/us/politics/05rights.html).

The repeated irony of *Ledbetter v. Goodyear* is that the jury, which for centuries has been recognized in Anglo-American history as the guardian of individual liberties, was thwarted in its decision of awards and punishments. This reversal represents the elite's desire to reduce lawsuits against corporations by making them uneconomic to pursue. Equally important, the jury's recognition of egregious discrimination was also ignored, thus thwarting the very foundation and philosophy of the jury's existence to find and apply justice. This is not to argue that juries should have unfettered freedom but neither should they be hindered in their basic duty.

The *Ledbetter* decision received much media attention and thus came to the attention of middle-class Americans. The public's reaction was similar to that of the original jury. As a result of middle-class angst on this issue, the Congress did take action. The House of Representatives passed legislation changing Title VII to include cases like Ms. Ledbetter's, but when it reached the Senate the new legislation could not muster the necessary sixty votes to avoid a filibuster and, hence, died leaving the Court's decision untouched.

With the election of a Democratic Congress and president in 2008, the legislation in question was finally passed into law. This did not give relief to Ms. Ledbetter but stopped similar discriminations in the future. The reaction to the *Ledbetter* decision is not only a good reflection of middle-class progressive republicanism but also demonstrates how the conservative republican system of government is established to support capital interests. It would be inaccurate to conclude that the middle class, in general, is liberal or progressive because of their reaction to the *Ledbetter* decision. Rather, it is more accurate to judge the American middle class as having a sense of justice derived from their veneration of the Founding documents.

When the American middleclass was beginning to reach majority status during the years of the Great Depression, it supported Roosevelt's reforms against the conservative establishment who opposed New Deal changes. These New Deal programs were viewed by upper-class Americans as threatening their wealth and the capitalist economy that provided and sustained their wealth (Domhoff 1970:156–250). The middle class viewed these legislative plans (e.g., workmen's compensation, social security, collective bargaining) as "pragmatic" not as a liberal or a socialist agenda. This is not to say that elements of the American elite were not active in the reform process; after all, Roosevelt was from the American elite. "[M]ost leaders within the power elite agree[d] with utilities magnate Samuel Insull that it is better to 'help *shape* the *right* kind of regulation than to have the *wrong* kind forced upon [you].' Or, as banker Charles G. Dawes put it, the problems of the 'great combinations and corporations' must be 'settled by conservative men' so that the solutions 'will not prove a barrier in the path of commercial and national progress'" (Domhoff 1970:158).

No matter how moderate, these reforms did move American society away from property rights dominance to a greater concern for the plight of ordinary Americans. With the "victory for democracy and freedom" fueling American passions after World War II and the American middle class becoming the largest, if not the majority, social class in the 1950s, it should come as no surprise that middle-class republican idealism became reflected in the society in a wide variety of ways.

Justice and the American Middle Class

The mid-twentieth century witnessed major changes in American justice and the justice system. On the surface, this was not surprising as American society and culture were undergoing a variety of salient transformations. The United States had just successfully concluded World War II, which lifted the society to the top of world power status while touting the qualities of democracy and a free society. New technologies and knowledge were becoming common and anticipated as a regular part of societal growth. The standard of living of average Americans was also rising rapidly and was expected as a normal feature of society, with each generation expecting to do better than the last. The middle class was expanding to majority prominence as the American economy began passing from an industrial to post-industrial society.

A rending change in the American social fabric was announced in 1954. In *Brown v. Board of Education* the Supreme Court (the new Warren Court) declared that "separate but equal" was no longer constitutional, thus overthrowing *Plessy v. Ferguson* (1896). As the racial integration of American society played out in schools, cafes, and buses, the Civil Rights Movement in its passion and horror was played out in American living rooms on the increasingly common television most affordable to the growing middle class. This social upheaval roiled into the anti-war movement, the women's movement, and the gay movement, and the "cultural wars" began. This cultural conflict was focused on justice in all of these various movements; a more just society was demanded for the general culture.[17]

On this sociocultural background, the criminal justice system experienced its own major changes. Most notable was the "Due Process Revolution" attributed to the Warren Court (1953–1969). At the center of this revolution was the "incorporation" of the Bill of Rights. With incorporation, Constitutional rights and protections were being applied by the Supreme Court to the states. Depending on their political view, Americans have either attributed these changes to the "activism" of the Warren Court or to the Courts redressing the injustices of the system. At the same time, American law enforcement was also undergoing radical changes in structure and philosophy as were the correctional and juvenile justice systems.

That all of these criminal justice institutions were changing during this tumultuous period in history was not coincidental. While no historical shift can be attributed to one factor, some factors like class conflict are worth noting and exploring even if others, for practical reasons, cannot be fully accommodated. In the past, American nationalistic history has been largely descriptive, explained by immediate ideas and conditions, putting the best face on America's past, and ignoring more critical long term trends. The history of American justice and the justice system has been no exception.

Not coincidently, the mid-twentieth century, with all its major changes, also ushered in the American middle class as a commanding force with its own particular culture and standard of living. Although no exact moment can be identified, sometime in the mid-1950s the American middle class became the largest social class in the society. The importance of this ascent, if not apparent, is likewise not fortuitous to the social turbulence and changes previewed earlier. The standing of the middle class at this moment in American history is easily understood if we ask, "How would American society have been different had the American working class maintained its majority?" Few would argue that the middle-class society of today is not significantly different from the blue-collar working-class society of the late nineteenth to mid-twentieth centuries.

The Due Process Revolution of the twentieth century, which played out prominently in the 1960s, was in a subdued way a middle-class driven revolution. As a highly-educated group, the American middle–class had a vision of justice, fairness, and individual rights they felt were backed by the Founding documents—The Declaration of Independence and the Constitution, including especially the Bill of Rights and the Fourteenth Amendment. There seems to be little doubt that these beliefs were enhanced by the democratic idealism playing out so principally in post-World War II America. This is not to say that all middle-class Americans were constitutionally and historically knowledgeable. But their education gave them a much clearer sense of what American society was supposed to represent and the importance of enforcing the vision as "a society of laws" in pursuit of a just way of life.

The rise of the middle class in American history has brought an important dimension to class conflict and the impact of this conflict on American history and justice. During the Founding, when American society was largely a division of two classes, the small middle class pressed, with some success, its case to be involved in the establishment of the nation. During the nineteenth century, as this middle class grew in size and wealth, its members involved themselves in a number of justice-driven movements such as Temperance, suffrage, abolition, and labor. Equally important was the middle class' involvement in pressing for compulsory and universal education. As American society approached and then passed into the twentieth century, middle-class political influence continued to expand.

Notes

1. For example see Ryerson's (1978:202) citation from the *New-York Gazetteer* that printed a letter from "an ill-tempered Tory."
2. "'Sorts' [as in "middling-sorts"] represented a relatively neutral representation meant to defuse growing resentments, between 'rich' and 'poor,' the 'big bugs' and the 'small fry.' Ben Franklin . . . , who like many parvenus aspired to become a gentleman, spoke for the 'poor' (tradesman) in this context. Social groups were in flux, and the middling sorts of average farmers, traders, and artisans [mechanics] were best known for their lack of noble attributes, including civilized manners, generosity, and high principles" (Bledstein 2001:5; also see Blumin 1989:17–18).
3. Thomas Young to John Lamb, June 19, 1774, Lamb Papers, N.Y.H.S.
4. "In early November 1765, a large gathering of importers and retailers formed an association to boycott British goods from January 1 to May 1, 1766, with the provision that if the Stamp Act were not then repealed, they should meet again to consider an extension of the ban. To execute this agreement, which had the most thorough support of any boycott in Philadelphia before 1774, the meeting chose two small committees, one of major importers, the other of shopkeepers. . . . This heroic effort was ultimately successful. In the fall of 1768, a crippled economy, the growing irritation with the new trade duties . . . brought the merchants to an agreement. Philadelphia's major tradesmen pledged to enter into an association in March if relief was not forthcoming from Parliament" (Ryerson 1978:27, 29).
5. "On May 23, Philadelphia's 'artisans, manufacturers, tradesmen, mechanics, and others' resolved 'to render the non-importation, as it now stands, permanent.' Deeply moved by a letter from Philadelphia's artisan-hero,

Benjamin Franklin, recommending the continuation of the boycott . . . a large number of mechanics attended the boycott subscribers' June 5 meeting. . . . In July, strong mechanic support was again crucial as the boycott committee persuaded the city's nonimportation subscribers to issue a public condemnation of New York's defection from the common cause. . . . A crucial ingredient in this victory was the resistance movement's second creation—a politically united, articulate mechanic class. The sudden coalescence of Philadelphia's artisans in May 1770 proved lasting. When the city's importers terminated the general boycott in September, mechanic spokesmen challenged the merchants' right to take this action. Because nonimportation vitally affected the public welfare, they reasoned, the subscribers' decision to alter the association should have been shared by all 'Tradesmen [merchants and artisans], Farmers and other Freeman.' On September 27, 'A Brother Chip' advised his friends to cast their votes wisely—for candidates favorable to and even of their humble class. . . . A craftsman ran for sheriff for the first time in years, and artisans won four of the ten city offices filled by election, an unusually strong showing. In an even sharper break with Philadelphia's elitist traditions, the mechanics put a tailor into the Assembly" (Ryerson 1978:31–33).

6. As Ryerson (1978:95) continues, "The mechanics' ticket was thoroughly radical in character." It must likewise be remembered what "radical" referred to: "Distinct tickets were brought out of nomination, and the freemen repeatedly preferred one kind of slate over all others. These electoral decisions sharply altered political life in Philadelphia by completing the transformation of the local resistance committee, which had first been an instrument of one occupational class [merchant elite] in 1765, and then a traditionally elitist representative of the whole community (June 1774), *into a new, aggressive advocate drawn from and speaking for, the middle classes that would soon politically dominate the whole community. In a microcosm that was both spatial and chronological, this transformation embraced America's gradual evolution from the corporate, class-based politics of the colonial era to the more egalitarian, individualistic politics of majoritarian democracy in the new nation*. . . . In the fall of 1774 . . . the occupational structure of the committees began to show a more radical change. The number of craftsmen, shopkeepers, and petty retailers—the 'mechanics'—swelled so greatly that it first cut into the strength of merchant committeemen, and then into that of the manufacturers and large-scale retailers. As long as the committees were still growing, merchant and manufacturer representation only declined relative to that of the mechanics, but in 1776 the number of merchant and manufacturer committeemen declined absolutely. The 'mechanics' tickets of 1774, 1775, and 1776 were both instruments to express mechanic and radical views, and vehicles on which craftsmen and shopkeepers, who for the first time were effectively organized to participate in public life, 'pushed their way into the political arena' of Revolutionary politics" (also see Ryerson 1978:179, 184–185. Also see 202–206; emphasis added).

7. "The protracted battles between Federalists and their Jeffersonian challengers had thoroughly politicized the very notion of social superiority. Those who found the jumbling of social place unsettling put up stiff resistance to translation of political values to social norms, but other

forces conspired to promote parity among white American men. . . . Colonial habits of deference had been a casualty of the Revolutionary War; notional acceptance of equality was a badge of patriotism,but more enduringly, Americans who succeeded in establishing a competence on farms, in trade, or through the new array of urban professions began to shape a new social order around their interpretation of American virtues" (Appleby 2001:34–35).

8. This definition is not meant to exclude other forms, forums, or institutions of class conflict. Nor does the two-party system represent a perfect cleavage between the haves and have-nots. The American two-party system is utilized here because it is a national institution that encompasses other class conflict mediums.

9. "Beset by democrats, demagogues, and disorganizers, the Federalists looked upon the President as their rock of salvation. To him they gladly assigned the responsibilities of leadership in both foreign and domestic affairs. 'It is upon the Executive we depend for the execution of the laws and for general protection,' declared a Federalist congressman. He is 'the cement of our Union, the representative of the whole people.' A Federalist was expected to construe the powers of the President broadly and to defend his prerogatives against legislative encroachment. In this regard, Fisher Ames set a model for his party: it was said that Ames seldom spoke without casting aspersions upon the House of Representatives and bestowing praise upon the President . . . the fear that the rule of Congress would mean the triumph of democracy—'it will play the mob at last,' Fisher Ames predicted—kept Federalist members of Congress loyal to the executive. Not only did they look with equanimity upon the aggrandizement of the executive—they cheerfully abnegated powers of Congress in order to ensure that he did not want [for] authority" (Miller 1988[1960]:115–116).

10. "Thus, despite the fact that Hamilton's objective was to promote the unity and national power of the United States, his policies led to the creation of two political parties representing the two dominant economic groups in the country: the planting-slaveholding-farmer interest and the mercantile-shipping-financial interest. By 1792, the opponents of the Secretary of the Treasury [Alexander Hamilton] had adopted the name [Democratic-]'Republicans,' leaving to the Hamiltonian residue the denomination of 'Federalists.' These parties were divided by economic and ideological differences greater than those which have generally existed between major American political parties" (Miller 1988[1960]:101).

11. "Being men of wealth and high social position, the Federalist leaders fell easily into the assumption that there was a close connection between the ownership of property and the possession of the talents necessary to the efficient administration of government. The men who had made good in trade, speculation, and the professions were the proper custodians of the national welfare; they alone possessed the ability, wisdom, sobriety, public spirit, and love of good order upon which the success of all government, especially republican government, depended. . . . [However] even within the party itself, the rank and file were never permitted to indulge the pleasing illusion that they were the social equals of the leaders" (Miller 1988[1960]: 108–109).

12. "Federalism was not a wholly static political philosophy: it changed with the times, but its progress was not in the direction of liberalism. Under the impact of the shattering events of the 1790's, conservatives tended to become archconservatives. The innovators of 1788 had by 1800 become the dedicated champions of things as they were. 'We have sailed round the world of novelty,' said John Ward Fenno, a Federalist newspaper editor, 'without making any discovery worth retaining, except that our discoveries are worthless.'... The authoritarian element became progressively stronger in the party; distrust of the people became more pronounced. Increasingly, Federalists revealed themselves to be more intolerant, more disposed to castigate 'popular delusions,' and more inclined to throw up their hands in despair at the iniquities of the times. Had the Federalists been in a position in 1800 to draw up a Constitution for the United States, it would have borne little resemblance to the frame of government which emanated from the Philadelphia Convention in 1787" (Miller 1988[1960]:117–118).
13. As Miller (1988[1960]:105) observes, "One of the most striking anomalies of American political history was the emergence of the great slaveholding planters of the South as the leaders of the [Republican] party which prided itself upon its liberalism, its devotion to republican institutions, and its concern for the welfare of the masses."
14. "Federalist elites could not be as complacent about these popular rites and rituals as their eighteenth-century colonial predecessors had been. The lower orders were not as lowly as they used to be; they were now composed ... of those who referred to themselves as 'middling sorts'—artisans, small farmers, shopkeepers, petty merchants, all those who made up the bulk of the Northern Republican party. And the Republicans seemed not at all interested in reaffirming the existing structure of authority; they meant to destroy it and bring down all of the 'aristocrats' who hitherto had dominated it. This linked them with their fellow revolutionaries across the Atlantic" (Wood 2009:179).
15. Gordon S. Wood (2009) has written an excellent book on this period in American history entitled, *Empire of Liberty. A History of the Early Republic, 1789–1815.*
16. As Wood (2009:319) notes, "Although Americans ... had never been very respectful of authority, the Revolution seemed to have emboldened many of them to challenge all hierarchy and all distinctions, even those naturally earned. Middling men began asserting themselves as never before. As one foreigner noted, 'The lowest ... stand erect and crouch not before any man' ... By what right did authority claim obedience? This was the question now being asked of every institution, every organization, and every individual. It was as if the Revolution had set in motion a disintegrative force that could not be stopped.... How could they not agree with foreign critics who declared that in the United States 'liberty and equality level all ranks?'"
17. The "culture wars" are usually conceptualized as specific movements and ideas. More generally, the culture wars represented "the establishment" versus "agents of change"; a broad challenge to the traditional American way of life. In addition to the commonly recognized movements in the 1960s and 1970s there was a more general demand by many for more tolerance

and an opening of the traditional way of life to new visions. This included greater secularization, more open sexual mores, less social class division, a more equitable division of income and wealth, and greater regulation and control of powerful institutions, especially of corporations but of authority in general. Significantly, it also included recognizing and including the cultural diversity of American society.

7

The Party-Democratic Period: 1830s to 1930s

A study of business leaders' views in the nineteenth century found that they believed political leaders to be "stupid" and "empty" people who go into politics only to earn a living. As for the ordinary voters, they are "brutal, selfish and ignorant . . . in this good, democratic country where every man is allowed to vote the intelligence and the property of the country is at the mercy of the ignorant, idle and vicious" (Domhoff 2010[1967]:205–206).

The middle period of American history, roughly from the time when the new middle class begins to appear until it commenced its political and cultural majority in the twentieth century, is referred to by Morton Keller (2007) as the "party-democratic regime." He describes this era as running from the 1830s to the 1930s. Keller (2007:67) observes that the "Democrats and Whigs of the 1830s and the 1840s had more in common with each other than they had with the Jeffersonian [Democratic-]Republicans and Federalists from which they claimed descent." Another way of describing this same period is to observe that class tensions that had been expressed between the two earlier political parties were curtailed when the upper class came to fully dominate both parties. "In fact, different factions within the power elite controlled both parties for most of their history . . . the Democrats were originally the party of the agrarian wealth, especially in the South, the Republicans the party of bankers, merchants, and industrialists" (Domhoff 2010[1967]:153).

With the defeat of the Federalist Party in 1800, the American polity turned toward the more rhetorically progressive republicanism of the Jeffersonian Democratic-Republican Party. This progressive idiom was much more appealing to average Americans as it appeared to encompass their needs and desires. "The Party-Democratic Regime not only created a new politics but transformed government and law.

The republican approach to governing in the early Republic assumed that elite rulers would disinterestedly serve the public interest. In the new regime, 'the democratic ideal of popular self-rule was translated into a reality of party government through the medium of yet a third concept—that of the rule of the majority'" (Keller 2007:88).

Becoming more democratic created its own problems (see Zakaria 2003). Majoritarian rule or democracy without constitutional constraints leads to spoilage, exploitation, and the abuse of minorities. It was not until the passage of the Fourteenth Amendment that guaranteed liberties began to reassert themselves against majoritarian abuse. Even then we do not see a full restoration of the Bill of Rights until the Warren Court and the Due Process Revolution in the mid-twentieth century.

With the continued failure of their agenda, Federalists took measures to regain their majority by regrouping as the Whig Party. The name "Whig" invoked the Federalists' victories of the Revolution and, thus, its more progressive republican rhetoric. The Whig Party modified the language of its conservative economics by suggesting that all hardworking and God-fearing men could obtain success under its sociopolitical program, an appeal aimed at "native-born" Americans.[1] As Domhoff (2010[1967]:2) observes, "Revolutionary leaders from the higher classes had to concede greater freedom and equality for common people to gain their support." Much of the inclusive free market ideology we experience today that associates the free market with democratic ideals and individual freedoms, and advocates a small and low-taxing government, was developed during this middle period to make the Whig program more attractive to the general populous.

The old Federalist elite encouraged the growing upper middle class to not only join their political agenda but adapt the elite cultural ethos. Most obvious was the inclusion of the middle class into the old Puritan churches (Presbyterian, Congregational, and Unitarian churches) that were anti-Catholic and anti-immigrant. Aside from its strong Calvinistic fatalism and Protestant work ethic (which theologically supported wealth holders as the "chosen"), neo-Puritan religion, as Gusfield (1986[1963]) argues, was used to set the standard as the indigenous or original American culture. Although Gusfield (1986[1963]) focuses his discussion on that part of neo-Puritan culture dealing with alcohol consumption, his point is that the old Federalist elite was making a substantial effort to maintain cultural dominance by assimilating a chosen group of (white, Protestant, male) Americans into its cultural beliefs and behaviors.

As Gusfield demonstrates in the case of the Temperance Movement, the old Federalist elite invited "native-born" Americans into their political ranks through social issues (Wilentz 1982:46). In addition to Temperance, other concerns included the abolition of slavery and more mundane issues like proper manners, dress, and material items considered "culturally appropriate" for a proper and moral life (Moskowitz 2001:170–184; Keller 2007:84–85). Similarly, the Republican Party today solicits members through "socially conservative issues" like abortion, and yet is still strongly Protestant and anti-immigrant. Indeed, much of the Federalist/Whig social agenda and strategy is alive and well in today's Grand Old Party.

For their part, the Democratic Party became less progressive and increasingly friendly to elite interests as the nineteenth century continued (Domhoff 2010[1967]:153). The earliest and most obvious such indication was the quick acceptance that the Jeffersonians conferred on the Constitution. This recognition assisted in shattering the Antifederalist movement and helped assure an elite-dominated government. As Keller (2007:68) and others have pointed out, the historical shift of parties in power from the Federalist/Whigs to the Jeffersonian/Democrats, though a progressive shift, did not include women, Native Americans, and most African Americans, and neither were these early Democrats strongly advocating a true universal suffrage. In Democratic administrations elite Americans continued to be overrepresented in appointed offices and in policymaking. For all their faults and failures the Democrats did move American society modestly toward democratic practices in this post-Federalist period.

The Jacksonian Democrats, who historically followed the Jeffersonian Party, perpetuated a reputation as being the party of the "common man." This too, in many respects, turned out to be more political rhetoric than actual progressive republicanism.[2] The Jackson Democrats did support and achieve more universal suffrage for white men, thus acquiring the common American's support and votes. This change seemed inevitable. As was already noted, both Federalists and Jeffersonians, to varying degrees, begrudgingly conceded that expanded suffrage for (white) men was probably going to happen with the expansion of an industrial work force that by the 1840s was becoming obvious.

While catering to common Americans through suffrage and western land expansion, the new Jacksonian Democratic Party nonetheless moved its practices in a conservative republican direction, thus ending hope for a true party of common people. In authentic Federalist form, the Jacksonians promoted a strong executive at the expense of the legislative and judicial branches of government. "On close examination, the leading Jacksonians were shown to be not champions of deprived workers and small farmers, but cold-blooded political entrepreneurs, often men of great wealth or men eager to become wealthy, whose main purpose was to get power and keep it. Jackson himself, as it turned out, was an inconsistent opportunist, a shady land speculator, a political fraud, and a strikebreaker to boot" (Wilentz 1982:45).

Except in rhetoric, the eventual outcome in this period was that political parties became much less ideological, especially concerning social class issues, and much more pragmatic and crass in serving wealthy interests. This had the result of dividing average Americans between two parties, neither of which had much concern for their plight, and of creating the malaise and cynicism that has since kept half or more of average Americans home during elections. For these reasons, equating social class with party in a two-party system became difficult except in the broadest and often cursory sense. If America had had a multiparty system the equation of class with party would be much clearer as we find in Europe. Instead, with class often neutralized, average Americans became susceptible to ethnic, racial, religious, and regional divisions. And, in turn, these latter divisions went a long way in neutralizing class interests.[3] The Democratic Party, which is often portrayed as the party of common people was, during the nineteenth century, controlled by the white Southerner elite.[4]

In other words, the wealthy elite were, and for most of American history has been, protected from class unification and the interests of ordinary Americans by their dominance of the two major parties and the exploitation of the diversity fractures in the social fabric. "[T]he social politics of pre-Civil War America rarely assumed the language or character of class conflict. Religious, ethnic, and sectional identity were far stronger predictors of social attitudes" (Keller 2007:102; also see 101–104).

Nineteenth-Century Class Conflict

You know, the regular well-to-do world should relax about us types. Us Lower sorts. You can never mount a true war of us against the rich cause the rich can always hire us to kill each other. Which they and us have done plenty, and with brutal dumb glee. Just toss a five-dollar bill in the mud and sip wine and watch our bodies start flyin about, crashing headfirst into blunt objects, and our teeth sprinkle from our

> *mouths, and the blood gets flowing in such amusing ways. Now, it's always just us against us – guess who loses? (Woodrell 1998:207).*

The early and mid-nineteenth century saw the release of class tension, often in a violent manner. As the antebellum period moved forward, the espousal of egalitarian and Revolutionary rhetoric led to organized forms of hostility. One prominent example is the Anti-Renter Movement of 1839 (Zinn 1995[1980]:206–208), similar to the renters' violence reviewed above (Chapter Two) during the Revolutionary period. In the Hudson Valley of the state of New York, a small number of interrelated and wealthy families owned nearly two million acres and rented to three hundred thousand farmers and their families. When the renters organized and refused to pay their rents, taxes, and obligations unless their concerns and objections were addressed, the sheriff was dispatched with five hundred mounted and armed men to confront the renters. " [B]ut [they] found themselves in the midst of shrieking tin horns, eighteen hundred farmers blocking their path, six hundred more blocking their rear, all mounted, armed with pitchforks and clubs. The sheriff and his posse turned back, the rear guard parting to let them through" (Zinn 1995[1980]:206).

Although the renters were well organized and the resistance continued for several years, often invoking the American Revolution and its language, several renters were finally arrested and found guilty of murder. "The judge sentenced four to life imprisonment and two to be hanged. Two of the leaders were told to write letters urging the Anti-Renters to disband, as their only chance to escape heavy sentences.... The power of the law thus crushed the Anti-Rent movement" (Zinn 1995[1980]:208; also see Christman 1945). Diverting the Anti-Renter movement into a voting movement, the small tenant farmers elected a governor who sympathized with the movement and pardoned the tenants who had been imprisoned. The battles between renters and landlords continued into 1869, though the structure of rich and poor remained intact.

In the same period we have the Dorr's Rebellion (1841–42) in Rhode Island, which concerned the right to vote (Zinn 1995[1980]:209–211). In Rhode Island only land owners could vote and as the nineteenth century proceeded, more and more Americans were engaged in non-agricultural and industrial pursuits. Being refused suffrage, the common people of Rhode Island voted for a shadow government that they recognized as the legitimate authority. Although many common Rhode Islanders were prepared to use violence to achieve voting privileges, this was largely avoided because of the threatened intervention of federal and state militia troops.

Labor unrest, which Dubofsky and Dulles (2010[1949]:20–24; also see Dray 2010) trace back to late seventeenth-century America, began in earnest as industrial manufacturing appeared in America during the early nineteenth century. By 1820 there were one hundred thousand laborers employed in cotton mills alone, living on substandard wages, working long hours under poor working conditions, and living in poor quality housing and communities. These unskilled workers were beginning to threaten skilled labor in skilled craft trades who had already organized their own trade societies, precursors to unions. As these trade societies became increasingly militant in protecting wages, working hours, and conditions, employers sought protection from the criminal justice system, urging that striking workers be arrested and charged with crimes.[5]

In 1810, Journeymen Cordwainers in New York were indicted for criminal conspiracy for a strike action. By 1822 aggressive unionism began to appear in the New England textile mills (Dray 2010:11–60) and in 1827 the Mechanics' Union of Trade Associations appeared, the first time that several craft unions came together to form a large umbrella union of diverse crafts. In 1834 a call went out across the country for a national organization that would include all the trades. Their demands became more universal and the union became involved in the political process nominating candidates for public office. "Ultimately workingmen's parties were established in at least a dozen states. As far west as Ohio, as well as along the Atlantic seaboard, local groups of farmers, artisans and mechanics named their own political candidates and in some instances elected them. For a brief time they were highly important, and sometimes held an actual balance of power between the major parties in local elections" (Dubofsky and Dulles 2010[1949]:33; also see Dray 2010:61–121).

By the end of Jackson's terms as President, both parties—Whigs and Democrats alike—had come to realize that with the expansion of suffrage, electoral politics was becoming increasingly dependent on attracting working men in industrial settings and the growing numbers of small independent farmers. Although women had also unionized in the mills and had become politically active, without the vote they could only be effective by supporting men's unions and union candidates

(Dray 2010:57). Early on, as might be expected from the Federalist/Whig philosophy, Democrats were more successful in supporting labor and gaining labor support in return. Democrats and labor parties were often splitting votes, which worked against a labor party for the next century and saw the efforts for a national labor party finally collapse in the early twentieth century even as labor's power continued to peak (Domhoff 1970:228).

The ultimate failure of a national labor party did not occur without significant political victories for more local labor parties of the early nineteenth century. One political victory for labor that clearly spelled out class conflict was labor's triumph in ridding the country of debtor's prisons and the criminalization of poverty, despite the opposition of business.[6]

Even though these early nineteenth-century labor organizations were short lived, they were nonetheless a clear indicator that class tensions existed in the American social fabric and the rhetoric of class conflict was commonly expressed by the unions. "During these years in which such marked progress was being made in social reform in the country as a whole, and particularly during Jackson's second administration from 1833 to 1837, union activity was more widespread and more militant than it would be again for several decades" (Dubofsky and Dulles 2010[1949]:48; 49–65; also see Zinn 1995[1980]:214–228). Jackson's second term witnessed so many trade strikes that it led the *New York Times* to exclaim that the only group left to strike were the editors.

> In increasingly active defense of their rights, trade union members did not hesitate either to threaten or actually go out on strike when their employers refused to meet what they felt were their legitimate demands. When the latter tried to hold down wages or bring in untrained workers at lower pay, there were turn-outs in almost every trade and in every city. Printers and weavers, tailors and coachmakers, masons and bookbinders walked out. . . .
>
> The girls working in New England cotton mills again went on strike. "One of the leaders mounted a pump," The *Boston Transcript* reported, "and made a flaming . . . speech on the rights of women and the iniquities on 'monied aristocracy' which produced a powerful effect upon her auditors, and they determined to have their own way, if they died for it." As in the first waves of strikes instigated by the original trade societies, such turn-outs were almost always peaceful, but they became so general that the business community

> became increasingly alarmed. Between 1833 and 1837 no less than 168 were recorded in contemporary newspapers (Dubofsky and Dulles 2010[1949]:54–55).

Much of this labor unrest was driven by hyperinflation, the result of speculation driven by an economic boom. "It was generally estimated that the cost of living increased some sixty-six per cent between 1834 and 1836" (Dubofsky and Dulles 2010[1949]:49), with the increase in wages lagging far behind. To break the trade unions, employers tried a number of tactics. They brought in untrained children and women whom they paid lower wages and the use of convict labor became widespread. As became all too common, business owners tried to blame labor unrest on the "outside" agitation of radicals, usually foreigners, thus playing to the prejudices aimed at immigrants. In response to workers' demands for a ten-hour work day, employers argued that a shorter work day "would undermine the workers' morals and foster intemperance. . . . [This] became the chief stock and trade of the conservative opposition to any change in the traditional sun-up to sunset system" (Dubofsky and Dulles 2010[1949]:54–55; Dray 2010:42–46, 53–56).

Violence and the threat of violence in these labor conflicts were not absent. Employers established "protective associations" that would act together against workingmen, women, and children. "In New York a group of Employers, Curriers and Leather Dealers took up arms against the General Trades' Union and mutually agreed that they would not employ 'any man who is known to be a member of that or any other society which has for its object the direction of terms or prices for which workmen shall engage themselves'" (Dubofsky and Dulles 2010[1949]:58).

As noted earlier, when employers could not defeat unions in any other manner they would turn to friendly state courts, charging that unions were conspiring in restraint of trade. This played out clearly in *People v. Fisher* (1835) when the New York Supreme Court held that the society of cordwainers did conspire to raise wages, which was seen to damage trade and commerce. The reaction to such decisions was so strong, not only by unions and laborers, but by some editors, that later juries and courts were swayed to support union rights. Nonetheless, trade unionism remained very active and recruited a membership estimated to be around three hundred thousand workers, a membership number not to be reached again for another fifty years.

In 1837, however, a depression struck that was so severe that it all but destroyed the union movement. By the 1840s the American industrial plant, which hired unskilled labor, was becoming increasingly competitive, thus driving down the living standards of its workers to abysmal levels. While the larger society was certainly aware of the harsh working conditions and the low wages and slum living that resulted, the organization of unskilled labor was largely stalled because of prejudice—the labor force being principally composed of foreign immigrants, a bias that continues to this day. Immigrant numbers were so large that the surplus population effectively kept wages low.

In the first fifty years after the Revolution, approximately one million immigrants entered the United States. Driven in part by the famine in Ireland, another three million immigrants flooded American shores in the decade from 1846 to 1855. Although the surplus population was sufficient to keep living standards and wages low, immigrants also faced snarling discrimination from the native-born because of the immigrants' religions (largely Catholic but also Jewish), their inability to speak English, or their foreign cultural practices. In addition, there were ethnic divisions within the immigrants themselves that pitted them against each other, thus helping to drive wages down to starvation levels.

While the depression and immigration flood retarded a resurgence of unionism, these conditions did motivate the birth of reform movements largely populated and often led by the growing new middle class (Blumin 1989; Bledstein and Johnston 2001; Dubofsky and Dulles 2010[1949]:72). This new American middle class was the product of industrialism itself, as the independent and successful mechanic became the white-collar employee of industry and related business. Motivated by religion and education, this new middle class saw it as their Christian and civic duty to help those in need. The carriers of reform were by and large women, as women and their families were often the focus of reform.

As the reform movements got underway, the middle class of antebellum America was being removed spatially and socially from their manually working counterparts. Small manufacturing shops where owners worked side by side with their workers and knew their families intimately were being replaced by factories where management was being removed from production into separate office and psychological spaces. The difference between manual labor and non-manual labor was increasingly recognized socially, with non-manual labor receiving higher status and pay; wages were differentiated from salaries, work dress between the groups was different, and lifestyle divergence became apparent. Likewise, the office workers and the factory workers were separating into different neighborhoods and communities that reflected the higher incomes and changing culture of the middle class.

This separation between the working and middle classes, while significant and complex, is never entirely complete, and while the new middle class moved significantly to emulate the manner and style of the upper class, there was never any doubt that the social distance between the upper and middle levels was much greater than the social distance between the middle class and workers. Indeed, the antebellum middle class "scoffed at the elitist authority of a Federalist bureaucracy, both in relationship to an intrusive administrative state and a tax-supported church establishment. They ridiculed the pretensions of deference to hierarchy where it appeared to impose arbitrary restrictions and regulations on common people" (Bledstein and Johnston 2001:103).

For all their growing differences, the new middle class was not historically distant from trade workers and numerous family ties continued to exist. Although the immigrant status of the many new unskilled laborers created significant social distance from the middle class, this distance was offset to an extent by religious beliefs and sociological education. "The 1840s were pre-eminently a period of vague, idealistic, utopian reforms, each one of which was held forth by its zealous advocates as a complete panacea for all the evils of the day. . . . The reformers themselves were forever seeking to win the support of workingmen for their various causes. They descended in droves upon every meeting or convention that might be summoned to consider labor issues, and sometimes succeeded in wholly dominating it" (Dubofsky and Dulles 2010[1949]:72).

These reform movements also included small farmers, involving what was known as "agrarianism." This movement claimed that the common people had a natural right to existing public lands—farm lots of one hundred and sixty acres—that could not be confiscated for the payment of debt. Through such a reform it was felt that the common working people would be assured of their share of the national wealth. This resurgence of reform on the part of working people and many middle-class reformers was, in part, a reappearance of labor interests after the economic collapse in 1837. This movement, though opposed by capital and employers, culminated in the Homestead Act of 1862 (Dubofsky and Dulles 2010[1949]:74–76).

As Applegate (2001:112) notes, "[T]he major movements that defined middle-class culture [were] temperance, abolitionism, domesticity, public education, spiritualism, and popular literature, to name only a few." Middle-class reformers "used sympathetic identification or empathy to institutionalize the concept of individual rights and extend those rights to the disenfranchised, to those who had been discriminated against on the basis of perceived difference" (Applegate 2001:114). Referring to Henry Ward Beecher, the famous nineteenth-century preacher of great influence in the middle class, Applegate (2001:115) continues, "Henry counseled sympathy for everyone, rich or poor, black or white. He offered, in the words of the newspaper editor, 'a rational and affecting appeal to men to "Put yourself in his place" and look at things from other people's point of view; to see the other side; to make allowances for differing circumstances and consequent opinions and sentiments; and so—in consonance with his theological and religious teachings—a plea for liberty of opinion with harmony of feeling.'"

The American middle class has often been depicted as conservative, individualistic, and self-interested, and there appears to be more than enough scholarship to support this conclusion. But Beecher's message represents a different side of middle-class values. What we find, then, is a contradiction in middle-class ideology that continues even today. On one hand the middle class embraces laissez-faire values but also feels compelled to extend individual rights universally. This latter position comes from the middle class' aggressive pursuit of education, which inevitably includes the Founding documents, which incorporates values deeply embedded in Western history. As we have already discerned, such rights have been historically asserted to control an elite that is trying to minimize the privileges of common people. For this reason, among others, the middle class is suspicious of the American upper class.

With the support of middle-class reformers, organized labor was making a fairly strong comeback just prior to the outbreak of the Civil War. "One strike toward the close of the period, breaking out early in February, 1860, awoke widespread concern and was to prove the most extensive yet recorded in American history. It was called by the shoemakers of Natick and Lynn, Massachusetts, and spread throughout New England. With the formation of mechanics' associations in some twenty-five towns, close to 20,000 workers were ultimately reported to have turned out" (Dubofsky and Dulles 2010[1949]:80–81; also see Dray 2010:61–73 and Foner 2010:116).

The Growing Labor Conflict of the Post Civil War

With the economic boom that came with the Civil War, organized labor experienced a continuing resurgence. Laborers were often subject to a draft that their wealthy counterparts could avoid by paying bounties, and workers also suffered from the inflation produced by the war economy. But trade union organizations thrived in no small part because they had President Lincoln's support. In the year 1863 to 1864 the number of trade unions rose from 79 to 270 with an estimated membership of some 200,000. In addition, there were 32 unions organized on a national basis. With the war's end, labor came forward aggressively, but the road ahead would turn out to be rocky.

Industrial growth, stimulated by the Civil War and war production, continued to grow rapidly at the war's end and to change almost all facets of American society. Production of many kinds, from farming to steel, became increasingly efficient (Zinn 1995[1980]:247). The results were many and wealth was becoming seriously concentrated in the hands of a few, in no small part at the expense of laborers engaged in the production process (Phillips 2002:37–46; Zinn 1995[1980]:250–289). It was not until the second half of the nineteenth century and the early twentieth century that industrial working conditions became so horrific in scale and the farmers' situation so subjugated, that social class became decidedly important in American politics. The post-Civil War period is one of the few historical periods when the social, economic, and political issues of average Americans were acknowledged.

On September 18, 1873 the postwar boom ended abruptly with the banking failure of Jay Cooke and Company, the country's top investment banker. With its collapse, thousands of businesses failed, including nearly a hundred railroads. Unemployment soared into the double-digits and wages were being deeply cut for those who were still working. Into this post-Civil War environment came the Great Strike of 1877 (Dray 2010:107–121), a general strike that has been all but forgotten in the American memory.

Beginning in the rail yard of the Baltimore & Ohio Railroad, on July 14, when railroad workers were informed that their wages were being cut, the strike, following the rail lines, quickly spread to Baltimore's Camden Station, then on to Pittsburgh, Chicago, Philadelphia, and St. Louis. As the strike spread, other unions and laborers joined the strike in the tens of thousands. In an attempt to stop the strike and reclaim privately-owned industrial properties workers were confronted by local police, state militia, and the federalized National Guard. These confrontations lead to multiple violent encounters where workers were injured and killed. Many police officers and soldiers were also injured.

In Pittsburg, units of the Pennsylvania National Guard were called in from Philadelphia, arriving in rail cars already battered by rocks and bricks as they passed through towns on their way to Pittsburgh. Armed with artillery and Gatling guns, the National Guard entered Pittsburgh and was immediately confronted by an angry crowd. "The troops, hemmed in by the infuriated crowd, fired into the air, but a second volley was far more lethal, mowing down scores of people and killing twenty, including an eighteen-year-old local militiaman. The wounded included women and small children" (Dray 2010:113).

As the strike reached Chicago the response by workers and unions had escalated to very serious heights. "The Chicago board of Trade, a committee of businessmen led by retailers Marshall Field and Levi Leiter, hired Pinkerton guards, organized private militias to keep watch over affluent residential areas" (Dray 2010:115). In St. Louis tens of thousands of strikers moved down the city's avenues singing the "La Marseillaise" and a speaker reminded the crowd of a time when the poor were so oppressed in France that the guillotine was employed against the elite (Dray 2010:118).

One telling indicator of how seriously capital and the government took the threats raised by this strike can be found in the expanded facilities and readiness of the National Guard. "Over the years Americans have come to think of these dour, substantial buildings as historic rallying places for troops in the case of foreign threats to U.S. soil, but their original purpose was to allow the rapid deployment of the militia to keep workingmen in check" (Dray 2010:119).

With a rapidly expanding industrial economy in the North and West, we might expect that labor would enjoy an increasingly higher standard of living. But nothing could have been further from the truth. Continuing immigration in massive volumes kept wages at poverty levels and working hours and conditions oppressive. From the end of the Civil War until the turn of the twentieth century an estimated ten million Europeans landed on America's eastern shores. The West experienced fewer numbers but some seventy-five thousand Chinese immigrants, about a tenth of California's population, were imported to work on the rapidly expanding railroads. Within this mass of immigrant labor was the exploited labor of children, some contracted by desperate parents or kidnapped and forced into slave labor. Child labor only made worse the surplus labor that already existed and it contributed significantly to the lowering of wages. "[I]n 1880 there were 1,118,000 children under sixteen (one out of six) at work in the United States." (Zinn 1995[1980]:261)

Between the vast amounts of concentrated capital and the immigrant-created labor surplus, American labor and farmers found themselves harshly restricted. Great wealth translated into corruption of the political process with the result that anti-labor laws and anti-labor court appointments ensured that labor remained under the thumb of capital, a situation that grew worse as the twentieth century approached. Also conspicuous in this regard were the strong biases of the courts in favor of wealth.[7]

During this same period between the Civil War and the beginning of the twentieth century, the American economy suffered two episodes of economic depression. Unlike the depression of 1837, which all but killed the early labor movement, these post-War depressions riled labor to greater heights of agitation. The difference between these two periods is that the labor movement had grown in size after the war and included increasing numbers of unskilled laborers. As the exploitation of workers by capital grew worse the protests of labor became more virulent and were met by the forceful intervention of the police and militia. The specific instances were many and included the Tompkins Square riot, which took place in New York City in January of 1874 when mounted police charged a peaceful crowd of workers. In the ensuing panic men, women, and children were beaten by the police. Others were trampled and injured by the crowd trying to flee the police.

In the same year, there were sometimes violent, but always contentious, strikes by eastern Pennsylvania coal miners who were promised higher wages and then ignored by mine owners. There were pitched battles between the miners and the private security officers of the coal-and-iron police. Finally, "the bitterly anti-labor head of the Philadelphia and Reading Railroad, which controlled many of the mines, took the initiative in this campaign. He hired a Pinkerton detective . . . to get proof of criminal activity" (Dubofsky and Dulles 2010[1949]:105–106). In the end this detective gave testimony that not only led to arrests and convictions of twenty-four strikers but also to the hanging of ten strikers for murder. These arrests, convictions, and hangings broke the back of the strike.

Though labor tension and violence diminished for a few years, labor dissatisfaction continued and boiled to the surface again in the 1880s as the society was gripped by yet another depression. During this decade the Workmen of the Knights of Labor alone achieved a membership of seven hundred thousand laborers (Dray 2010:125). "[S]o many strikes broke out that the period has been called . . . the Great Upheaval" (Dubofsky and Dulles 2010[1949]:102).

By 1886 the movement for an 8-hour day had gained considerable momentum following the call by the Federation of Organized Trades and Labor Unions to make May 1, 1886 the date that the 8-hour work day would become the standard. As this day approached the American Federation of Labor called for a nationwide strike to support this demand. "So, 350,000 workers in 11,562 establishments all over the country went out on strike. In Detroit, 11,000 workers marched in an eight-hour parade. In New York, 25,000 formed a torchlight procession along Broadway, headed by 3,400 members of the Baker's Union. In Chicago 40,000 struck, and 45,000 were granted a shorter working day to prevent them from striking. Every railroad in Chicago stopped running, and most of the industries in Chicago were paralyzed. The stockyards were closed down" (Zinn 1995[1980]:264).

Such labor activities led to the all too common response by the business community who invoked police and militia violence toward strikers. In response, three days later, on May 4, 1886, a rally was called in Haymarket Square to hear a number of speakers. When a bomb was thrown—the perpetrator was never known—a police riot ensued. With a large number of injuries reported on both sides, eight police officers and four or more workers were killed. The police arrested eight labor leaders who were connected directly or indirectly to the rally and its anarchist organizers. In the end, all were found guilty and four were eventually hung; a fifth committed suicide. The Haymarket riot set off an international reaction condemning the authorities and elevating the defendants to celebrity status. As Rayback (1959:168) notes, "In the public mind the Haymarket affair was a climax to ten years of labor violence" (also see Dray 2010:143–159).[8]

In 1889 the Interstate Commerce Commission reported that some twenty-two thousand railroad workers had been killed or injured because of the lack of safety precautions by the railroads companies (Zinn 1995[1980]:250). Predictably, radical elements gained a strong footing in the labor unrest and socialistic ideas not only gained popularity but came into practice in some political jurisdictions, thus openly challenging the hegemony of capitalist rule in the context of a class struggle. "Thus, the eighties and nineties saw bursts of labor insurrection, more organized than the spontaneous strikes of 1877. There were revolutionary movements influencing labor struggles, the ideas of socialism affecting labor leaders. Radical literature was appearing, speaking of fundamental changes, of new possibilities for living" (Zinn 1995[1980]:275–276).[9]

The Progressive Era: Populism, Socialism, and Reform

Not commonly recognized by most Americans, the working conditions and violence of the nineteenth century, the most extreme in American history and at times bordering on a national violent insurgency, has been well described and documented, all within the language of class conflict. The American two-party system could no longer accommodate this strife and violence, and third-party movements aimed at representing a growing industrial working class and populist farmers became a reality in the late nineteenth and early twentieth centuries, seriously challenging the hegemony of the two-party system. The dissatisfactions of common Americans had reached a point that could no longer be ignored by capital and the elite social strata. Although political and violent suppression of working and farming Americans continued, an awareness by some elements of the higher circles that they might, at the very least, see continuing disruptions to their business activities and, at most, lose their power and wealth, led them to a series of reforms designed to appease common Americans while leaving private capital and power largely intact. This turn-of-the-twentieth-century-period-of-appeasement has become known at the Progressive Era.

Though reform, even radical or revolutionary reform, had been on the lips of some farm and labor leaders since the Revolutionary War, the Populist Movement (and later Populist Party in 1892) achieved enough success at the end of the nineteenth century to move capital and the sociopolitical elite toward reforms aimed at alleviating common American farmers and laborers from abusive and corrupt economic policies and practices. The first document of the Populist Movement—i.e., the "Cleburne Demands"—asked for "such legislation as shall secure to our people freedom from the onerous and shameful abuses that the industrial classes are now suffering at the hands of arrogant capitalists and powerful corporations" (in Zinn 1995[1980]:280).

Though strongly supportive of the urban industrial labor movement, the Populist Movement was largely an agrarian farmer's faction.

Among other things, farmers wanted regulation of railroad rates, heavy taxes imposed on land held only for speculation, an increase in the money supply, and an end to foreclosures. Well organized, the Populist Alliance had two hundred thousand members in three thousand sub-alliances by 1887. Five years later, Populist speakers had covered most states and had reached some two million farm families. "It was a drive based on the idea of cooperation, of farmers creating their own culture, their own political parties, gaining a respect not given them by the nation's powerful industrial and political leaders" (Zinn 1995[1980]:280). By 1889, the National Farmers Alliance had gained some four hundred thousand members.

The Populist Movement and Party were class-conscious entities. As Dubofsky and Dulles (2010[1949]:162) observe, "[P]opulism challenged the whole concept of government by organized wealth. In very much the same pattern as Jacksonian Democracy, it strove to recover for the common people the political power that was felt to have been usurped by the business community. The Populist Party ... accepted as its basic premise the idea that wealth belonged to those who produced it, and called for a union of all the laboring elements in the nation to uphold their rights."

A broader statement of the Populist ideology can be found in the party's platform—actually called the People's Party—stated at their first convention in 1892:

> We meet in the midst of a nation brought to the verge of moral, political and material ruin. Corruption dominates the ballot box, the legislatures, the Congress, and touches even the ermine of the bench. The people are demoralized ... the newspapers are subsidized or muzzled; public opinion silenced; business prostrate, our homes covered with mortgages, labor impoverished, and the land concentrating in the hands of capitalists. The urban workmen are denied the right of organization for self-protection; imported pauperized labor beats down their wages; a hireling standing army ... established to shoot them down. ... The fruits of the toil of millions are boldly stolen to build up colossal fortunes. ... From the same prolific womb of governmental injustice we breed two classes—paupers and millionaires (in Zinn 1995[1980]:282–283).

The People's Party had some electoral successes, electing local and state officials as well as some Congressmen. In the Presidential election of 1896 the Populists joined with the Democratic Party, running William Jennings Bryan as the Democratic candidate who was defeated by William McKinley. Certainly motivated by fear, the Republican Party, representing wealth and corporations "mobilized, in the first massive use of money in an election campaign. Even the hint of Populism in the Democratic Party, it seemed, could not be tolerated, and the big guns of the Establishment pulled out all their ammunition, to make sure" (Zinn 1995[1980]:289). When McKinley was assassinated in 1901 and the presidency passed to Theodore Roosevelt, wealth and capital were now ready to take a less violent and strident path in dealing with farmers and labor.

Less violence, however, did not mean that the tactics of violence or the threat of violence and intractability were over. Rather, ruthlessness and offers of reform were used in tandem to demonstrate capital's resolve, should reform as they envisioned it fail. Domhoff (1970:156–250) has further explained that the American economic and corporate elite was divided into two, but not distinct, camps. In one camp were the moderate conservatives represented by the National Civic Federation. This faction was willing to talk to labor and consider social reforms and concessions to unionization that would temper some of the harshness of the American capitalist system. In the other camp were the ultraconservatives represented by the National Association of Manufacturers and the Chamber of Commerce who were unwilling to consider concessions to labor or give any support to social reform.

Although the moderates among the elite were alarmed by past farm and labor history and its recent culmination in the Populist Movement and Party, they were even more alarmed by the momentous appearance of the growing American Socialist Movement. The shrill refusal by American capital to consider any reform in response to the farm and labor upheavals of the nineteenth century only resulted in a fiercer reaction by many common Americans. Rather than asking for reforms, the Socialist Movement was advocating a new economic and political system that would corral and control capital, reducing personal wealth and power.

While there was an American Socialist Party, the Socialist Movement was conceptually broader and included radical reformers of many stripes, including anarchists and Marxists of various forms and umbrella groups like the Industrial Workers of the World (the IWW or "Wobblies"). The movement included Eugene Debs, labor organizer and presidential candidate of the Socialist Party, who won about four hundred fifty thousand votes in the 1908 election and nine hundred thousand in the 1912 election. But there were also many popular figures like Upton Sinclair, Jack London, Mother Jones, Susan B. Anthony, and Helen Keller. The socialists accomplished a number of electoral victories, "In 1910, Victor Berger became the first member of the Socialist party elected to Congress; in 1911, seventy-three Socialist mayors were elected, and twelve hundred lesser officials in 340 cities and towns. The press spoke of "The Rising Tide of Socialism" (Zinn 1995[1980]:346).

Perhaps most notable, the Non-Partisan League (1915–1922) was organized in 1915 by a number of socialists who felt that the Socialist Party was not attending to the requirements of farmers. Their platform called for state-owned grain elevators, a state bank, and state-owned insurance companies providing crop and fire insurance to farmers. "By the election of 1918, the League had captured the control of the Republican Party in North Dakota, elected the Legislature, and elected their candidate as governor in North Dakota. In a single session of the State Legislature, they enacted all five planks of the platform of 'State Socialism,' including the foundation of the state-owned Bank of North Dakota, which continues to this day" (Evans 2009: 1–2).

The spread of socialism in American society was being driven by a number of factors. Working Americans were not finding satisfactory answers to their problems through the two-party system. In part, this had to do with the nativism and racism that existed in both established parties but also involved the classist attitudes reflected in the opening quotation to this chapter. Working Americans were not only striving for better working conditions and adequate social programs, but were also determined to achieve a status that would make them deserving, franchised citizens.

Just as immediately, socialism became popular because the abuses of the workplace had not abated. By the early twentieth century, when socialism came into its own, there was a large and growing working class making resistance to abuses easier and more universal. Corresponding to the large numbers of workers was a society with better transportation and communications; the nation and world could more quickly know about and respond to corporate mistreatment. Likewise, there was a growing sense that the existing sociopolitical and economic systems could not deal with these abuses since such ill-treatment had been present for nearly a century and was growing in intensity. Examples of maltreatment and neglect by American capital were numerous and easily revealed.

The fire at the Triangle Shirtwaist Company is one of the better known incidents and has been kept alive by the early pictures that still circulate of dead young women who jumped from the building to keep from being burned alive.

> On the afternoon of March 25, 1911, a fire at the Triangle Shirtwaist Company that began in a rag bin swept through the eighth, ninth, and tenth floors, too high for fire ladders to reach. The fire chief of New York had said that his ladders could reach only to the seventh floor. But half of New York's 500,000 workers spent all day, perhaps twelve hours, above the seventh floor. The laws said factory doors had to open outward. But at the Triangle Company the doors opened in. The law said the doors could not be locked during working hours, but at the Triangle Company doors were usually locked so the company could keep track of the employees. And so, trapped, the young women were burned to death at their worktables, or jammed against the locked exit door, or leaped to their deaths down the elevator shafts. . . . When it was over, 146 Triangle workers, mostly women, were burned or crushed to death (Zinn 1995[1980]:319).[10]

Another well-known incident, which received national and international attention and stoked the passions sympathetic to socialism, was the Ludlow Massacre of 1914. Considered the culmination of Colorado's "Thirty Years War," the Ludlow Massacre is believed to be one of the most violent labor conflicts of the Progressive Era. The relationship between coal miners and mining corporations had been very bad for more than a decade when the United Mine Workers began organizing the Colorado miners. John D. Rockefeller's Fuel and Iron Company and other mine owners, refused to recognize the miners' union and their demands for a 10 percent wage increase, a thorough enforcement of state laws, and an 8-hour work day. In response, a strike of some 8,000 miners was called for in the fall of 1913. The mining companies then evicted the miners and their families from company-owned housing and the miners set up a tent city.

Violent clashes between miners and the companies' security forces, aided by the state militia, began to occur and lasted over several months. On the day of the massacre, April 20, 1914, mine security and the state militia invaded the tent city shooting miners, women, and children and setting fires to the camp. When the battle ended two women and eleven children were found suffocated in a burned-over tent that had a pit dug in its floor for security from gun fire.

The miners retaliated but, by the end of April, President Wilson ordered in federal troops to put down the violence. In all, about seventy miners, women, and children were killed by mine company forces and federal troops. After another six months of unsuccessful mediation the miners called off the strike and returned to work. The Ludlow Massacre became a rallying event for labor and the socialist movement (answers.com/topic/Ludlow-massacre;libcome.org/history/1914-the-ludlow-massacre).

Only seven years later, in August and early September of 1921, an even more violent encounter, known as the Battle of Blair Mountain, occurred between miners and mine owners in Mingo County, West Virginia (Shogan 2004). The miners and their families lived under the oppression of a company town system. The hired detective agents of the mining operators maintained order and kept out union organizers through intimidation, harassment, espionage, and murder. In their attempt to organize a union (United Mine Workers), ten thousand miners took up arms to protect themselves and their families and push their efforts to unionize against an armed and aggressive private army led by the sheriff of Logan County and paid for by the mine operators. The mine operators, with the support of local law enforcement, private security, and federal troops, fought the miners and their union in an open armed conflict.

It has been estimated that tens of thousands of rounds were exchanged between the two sides, thus constituting the largest labor uprising and armed insurrection since the Civil War (Shogan 2004:4). The operator's agents not only used a heavily armored train, which fired on men, women, and children, but also hired an airplane to drop World War I surplus bombs on the miners. Facing a miner's army of more than ten thousand armed men, federal troops were called in. Against this federal force the union leaders urged miners to go home and the battle ended. In the aftermath almost a thousand miners were arrested and indicted for murder, conspiracy to commit murder, accessory to murder, and treason against the State of West Virginia.

Although the Triangle fire, the Ludlow Massacre, and the Battle of Blair Mountain were dramatic events that came to symbolize the plight of the American worker and the nature of American capital, the everyday facts were that in the late nineteenth and early twentieth century, workers by the tens of thousands were being killed or injured each year in American industrial plants. In mining alone some twenty-six thousand miners were killed on the job between 1890 and 1917. In this same time period about twelve thousand miners were injured each year. Because of poor working conditions and low pay, tens of thousands of work actions occurred each year. Shogan (2004:3), for example, reports that in the year 1919 alone there were more than three thousand walkouts involving more than four million workers. Even today, American industry still leads the developed world in work-related deaths and injuries. However, by the time of the Blair Mountain Battle the socialist movement was reaching the peak of its popularity in American society. Capital, through its progressive agenda, was beginning to split the more moderate elements of the labor movement from those considered radical.

The National Civic Federation, the American Association for Labor Legislation, and the Defeat of Radical Labor

It is better to "help shape the right kind of regulation than to have the wrong kind forced upon [you]"
Samuel Insull (in Domhoff 1970:158).

In the early twentieth century, laborer's political counterpart, American capital, could be broadly configured as two, though not totally separate, groups: the ultraconservatives represented by the National Association of Manufacturers (NAM) and the Chamber of Commerce, and the moderate-conservatives (or "Progressives"—whose titular head was Theodore Roosevelt) represented by the National Civic Federation (NCF), the American Association for Labor Legislation (AALL), and other similar groups (see Domhoff 1970:170–249).[11] The moderate-conservatives, or Progressives, were composed largely of two social classes—members of the American upper class and groups from the American middle class. The upper-class moderates provided political clout for reform while their middle-class members gave the movement numbers or moderately minded foot-soldiers (Domhoff 1970:177). The ultraconservatives of the American upper class were not interested in dealing with labor and continued to oppose it harshly. Because the ultraconservatives, represented by NAM and the Chamber, continued to stubbornly resist labor, often with heavy-handed and violent tactics, efforts by the Progressives to come to terms with labor were complicated.[12]

The uncertain and often contradictory practices of capital were confusing for labor, creating distrust and inevitably postponing any progress towards a resolution. It appears that elite moderates were willing to fight radical and socialist labor to the point where radical labor might win reform and then step back and undercut radical labor's efforts by offering more moderate reforms. In others words, capital would give nothing until there was no other choice and then give only what it had to in order to calm labor turmoil. "In short, carrot and stick was the moderate policy, stick was the conservative policy . . . it is hard to escape the impression that most corporate leaders are coldly calculating in their relations with labor. This does not deny that some elite are more nobly motivated, but it seems that the benevolent have little success in persuading their corporate brethren except in times of crisis" (Domhoff 1970:220, 221). It has been noted by many that labor made the most gains during times of crisis: during wars, economic recessions, and depressions.

Socialist labor, its political party, and its labor movement, reached its peak of power just before World War I. Though it would continue to be a force in labor and would have some resurgence during the Great Depression, the American elite and their Progressive movement was able to neutralize radical labor by refusing to deal with it while at the same time negotiating moderate and conservative reforms with the moderates of labor like Samuel Gompers. Indeed, the writing was on the wall as early as 1902 when the moderates of capital were able to convince the moderates of labor to refuse to vote for the creation of a labor party at the American Federation of Labor (AF of L) convention—defeated closely 4,897 against to 4,171 in favor (Domhoff 1970:228).

Certainly, the socialists and radicals of the labor movement seriously scared American capital. The American elite had only to look to their European cousins to see what could happen should the socialist-labor coalition successfully form a labor-social democratic party (Domhoff 1970:158–161). Or, even worse for capital, were the Russian Revolution and the spreading communist influence among laborers and peasants throughout the world. Although America was not a parliamentary system where third parties could easily get traction, the American moderate-elite, while still dominating the courts, grudgingly gave in to modest reforms that would give credibility to the moderates in labor and keep the main working force from all-out rebellion. Four of the most contentious issues at the time between American capital and American labor were protective labor legislation (including workmen's compensation), the regulation of business, social security, and the recognition of labor unions. Supporting these reforms, "The AALL fought on five major fronts: industrial disease, industrial accident (workmen's compensation), unemployment, old age pensions, and health insurance" (Domhoff 1970:174).[13] Through the efforts of AALL, the NCF, and other Progressive organizations, legislation addressing these issues was forthcoming (Domhoff 1970:174–176). Of specific importance to capital was the issue of having uniform laws so that the industries of one state would not have an advantage over their competition in other states. With a level playing field, industry could then pass along to consumers the costs of these reforms, an important principle that remains today.[14]

Protective Labor Legislation, Business Regulation, Social Security, and the Recognition of Labor Unions

Though the moderate elite and their Progressive Movement organizations were able to pass many pieces of social and regulatory legislation, this legislation was restrained and did not reflect the more robust reforms being demanded by labor. Workmen's compensation is a good case in point. Workmen's compensation as it was proposed by the Progressives was opposed by labor and yet was passed by the moderates of capital only grudgingly.

As is well known, working conditions in many work places in the early twentieth century were reprehensible. Accidents, injuries, and deaths were much higher than in industrial Europe—which is still true today—and provisions for the injured or families whose support members were permanently disabled or killed were all but nonexistent. A European worker, on the other hand, had broad benefits. Injured American workers had little recourse except through the courts, and, though they usually lost such claims, capital was uneasy because of the uncertainty of the outcome of litigation. In addition, the increasing political clout of organized labor was having effect in some states as they began to pass legislation favorable to labor. Finally, industrial working conditions were a major factor creating unrest among workers.

For these kinds of reasons the National Civic Federation came forward with a plan for compensating injured workers that would be administered by the various states. Organized labor opposed this plan because it did not trust the states but finally capitulated in 1909 followed in 1910 by support from the National Association of Manufacturers. By 1920 all but six southern states had passed workmen's compensation. "[T]he pressures of the very active Socialist Party . . . helped to drive compensation rates above 50% of weekly pay, even though the businessmen favored 50% or less. The socialists had demanded 100%" (Domhoff 1970:200). Although it was not everything labor wanted—and working conditions only slowly changed, remaining relatively hazardous in American work places—workmen's compensation was a victory for common Americans. It required many years of often violent protest and the serious threat of socialist reform, however, to get an even modest compensation package.

During this same period of time the Federal Trade Commission (FTC) was formed in 1914. As with workmen's compensation, the idea for the FTC came from the National Civic Federation (NCF), even though their earlier attempts were successfully opposed by the National Association of Manufacturers representing small and medium-sized business associations. As time passed more elements of big business supported the Federation's proposal.[15]

As has become the common pattern, regulatory agencies are dominated by the very businesses that the agency is meant to regulate. So in the face of demands by common Americans for business regulation, capital created the agency through its own private policy groups like the NCF and then had the political clout to have its own people appointed to oversee the formation and application of the regulations.

The most famous social legislation, the one that still represents the gold standard, is the Social Security Act of 1935. The enduring force behind a social security plan was the American Association for Labor Legislation (AALL) with the support of other Progressive organizations supported by moderate-elite capital. By 1921, a middle-class organization, the Fraternal Order of Eagles (FOE), joined AALL in support of this legislation. AALL began its push for social insurance (e.g., unemployment compensation and old-age pensions) in the years just after 1910. As with the two previous cases, American capital was fearful that demands by labor, supported by common Americans, might be enacted. The Townsend Plan, for example, called for a two hundred dollar monthly pension for everyone over the age of sixty, a plan that became very popular with many of the distressed sufferers of the Great Depression.

AALL and its partner organizations had some success in getting individual states to pass their unemployment and pension programs in the 1920s. This was often frustrated by the state courts declaring such legislation to be unconstitutional. But with the onset of the Great Depression and the clamor by organized labor, radicals, and common people for economic relief, capital finally supported a watered-down version of a government-sponsored old-age pension, the Social Security Act of 1935. The bill was opposed by the National Association of Manufacturers and several other institutional fellow travelers, even to this day (Domhoff 1970:213). As a result of this opposition, the bill had a difficult time passing through the Congress.

Domhoff (1970:216–218) notes on this account that,

> The Social Security Act, not particularly impressive to begin with, was even less impressive as it was finally passed. Benefits were minimal, with workers contributing half of the old-age pension funds, the employers paying for all of the unemployment compensation. In practice, the big corporations paid little or nothing, passing most of their costs along to the consumer.... Nor were the rich taxed personally to help pay for the program (only the first $3,000 of a salary was taxed). The masses ... were being forced to save part of their incomes for a rainy day.... "It is hard to escape the impression that the Committee on Economic Security, correctly anticipating hostility in Congress and the courts ... felt obliged to adopt the least good of the plans of unemployment compensation ... [It] left millions of old people uncovered, and in any case payments under old-age insurance would not begin till 1942" ... The act was a far cry from what had been hoped for or demanded by the extremists, but it was probably their pressure that activated the moderate members of the power elite and enabled them to effect an improvement in the situation.... [I]t is also true that the result from the point of view of the power elite was a restabilization of the system ... and directed political energies back into conventional channels.

Labor's right to organize and bargain collectively was the last of the four major Progressive reforms. The legal recognition and protection of unions culminated in the passage of the Wagner Act in 1934 and the Supreme Court's decision to uphold this legislation in 1937. Although Domhoff (1970:218–219) gives the National Civic Federation (NCF) and the moderate conservatives of capital credit for nurturing this legislation from its beginning in 1900, it must be remembered that by the time the Wagner Act passed labor had been struggling, often violently, for this recognition and the right to collective bargaining for a hundred years. This recognition might have come earlier had the ultraconservative National Association of Manufacturers not vigorously opposed it with aid from the courts. Indeed, NCF was not always enthusiastic about the rights of organized labor and both organizations had used arguments focused on property rights to defeat labor on numerous occasions.

NCF, understanding that continuing labor unrest was bad for business and might lead to radical political changes, set about to encourage the growth of the moderate elements of the labor movement. "They sought to mold and strengthen conservative trends that were contending with socialistic ones. NCF members and the economists such as Commons who advised them were aware even then of what a recent account makes clear in retrospect: 'The unionism that emerged was a mosaic of selfish sectional-minded groups, loosely organized in a relatively weak federation, hostile to the state, wedded to collective bargaining as the exclusive method of change, and frankly predicated upon a permanent acceptance of the capitalistic order'" (Domhoff 1970:219).

It should be noted that the Wagner Act passed into law during the crisis of the Great Depression, an atmosphere in which common Americans could make some progress toward a more equitable life. Only a few years later, in 1947 when the crises of the Depression and World War II had passed, the Congress, over the veto of President Truman, rescinded much of the Wagner Act with the passage of the Taft-Hartley Act. Perhaps the most damaging part of the Taft-Hartley Act was the union security clause that allowed states to institute right-to-work laws. Currently, under this clause twenty-three states now prevent unions from negotiating contracts or requiring workers to join the union. In effect, Taft Hartley allows states to all but kill unions, thus placing workers in a position of being fired without cause regardless of the length of their tenure. As a result, wages and working conditions in these states are far worse than in union states.

Notes

1. "Native-born" Americans refers here to Americans of European descent (especially northern Europeans) who were born in America, as opposed to immigrants who were increasingly coming from southern and eastern Europe (and other parts of the globe) and were largely Catholic.
2. "The [Democratic] party sought also to identify itself with a more radically egalitarian creed. In 1840 it formally adopted the name Democratic, instead of calling itself Republican in homage to Jefferson. Jacksonian class-warfare rhetoric appeals to historians in search of historical validation for a liberal-left tradition in American politics. . . . But Jacksonian anti-capitalism was encased in an agrarian-yeoman ideal far indeed from a social democratic state. Further muddying the ideological waters was the widespread readiness of the Democrats to temper their populist rhetoric with a healthy respect for enterprise and moneymaking" (Keller 2007:83).
3. "Like their Federalist and Republican predecessors, the new parties relied on complex sets of cultural and policy positions, keyed to core constituencies defined by location, religion, ethnicity, economic interest, and family tradition. The Democrats appealed to subsistence farmers, immigrants, Catholics (up to 90 percent of the Catholic vote in the large cities was Democratic), and anomalies such as Dutch and German farmers in New York

and Pennsylvania who were well enough off to be Whigs but were repelled by what they saw as that party's threat to their religious and social values. The Whigs were strongest among evangelicals, the commercial classes, and the prosperous agricultural counties (though not in profoundly Republican Virginia)" (Keller 2007:83).

4. "The characterization of the Democratic Party as a coalition of outgroups even fits the slaveholders who controlled the party in its first sixty-nine years because they were agrarians in an industrializing society, slaveholders in a land of free labor. Although they controlled the presidency in thirty-two of the first thirty-six years of the country's existence by electing slave owners like Thomas Jefferson, James Madison, and Andrew Jackson, the plantation capitalists were on the defensive, and they knew it. Following the Civil War, the Democratic Party became even more completely the instrument of the Southern segment of the upper class when all white Southerners moved into that party. They correctly saw this move as the best strategy to maximize their impact in Washington and at the same time force the Southern populists to accept marginalization within the Democratic Party or else start a third party that could go nowhere.

   After the Civil War, the white Southerners gained new allies in the North with the arrival of millions of ethnic Catholic and Jewish immigrants, who were often treated badly and scorned by the Protestant Republican majority. When some of these new immigrants grew wealthy in the first half of the twentieth century, they became major financial backers of urban Democratic organizations (called "machines" in their day). Contrary to ultraconservatives and liberals, the liberal-labor coalition that developed within the Democratic Party in the 1930s [representing common Americans] was no match for the well-established Southern rich and their wealthy urban ethnic allies" (Domhoff 2010[1967]:154).

5. "The first of such actions was the prosecution, in 1806, of the Journeymen Cordwainers of Philadelphia. The case grew out of one of the recurrent strikes for higher wages on the part of these aggressive shoemakers, and the trial judge proved to be a sympathetic supporter of the employers. In his charge to the jury he characterized the strike as 'pregnant with public mischief and private injury' and left the twelve good men true little choice as to the verdict he expected them to bring in.

   'A combination of workmen to raise their wages,' he declared, 'may be considered in a two-fold point of view; one is to benefit themselves... the other is to injure those who do not join their society. The rule of law condemns both... ' The grounds for such a decision were found in the old common law principle that wherever two or more persons conspired to do something jointly, even though they were individually entitled to take such action, the public interest was endangered" (Dubofsky and Dulles 2010[1949]:28).

6. "The antiquated practice of throwing a man into jail when he could not meet his financial obligations was still in almost universal effect in the 1820's. The Boston Prison Discipline Society estimated, at the close of the decade, that some 75,000 persons were being imprisoned annually for debts, and that in at least half of the cases, the sums involved were less than $25. In one instance, a woman was taken from her home and the care of her two children for a debt of $3.60, and in another a man was thrown into jail for

a $5 debt owing his grocer, even though it had been contracted while the debtor was ill. Thirty-two persons were found in one prison for debts which in every case were less than $1.

Obviously this system bore most heavily on the poor and its injustice rankled deeply. 'A law that makes poverty a crime,' one workingman political candidate declared, 'and a poor man a felon, after these very laws have made poverty inevitable, is not only cruel and oppressive, but absurd and revolting.' Adding to the miseries of the situation, the debtor's jails were shockingly overcrowded and insanitary, and there was often no provision for feeding the prisoners, who remained wholly dependent upon private charity. In New Jersey, according to one report, there were 'food, bedding and fuel: for criminals, but for the debtors only "walls, bars and bolts"' (Dubofsky and Dulles 2010[1949]:45–46).

7. In a long passage, Phillips (2002: 237; also see Domhoff 1970:221–223) describes the activism of the courts in pursuing favoritism for business, often by blocking government reforms in favor of common Americans by declaring such reforms unconstitutional.

"Federal and state courts took on a strongly conservative and pro-business bias by the 1880s after decades of appointment of judges from business and commercial practices. By the end of the nineteenth century their interpretations sent the law in pursuit of one innovation after another, without which the fortunes of the Gilded Age would have been considerably slimmer. Take the humdrum sounding issue of judicial review by state courts of legislative acts. State judicial decisions voiding laws as unconstitutional, rare before 1850, became common between 1861 and 1885. Then between 1885 and 1899 over a thousand such rulings were delivered. The Minnesota Supreme Court alone struck down seventy-seven.

Many of these decisions came under the statement in Article V of the U.S. Constitution that citizens may not be deprived of life, liberty, or property without due process of law. In 1877, U.S. Supreme Court justice Samuel Miller observed that from 1789 to 1868, when the due process constraint applied only to the *federal* government, cases were few and far between. But after 1868, when the Fourteenth Amendment applied Article V protections to the states, all of a sudden the dockets of the high court became crowded. The Fourteenth made the due process guarantee into a sword conservative judges could use to cut down state and federal legislation for 'unreasonably' interfering with property contracts. Judicial activism was further expanded in the 1880s by the Supreme Court's far-reaching holding that corporations, not just individuals, were 'persons' within the protection of the due process clause. This, too, was an enormous stretch. It soon meant, for example, that railroads and utilities would be protected against states empowering regulatory commissions to make final determinations on the reasonableness of rates. Finality could only come from the courts.

The judicial inventions of the late nineteenth century were so laden with specious property rights theory that U.S. Supreme Court justice Oliver Wendell Holmes was driven to his famous protest: that the Constitution did not embody laissez-faire or any other economic theory, and that 'the Fourteenth Amendment does not enact Mr. Herbert Spencer's *Social Statistics*.' Holmes also pointed a stern finger at the supposed 'dogma,

Liberty of Contract . . . which is not specifically mentioned in the text of the Constitution which we have to construe'" (Phillips 2002:237).

8. "While the immediate result was a suppression of the radical movement, the long-term effect was to keep alive the class anger of many, to inspire others—especially young people of that generation—to action in revolutionary causes. Sixty thousand signed petitions to the new governor of Illinois, John Peter Altgeld, who investigated the facts, denounced what had happened, and pardoned the three remaining prisoners. Year after year, all over the country, memorial meetings for the Haymarket martyrs were held" (Zinn 1995[1980]:266).
9. "It seemed that despite the strenuous efforts of government, business, the church, the schools, to control their thinking, millions of Americans were ready to consider harsh criticism of the existing system, to contemplate other possible ways of living. They were helped in this by the great movements of workers and farmers that swept the country in the 1880s and 1890s. The movements went beyond the scattered strikes and tenants' struggles of the period 1830–1877. They were nationwide movements, more threatening than before to the ruling elite, more dangerously suggestive. It was a time when revolutionary organizations existed in major American cities, and revolutionary talk was in the air" (Zinn 1995[1980]:258–259).
10. The New York *World* described the scene, "[S]creaming men and women and boys and girls crowded out on the many window ledges and threw themselves into the street far below. They jumped with their clothing ablaze. The hair of some of the girls streamed up aflame as they leaped. Thud after thud sounded on the pavements. It is a ghastly fact that on both the Greene Street and Washington Place sides of the building there grew mounds of the dead and dying. . . . From opposite windows spectators saw again and again pitiable companionships formed in the instant of death—girls who placed their arms around each other as they leaped" (in Zinn 1995[1980]:319). The political cartoon, "The Locked Door," presented on the front cover depicts the Triangle Shirt Waist Factory fire (Hearst Communications, Inc./Hearst Newspapers LLC.).
11. Domhoff (1970) uses the National Association of Manufacturers (NAM) to represent anti-union forces and the National Civic Federation (NCF) to represent the moderates in capital who were willing to talk to and deal with labor.
12. "The conflict between moderate and conservative approaches was to continue throughout the pre-World War II decades. It is best exemplified by a court case in 1907 . . . in which some of the richest and most powerful members of the NCF financed and defended AF of L president Samuel Gompers in the Supreme Court against a suit brought by the president of the NAM.

    And yet, to state the NCF/NAM split so cleanly and simply is to immediately blur reality. First, many NCF members were also in the NAM, and many of them seemed to say one thing and do another. According to Commons, for example, Mark Hanna played fair with labor, but some of his fellow NCR members and company-dominated unions in their plants fought unions by every means available. Thus, in actual practice, and from the point of view of the common worker, there was often very little difference between moderate and conservative approaches. Examples can be found of members of both groups who dismissed workers for joining unions, hired thugs to beat up striking workers, hired spies to report union organizers, and indulged in other ugly practices that call into question the image most members of the upper class like to hold of themselves. However, the important point here is that the moderate mentality was willing to concede certain points *if* labor really showed major strength" (Domhoff 1970:219–220; also 163–168).

13. "The only failure was on health insurance, where moderate forces within the power elite had to do battle with the insurance companies and the American Medical Association in addition to their usual protagonists, best symbolized by the National Association of Manufacturers" (Domhoff 1970:174).

14. Ironically, and because of labor's mistrust of capital, organized labor was not involved in the reform movement of the Progressives. "There is only one group that did not play a key role in the fight for protective labor legislation, and this is organized labor itself. Several accounts make this clear, even if the one by Brandeis' daughter calls the AALL 'middle class' in making its point. Labor was not in the forefront in these fights because it had considerable suspicion of reformers, because it feared that such paternalistic measures would weaken the union movement, and because it feared the use of the state as the instrument of such reform. Organized labor had to be convinced by the AALL and similar groups to go along with many of the reforms. When the AALL drafted a bill in 1915 to create a state industrial commission for New York . . . Gompers was so angry that he resigned from the association, calling it an association for the assassination of labor. 'Conditions,' and the fear of future trouble, not the pressure of organized labor, led to the reforms in which the AALL took a leading role" (Domhoff 1970:177–178).

15. "The NCF had been concerned about the *proper* regulation of business from its earliest years. There were a number of reasons for this concern. First there was the uncertain legal status of big corporations following the Sherman Act and various court interpretations. Second, there was the problem of dealing with cutthroat competition, that is, with regulating disputes within the big business community. Third, there was the problem of dealing with socialist and muckraking agitation. Finally, regulation varied from state to state, and the corporations were eager to see such functions taken over by the federal government, probably for reasons of simplicity, efficiency and ease of control. The problem for the NCF, then, was to find a way to take care of all of these problems with as few concessions as possible. History suggests that it succeeded admirably. The legal status of the corporations is secure, competition is nicely regulated, and no one argues against the trusts" (Domhoff 1970:202; emphasis added).

8

The American Justice and Due Process Revolutions

The Bill of Rights is by no means the exclusive source of constitutional rights and liberties; that the term "liberty" as used in the Fourteenth Amendment comprehends all fundamental rights (Konvitz 2001:106).

At this point justice has been identified and examined as tied to the history of class conflict in American society. For most of this history the conflict had been between the haves and have-nots, with common citizens frequently being denied justice in lieu of elite interests. If common Americans had had a greater voice in shaping the political system, it seems likely that they would have constructed a more expansive and progressive republicanism mixed with a more decentralized governmental structure. At least in the beginning, average Americans felt safer from elite domination by maintaining local political control, stressing universal suffrage with a more aggressive egalitarianism.

Even though a small middle class appeared as early as the Revolutionary Era as a social class that had noticeable impact in particular situations (Ryerson 1978), it remained a relatively small presence in American society. It is not until well into the nineteenth century that we can take some note of the middle class as being particularly and meaningfully involved in political movements and policy. Included, but not exhaustive, was middle-class involvement in suffrage, the women's movement, the abolition of slavery, prison reform, educational reform, and Progressive social and labor reforms. By the mid-twentieth century the middle class was becoming a majoritarian political force, and their part in the shaping of American justice needs to be more closely examined.

The middle class has never solidified in a manner similar to that of the working class and organized labor but instead realized its influence in the hegemony of a rising class culture configured around increasing wealth, educational attainment, white-collar occupations, and membership in what can be broadly identified as voluntary organizations. These voluntary organizations were encapsulated in reform movements like those identified above but also included middle-class churches and civic organizations (Blumin 1989:192–229). Education, beginning with public education and the pursuit of an active literacy and ultimately focused on the attainment of higher education, gave the middle class a social center around which their ideas and values could coalesce. As already noted, this would include an earnest dedication to constitutional liberalism as embedded in documents like the Declaration of Independence, the Constitution with its Bill of Rights, and the Fourteenth Amendment.

With their higher incomes, the middle class could live a quality of life that was better than their working-class counterparts but not nearly as good as the American elite. As would be expected, the middle class began to form middle-class neighborhoods in the nineteenth century when major purchases like housing and furnishings became a part of their identity and helped standardize their way of living (Blumin 1989:138–191). This class formation had a feedback effect in that the middle class had discretionary money and the market responded by creating material items and activities designed for middle-class consumption. This, in turn, further created and reinforced their middle-class identity. Their distinctiveness was additionally strengthened by the middle classes' dissimilarity from the social top and bottom; their social betters looked down on them with frequent ridicule and disdain and their lessers looked up to them and wanted to be included in their ranks. This created a kind of mirrored press that socially compressed the middle class while reflecting their identity to them from both sides of the social class spectrum.

By the mid-twentieth century, middle-class subsidies—beginning with veteran's benefits after WWII, including the GI Bill and low interest home loans to veterans—continued this class' coalescence and encouraged a common political agenda. Being well informed and educated, a circumstance meaningfully reinforced by the introduction and common use of radio, television, and rapid transportation and communication, the middle class came to project its values and ideas through the political process. This, in turn, provided a positive and rapid feedback; as politicians came to realize the significance of the middle class, they solicited middle-class votes by providing middle-class programs and subsidies. In this same manner, American society realized a middle-class driven reformation of justice unprecedented since the Revolution itself.

Against a backdrop of highly acclaimed democratic values encouraged by World War II and an increasingly college-educated aggregate, the American middleclass was engaged by current events and measured the society's response against a standard of justice resting in many cases upon constitutional liberalism. We can see this middle-class standard reflected earlier in a number of First Amendment cases including particularly *Gitlow v. New York* in 1925 (Irons 1999:265–293). The incorporation of the Bill of Rights, reflecting a movement toward progressive republicanism, began with the First Amendment. This coincided with the founding of the American Civil Liberties Union in 1920, and this kind of progressive justice is marked later in *Brown v. Board of Education* (1954). History commonly credits the Supreme Court with these decisions, but underlying such judgments was a commanding cultural context of middle-class values and support, perhaps more visible as the society actually began desegregation and progressed on to the Civil Rights Movement.

As examined in Chapter Six, the mid- to late twentieth century witnessed a major transformation in American justice beginning with the social progressivism of the New Deal. This was followed by other salient changes. The nation successfully concluded World War II trumpeting the qualities of democracy. New technologies and knowledge were appearing at an increasing rate and the standard of living of average Americans was growing rapidly. On this rising tide the middle class was expanding to majority status in the class structure.

As acknowledged above, a salient change in the American social fabric was announced in 1954 with *Brown v. Board of Education.* As the racial integration of American society took hold and spread across the country, the Civil Rights Movement, in its passion and shock, was played out in American living rooms. This social upheaval cascaded into the anti-Viet Nam war movement, the women's movement, the gay rights movement, and the Due Process Revolution, which incorporated much of the Bill of Rights. The backlash to these social changes created the "culture wars," which have been significantly focused on the meaning of justice in all of these various social movements and have broadly engaged the middleclass.

While no major historical shift can be attributed to just one factor, it seems unlikely that the numerical and political emergence of the middle class was just a historical coincidence with the turmoil and change of the same period. As the American middle class grew in magnitude and affluence, it increasingly became a major political and cultural force. Although this mid-twentieth-century historical episode is not usually viewed as a result of class conflict, it is likewise not a coincidence that during this same period there was also a revival of American conservatism. Resistance by the conservative establishment to middle-class sociopolitical demands was directly aimed at the social and liberal constitutional reforms cited above. Just as the Federalists had resisted a bill of rights for fear of losing control to the "democratic mob," modern corporate-financed conservatives criticized every move of mid-twentieth-century social reform with similar fears.

The Due Process Revolution and its fellow traveling social movements of the mid-twentieth century represented a resurgence of New Deal philosophy toward constitutional liberalism, progressive republicanism, and social justice more generally. It was part of a more progressive attitude that was comfortable with the redistribution of wealth and the leveling of society. This neo-New Deal attitude envisioned a society with better education, universal health coverage, subsidized child care, subsidized housing for the poor and elderly, training programs for the unemployed, subsidized school lunches for the children of the poor, and more stringent regulation of corporate behavior, as well as public funding for consumer protection and environmental initiatives, among others. The cost of these kinds of programs and policies threatened the American establishment in a manner similar to the fear created for them by the New Deal.

An association between the Constitution and Bill of Rights and progressive social programs had been made by Franklin Roosevelt in his "Second Bill of Rights" initiatives presented in his State of the Union address on January 11, 1944. Citing many of the liberties in the Bill of Rights, Roosevelt made the point that, "these political rights proved inadequate to assure us equality in the pursuit of happiness." Continuing, Roosevelt stated that,

> We have come to a clear realization of the fact that true individual freedom cannot exist without economic security and independence.... In our day these economic truths have become accepted as self-evident. We have accepted, so to speak, a second Bill of Rights under which a new basis of security and prosperity can be established for all—regardless of station, race or creed. Among these are "[t]he right to a useful and remunerative job in the industries or shops or farms or

> mines of the nation; The right to earn enough to provide adequate food and clothing and recreation; The right of every farmer to raise and sell his products at a return which will give him and his family a decent living; The right of every businessman, large and small, to trade in an atmosphere of freedom from unfair competition and domination by monopolies at home and abroad; The right of every family to a decent home; The right to adequate medical care and the opportunity to achieve and enjoy good health; The right to adequate protection from the economic fears of old age, sickness, accident, and unemployment; The right to a good education." (in Rosenman 1950:40–42).

The spirit and letter of Roosevelt's remarks were continued in President Kennedy's "New Frontier" and Lyndon Johnson's "Great Society." These programs were strongly supported by America's middle class as witnessed by Roosevelt's and Kennedy's popularity and Johnson's overwhelming election in 1964. Just as strongly, these programs were opposed by neoconservatives representing American wealth. This broad republican movement and related governmental programs required taxes on wealth, both individual and corporate, and a redistribution of wealth historically most feared by the American elite.

In response to the support for a considerable redistribution of wealth, the American elite reacted by increasing support for the ultraconservative elements of its membership. As we saw in previous chapters, this element has been represented by the National Association of Manufacturers and the Chamber of Commerce of the United States. Ultra-right reaction likewise included such think tanks as the Heritage Foundation, the Hoover Institution, and the American Enterprise Institute (Domhoff 2009:102–103;1978:81–87). Most telling, perhaps, the ultraconservative backlash included the shrill and strident ultra-right media that stirs hate and fear to protect ultra-right interests and specializes in anti-tax (redistribution) messages.

With American upper-class support through corporate donations and other right-wing institutions, the conservative movement captured the Republican nomination in 1964 and the presidency from 1968 thru 1976 and then again in 1980 with the two-term election of Ronald Reagan and then in 1988 with the one-term election of George H.W. Bush. Bill Clinton, a "New Democrat" elected president in 1992 with a Republican Congress for most of his tenure, could do little to stop the reversal of the distribution of wealth from the bottom and middle classes back to the top that continued in the two terms of George W. Bush from 2000 thru 2008. Through tax cuts, tax benefits, governmental subsidies, and outright governmental purchases from corporations, these Republican administrations were able to reverse the distribution of wealth, which had the effect of stagnating and even shrinking the middle class (Wolfe 1998:7). Likewise, the American right was able to stifle social reform and to push back on the Constitutional and social changes of the mid-twentieth century. In this important sense, then, the interests of the upper class were in conflict with the middle and lower classes of the society (Phillips 2002:127–138).

Middle-class optimism that things would get better each exceeding generation was stymied in the three decades beginning about 1980. The middle-class faith that their status "was like academic tenure: once you got it, no one could ever take it away" (Wolfe 1998:7) turned out to be untrue. As the numbers of middle-class jobs shrank, salaries languished, and middle-class occupations slipped in status, the middle class literally became more conservative, hunkering down to preserve what they had gained in decades past by opposing taxes and the social programs that required new revenue. Middle-class progressive values were sorely tested and found wanting, though the loss in one's standard of living could certainly include serious crises including the reduction and even loss of health insurance, the foreclosure on one's home, or the need to file for bankruptcy, all of which might be related to job loss or downgrading. Even those spared such fates could hardly help worrying and certainly felt the stress of the social class decay around them.

The conservative movement appeased the fears of the American elite by stopping, and even reversing, the distribution of wealth in the latter twentieth century and early twenty-first century. This conservative movement also had a social agenda that was hostile to the social justice movement ostensibly supported by the middle class. There is little evidence that the American elite cared, per se, about conservative social issues except as a way of recruiting social conservatives, notably the religious right, to their economic interests (see Kuo 2006).

Distracted by the economic crises of the 1970s, early 1980s and 1990s, the middle class with its social agenda was hardly back on its feet when the Republicans stole the national election of 2000. With the end of George W. Bush's administration and the election of Barack Obama in 2008, the middle class' social agenda once again began to get traction only to suffer another setback due to another and more serious recession brought on by a lack of corporate and business regulation during the Bush administration.

At the same time, the financial crisis and recession inherited by the Obama administration brought out more clearly the class conflict between the middle and upper classes. A revealing instance of this conflict was depicted on the *News Hour* with Jim Lehrer in a discussion between Michael Gerson, a conservative *Washington Post* columnist, and Mark Shields, a liberal syndicated columnist, related to the profits and top-level compensation enjoyed by financial institutions that had been responsible for the current recession yet were bailed out with taxpayer money. The following is a partial excerpt from this *News Hour* segment aired on October 16, 2009:

> JIM LEHRER: Mark, is it . . . fair to say that a lot of average Americans are really upset about the huge profits and the huge compensation that has already begun to return to Wall Street: Do they deserve to be upset?
>
> MARK SHIELDS: They deserve to be upset.
>
> Wall Street has earned the rage and the fury of ordinary Americans. Just two firms, Citigroup and Merrill Lynch, last year lost $54 billion. American taxpayers, firefighters and nurses, and teachers and hairdressers came up with the money. They . . . knew that it was important to keep them in business [and] came up with $55 billion.
>
> As they are losing $54 billion and borrowing $55 billion from the American people to keep their doors open, they award $9 billion in bonuses to their own people. Is that a sense of outrage? Is it justified, at the same time, Jim, that 14,000 Americans every day are losing their health insurance, when 5.5 million Americans have been out of work for more than six months, and we can't even get the Congress, the Senate in this case, to extend unemployment benefits to these folks, with 424 Americans every hour having their homes repossessed?
>
> Yes, there is a sense of rage, and it is totally justified.
>
> JIM LEHRER: Totally justified, Michael?
>
> MICHAEL GERSON: Well, it's certainly there. You know, and it's hard to argue with that sort of attitude. And many Americans feel it, left, right and center.
>
> MARK SHIELDS: That's right.
>
> MICHAEL GERSON: This is not a particularly big ideological issue. People feel like there is a different set of rules for the wealthy and for the middle class. I think that's true.

. . . [T]he fact is that a lot of executive compensation on Wall Street and other places is done through bonuses and stock options. It's not done with salaries. That's the way they compete for workers and, you know, keep people in jobs. That's the way Wall Street works.

And—you know, and a lot of Americans are angry, but a significant number are happy when they see the market over 10,000, which is also helping some of these firms as well. And, you know—and I think, if you look at the facts, the compensation strategies of banks in the research doesn't really correlate very well with the performance of the banks. It's not the key factor.

Greed is not the main factor here, but it is certainly a cause for a lot of resentment.

JIM LEHRER: Yes. And do you see that resentment waning, or is it going to continue to be there until this whole thing, or—I don't mean the whole thing, but much of the economy recovers? As long as the people are still hurting out there, they are going to see these headlines, they're going to see these reports and get upset.

MICHAEL GERSON: Well, there is a diversion right now, or a division, in America between those who are benefiting from the fact that the economy at its highest levels is coming back to some extent.

But unemployment is very high. You know, business startups are very low. The real economy out there is lagging behind our—you know, the economy at the heights. And I think that is going to cause some tensions.

JIM LEHRER: You agree with that, too, do you not, Mark? I mean, it's—while, in some strata of the economy, nothing is changing, except it is either remaining flat or it's negative, while, at the top, it's doing well.

MARK SHIELDS: Yes. It's socialism for the rich.

I mean, obviously, the people having their houses repossessed are not too big to fail, or the people losing their jobs. We're laying off teachers in this country. I mean, and 75 years ago, Franklin Roosevelt said the measure of our progress is not whether we add more to the abundance of those who have much, but whether we provide enough for those who have too little.

And, I mean, I just think this thing has turned totally upside down. And I think there is a political rage. I think Michael is right that it's not left, right or center. I just think it—we came to the rescue of these folks. Yes, they put the economy at risk. And now we—and they talk about the pay for performance.

> They got paid handsomely when they were profitable. They got paid handsomely when they weren't profitable. And they got paid handsomely with our money.

Such conversations, recognizing class conflict between common Americans and Americans of wealth are currently very common and regularly appear during economic crises. As both of the above commentators agree, the conflict is not just ideological but a class conflict.

Justice and the American Middle Class: Wolfe's "Class Morality Project"

Alan Wolfe, who wrote *One Nation, After All: What Middle-Class Americans Really Think About* (1998), does an excellent job giving a face to the American middle class through his "Class Morality Project." Wolfe (1998:3) defines the middle class as "a cluster of attitudes, beliefs, practices, and lifestyles" and a class with constant "moral and cultural meanings." Clarifying this definition, John F. Kennedy "used to say that ours was basically a conservative country, but that people wanted progress" (Kennedy 2009:408). Completing this definition, Wolfe (1998:4) cites one of his research subjects who stated, "'We are Americans. We have enjoyed many of the benefits of that, and for that we have many responsibilities.' For her, those responsibilities begin with the voluntary organization Habitat for Humanity. . . . 'I just believe that we were put here by God to love and care for each other and to make a difference in this world.' That is why, although proud of being a Republican, she cannot bring herself to agree completely with the way 'these tough, right-wing talk show hosts' talk about the poor. . . . It bothers her that the gap between rich and poor in America seems to be increasing."

Middle class and average Americans, as Wolfe notes, believe that one deserves what one earns, and one earns what one deserves. This element of self-reliance is deeply entrenched in middle-class culture as well as in progressive republicanism. This republicanism does recognize class differentials but advocates that a person's place in society should be determined principally by their achievements, not by their birthright, and that all persons, regardless of achievement (or the lack thereof) have some basic "natural" or "God given rights," which should be judicially guarded by their elected government. Opportunity should be open to all and should be equal, as has often been expressed in terms of universal access to public education. This progressive republicanism has also advocated various restrictions on wealth, including the inheritance of wealth, to prevent the development of a ruling class. Continuing, Wolfe (1998:3) states that, "Unlike being rich, to be middle class is to believe that what one has achieved is due not solely to family advantage—although within reason that is never to be spurned—but to one's own hard work and efforts."

Wolfe's characterizations of the middle class, which underscore its sense of justice, are many but he reminds us that the middle class is not a homogeneous aggregate but is divided along many lines, the most important being cultural-political—a divide noted above as the "culture wars." More traditionally we recognize this divide as a liberal-conservative separation.[1]

Though this depiction is oversimplified, the diversity of the middle class should not be forgotten. From the perspective here, we are more interested in the values the middle -class commonly shares, in the same sense that we find in Blumin's (1989) and Bledstein and Johnston's (2001) depictions of the middle class. In a value sense, the middle class has become more conservative in the last three decades while still being connected (or "touched," as Wolfe puts it), to the 1960s. As Wolfe (1998:278) concludes, "I have found little support for the notion that middle-class Americans are engaged in bitter cultural conflict with each other over the proper way to live."

Since Wolfe's research is on morality and the focus in this text is on justice, Wolfe's observations will not always be congruent with the subject discussed herein. But it is not unreasonable to conclude that morality informs justice, and the two social facets clearly overlap. Reviewing Wolfe's account and conclusions on middle-class morality should help achieve a common idea of the middle class' sense of justice.

Middle-class religion and morality are practiced through a worldview of modernism (Wolfe 1998:9–11). Modernism is a rejection of traditionalism as realized through the late nineteenth-century Victorian perspective—an absolutism or rigidity in thinking, morality, and behavior now embraced by socioreligious conservatives. Although middle-class traditionalists certainly exist, Wolfe's survey revealed that the American middle class is characteristically modern, especially emphasizing individualism or self-realization. "The freedom associated with modernity is the freedom to construct one's own life as one best sees fit" (Wolfe 1998:9). Personal liberty, as guaranteed by law, is essential as a person builds his or her own character through his or her own thoughtful determinations of right and wrong.

Religiously this means a personal relationship with God, as opposed to the need for a mediating organized religious entity. Likewise, modernity and its political liberalism mean a toleration of others' religions and individuality, including their pursuits and outcomes, although the middle class has difficulty accepting intolerant and extremist religious groups.

Somewhat ideologically wary of the welfare state (Wolfe 1998:196–204), the middle class' work ethic and self-help attitudes comprise their fundamental humanism. A respect of another's pursuits in self-realization necessarily means a fundamental respect for other persons. If human life has an inherent value then it is only realistic to recognize that some people will sometimes need help as they develop themselves on a life path. In this respect, Wolfe (1998:10) found that middle-class Americans are not only generous (often realized through voluntary organizations) but are also egalitarian. This sense of equality tends to be absolute in terms of individual worth but less so when it comes to economic status—after all, wealth is an individual accomplishment. Nonetheless, the increasing gap between the rich and poor is a concern to the middle class in that wealth at some point can compromise liberty and the ability to realize a person's own pursuits. This is an attitude found early among common Americans of the pre- and post-Revolutionary periods.

To temper middle-class idealism, Wolfe (1998:76) reminds us that to tolerate is not always to condone: "[N]early three times as many respondents condemned homosexuality as accepted it." This kind of libertarian thinking can be confusing from the outside. When social scientists ask Americans what they think, their tolerance for what they condemn can be mystifying. But this is an essential key for understanding the American middle class and their effect on justice. They feel obligated, in principle, to support the Civil Rights Movement, while personally rejecting, in some cases, integration (such as with school busing), affirmative action, or what they stereotypically think of as African American lifestyle. The same kinds of dualistic and contradictory positions can be taken with feminism, abortion, welfare programs, gay rights, immigration, and due process incorporation. In the latter case, an appreciation for middle-class duality is easier for many to understand. For example, one can view the First Amendment as sacrosanct while still not condoning, at times, what is being said or being uncomfortable with another's religious practices, not liking political demonstrations, or being cynical about the press because

First Amendment guarantees are absolutely necessary if a person is to be free to pursue an individual life.

Wolfe (1998:236–250) also describes in various ways the class conflict between the middle and upper classes—an upper class that the middle rightfully and commonly associates with corporations and capitalism:

> If middle-class Americans can be described as indifferent to unions, they are also increasingly hostile to corporations. . . . Americans adhere to an ideal that can be described as balanced capitalism. . . . Companies have, in their view, simply become too ruthless. . . . Extremely high salaries and unjustifiable perks violate a moral as well as an economic ideal. Very few middle-class Americans say what Trent Tartt [an interviewee in Wolfe's study] did: that he wanted to be rich. For the rest, too much wealth is like too much of anything else: a bad thing. People with too much money violate a deeply held middle-class belief in proportionality; their lives, however glamorous, are to be pitied more than envied (Wolfe 1998: 236, 237, 239, 246).

It is natural to the middle class that their worldview would be realized through the law. Personal liberties are prescribed by the law, everyone is equal under the law, and people correctly obey the law—"we are a society of laws." It is through this philosophy, the middle class believes, that a person is secure and safe. But more than that, the law represents legitimacy; it is the highest standard. If change is required, then there are proper legal processes (themselves defined by law), on how those changes are legitimately achieved—all based on liberal constitutional democracy (Wolfe 1998:111–273).

A passion for principle and law, rather than tradition, is the key to understanding the changes in "justice-thought" during the mid-twentieth century. The middle class could reject traditionalism because they were not part of that tradition and tradition would have been contrary to their life experience and its resulting worldview. The dominance of modernism, through the medium of the middle class, set the cultural stage for the Constitutional Revolution of 1937, the Due Process Revolution of the Warren Court, and other major social justice issues as the middle class matured demographically and politically. To try and review all of the social justice issues of the mid-twentieth century in pursuit of an understanding of how the middle class influenced American justice is too large a task. Rather, we will focus on the Due Process Revolution and related criminal justice system changes to understand the middle class' impact on justice more generally. The

Due Process Revolution and its sway on American justice were unprecedented since the American Revolution itself and built a foundation for many of the other social justice issues of the same period.

Incorporation of the Bill of Rights: The Due Process Revolution and the Projection of Social Justice

> *Before 1925, when the Court began in earnest the process of First Amendment incorporation, free speech had never prevailed against a repressive statute in the United States Supreme Court. (And although no case ever reached the Supreme Court, we should recall that no federal judge in the 1790s ever invalidated the infamous Sedition Act of 1798. With a few years of incorporation . . . freedom of expression and religion began to win in cases involving states. . . . Not until 1965 did the Supreme Court strike down an act of Congress on First Amendment grounds (Amar 1998:290–291).*

Modern scholars often explain the incorporation of the Bill of Rights with a descriptive recounting that strongly suggests that particular individuals and Courts acted from character, principle, and immediate circumstances to lead the country to a better realization of Constitutional ideals. While individual justices, Courts, and their economic and political contexts should by no means be dismissed (see Irons 1999), it is proposed here that sociohistorical forces, operating behind these more immediate causes, were working to bring major change and that the appearance of the middle class and a middle-class culture was also providing a compelling progressive republican mood within which the Court was changing. It cannot be a mere coincidence that incorporation arose and culminated with the rise and ultimate cultural hegemony of the middle class.

During the twentieth century, against this sociocultural middle-class background, the American justice system experienced major changes in Constitutional jurisprudence. Notable in this context was the Court's movement, beginning in 1925, to incorporate the First Amendment. A little over a decade later came the Constitutional Revolution of 1937 when the Court began to compromise its previous unyielding defense of property rights as the first principle of the Constitution and allow the government a larger role in regulating the economy for humane reasons. Brinkley (2010:1) continues, recognizing that "[t]he Court also became more active in incorporating new, but far from universal, social and cultural norms into its reading of the Bill of Rights and the Fourteenth Amendment." This change in the Court was followed by *Brown v. Board of Education* in 1954, a reversal of *Plessy v. Ferguson* (1896), which had a profound impact on the cultural fabric of the United States. Along with the reversal of *Plessy* came the Due Process Revolution customarily attributed to the Warren Court. Clearly, at the center of the Due Process Revolution was the incorporation of the Bill of Rights—those rights spelled out in the first Ten Amendments to the Constitution meant to protect citizens against governmental power and to ensure fundamental liberties. In the 1960s, these Constitutional protections were being extended to citizens of the states by the Supreme Court.

Conservative Americans have attributed these changes to the activism of the Warren Court, while liberals believed the Court was redressing the injustices in the system. These principal changes in American justice were not accidental but have a compelling historical context driven by social tensions that predate the beginning of the American Republic. More specifically, the criminal justice revolution, focused mainly in the 1960s and 1970s, was a major victory for individual rights and constitutional liberalism that had long been impugned by a small conservative elite establishment.

Although not necessarily liberal, the middle class supported these changes on principle and as legitimate. Constituting a large and active voting bloc, the post-war middle class created a political environment and culture that was conducive to progressive republicanism. It is not surprising that the Court would come to reflect this sociocultural environment. This milieu also accounts for the politicization of the Court in more recent history. Franklin Roosevelt certainly understood the value of progressive political choices to the Court, which provided a Court friendly to his legislative agenda. Political choices were brought home to conservatives with the activism of the Warren Court, something they still grumble about and fear to this day.

Since the time of the Warren Court, candidates for the Supreme Court have been thoroughly and contentiously vetted for the political nature of their past decisions. Largely because of the required supermajority in the Senate and because Republicans have dominated the Senate and White House for much of the past thirty years—and partly due to the randomness of events—the Court, by a slim margin, has been reconstituted as the historically conservative Court known for most of American history. Indeed, Court appointments have been drawn significantly into presidential and Senate politics.

As it has been from the inception of the country, the American sense of justice is still being contended. But we can get a good sense of the middle-class justice permeating the country by reviewing the history of incorporation. It has been commonly argued that the First Amendment did not apply to the states as this amendment specifically addresses what the US Congress could not do: "Congress shall make no law..." This was interpreted to mean that Constitutional Amendments applied only in federal jurisdictions, not to the states. Even if this translation were correct, this reasoning should not have applied to the other liberties addressed in the other Amendments as they do not specify Congress as the body to be restrained. Nonetheless, because of *Barron,* none of the liberties specified in the Bill of Rights were applicable to state jurisdictions until the twentieth century even though the restraint of state transgressions should have been obvious in 1868 with the passage of the Fourteenth Amendment.

However, for all its eloquence and clarity the Fourteenth Amendment was ignored by the body politic and the courts before the ink was hardly dry on the new Amendment. The *Slaughter-House Cases* (1873)[2] effectively neutralized the Fourteenth Amendment, and as late as *Prudential Insurance Co. v. Cheek* (1922) the Court was still holding that "neither the Fourteenth Amendment nor any other provision of the Constitution of the United States imposes upon the states any restrictions about 'freedom of speech'"(Irons 1999:198–201).

In the atmosphere of the Progressive Era, when socialist and labor agitation was near its height, Benjamin Gitlow, a socialist, was arrested and convicted by the state of New York for publishing left-wing materials. In *Gitlow v. New York* (1925) and later in *Near v. Minnesota* (1931), the Court employed the Fourteenth Amendment to extend free speech and press protections to citizens in state jurisdictions. These decisions quickly became the precedent for levering the incorporation of other liberties and provisions of the First Amendment.[3]

The right "to keep and bear arms" of the Second Amendment has been incorporated (*McDonald v. Chicago* [2010]) and has been the subject of some controversy between the gun-rights and gun-control constituencies with the latter arguing that this right is attached and restricted to the right to maintain a militia. As a mainly suburban population, this is also the position taken by many of the middle class. It is largely rural America that still stands staunchly behind the individual right to bear arms and supports its incorporation.

In earlier chapters, we often saw that common Americans had their grievances heard by the authorities only because they were armed and posed a threat if ignored. It seems likely that this memory was still fresh in Antifederalists' minds when a bill of rights was being demanded in conjunction with the passage of the Constitution. In this same regard, personal arms played a significant role in the Revolution, in following rebellions, and for protection and hunting on the western frontier. It was not until the turn of the twentieth century that gun control laws were finally passed in New York City.

The Third Amendment, prohibiting the government from quartering soldiers in citizens' homes has not been incorporated by the US Supreme Court, probably because it has not become an issue. However, property rights and privacy issues certainly seem implicit in the Third Amendment, and the Fourteenth Amendment would imply that incorporation should occur.

Violations of Fourth Amendment protections "against unreasonable searches and seizures" was made binding on the states in *Mapp v. Ohio* in 1961. This included the application of the exclusionary rule. Although there has been some debate on whether the Fourth Amendment can be generalized as a "right to privacy," certainly Americans have, and expect, a broad circle of sanctuary free from the intrusion of governmental invasion. This is not just a middle-class expectation but an expectation that reaches across most segments of society.

From its inception, Fourth Amendment protections seem to have disconcerted the American elite in their exertion of authority. We can see this historically in the general reluctance to include a bill of rights in the Constitution. Up until the twentieth century, law enforcement practices ignored the Fourth Amendment. In the Progressive Era there was a push back from the people in *Weeks v. United States* (1914) indicating that intrusions by the government had become so bothersome that the Court created the exclusionary rule. Originally, the exclusionary rule forbade the use in federal court of any evidence illegally obtained by federal agents. When Fourth Amendment abuses continued at the state level, the *Mapp* ruling extended the exclusionary rule to state courts. In 1983 a more conservative Court produced three "good faith exceptions" to the exclusionary rule, which many felt compromised the original intent of the exclusionary rule and the Fourth Amendment.

Then in 2001 the Patriot Act was passed by the Bush administration and a Republican Congress in response to the September 11 terrorist attack on the Twin Towers in New York City. This Act further compromised the Fourth Amendment and the exclusionary rule by allowing federal agents to make certain kinds of searches without a warrant or probable cause and without being responsible to the courts, thus eliminating much of the established protections. Although the Court has found parts of the Act unconstitutional it still contains many suspect provisions.

The Fifth Amendment contains four individual protections. The first, the right to a grand jury indictment, has not been incorporated. The excuse has been made by the Court (see *Hurtado v. California* [1884]) that since most states provide for a grand jury indictment in the case of serious crime, incorporation is unnecessary. This excuse seems thin as the jury (both grand and petite) has been historically viewed as the guarantor of all other rights. To have a jury of peers overseeing the states' process of indictment would seem especially important for the poor who are frequently compelled into plea bargains by the threat of jail time while they wait for trial and the threat of heavy sentences if found guilty at trial. Combined with the lack of incorporation to protect individuals from excessive bail and fines, the lack of incorporation for indictment by a grand jury seems particularly onerous and contrary to middle-class values. Its lack of immediacy for the middle class may explain, in part, why this protection has not been incorporated.

The protection against double jeopardy—from being tried for the same crime more than once—was incorporated in *Benton v. Maryland* in 1969. In some respects this protection has depth in that jeopardy attaches once a jury is sworn in, or a witness is sworn in at a bench trial. However, double jeopardy does not apply and does not prevent additional trials when several crimes can be charged for one criminal incident or the prosecution has evidence of other crimes that have not been charged or the federal court decides to make a charge when a trial fails in a state court or vice versa. Nor does double jeopardy prevent a civil trial when a criminal trial has or will occur, even if the person has been acquitted in the criminal case.

The Fifth Amendment is best known for its protection against self-incrimination and in 1964, in *Malloy v. Hogan,* the Court incorporated this provision. The protection against self-incrimination was further extended in *Escobedo v. Illinois* (1964) when the Court ruled that people accused of crimes have the right to have an attorney present during interrogation. In 1966, *Escobedo* was expanded in *Miranda v. Arizona* requiring that suspects of a crime be informed of their Constitutional rights (i.e., the right to remain silent, that anything they say can be held against them in a court of law, to have an attorney present during questioning, and that an attorney will be provided if the suspect cannot afford one).

The Sixth Amendment defines seven rights that deal specifically with criminal court procedures, all of which have been incorporated. The right to a speedy trial was incorporated in 1967 in *Klopfer v. North Carolina. In re Oliver* (1948) incorporated the right to a public trial. The right to trial by an impartial jury was incorporated in *Duncan v. Louisiana* (1968). Contrary to common understanding, the Court ruled that juries can be as small as six members, but even where there are twelve members only nine votes are necessary for a verdict. Within those guidelines states can write their own rules on jury size.

The right of a person to be informed of the nature and cause of the accusation(s) against him or her, to be notified of such, and to have a hearing was incorporated in *Twining v. New Jersey* (1908) and later reaffirmed in *In re Oliver* (1948). The right to confront opposing witnesses was incorporated in 1965 in *Pointer v. Texas.* Subpoena power—the right to a compulsory process for obtaining favorable witnesses—was incorporated in *Washington v. Texas* (1967). Finally, the Sixth Amendment's right to counsel was incorporated in two cases. In *Chandler v. Fretag* (1954) the Court held that the right to a privately attained attorney is "unqualified." In *Gideon v. Wainwright* (1963) the Court granted the right to state-compensated counsel for indigent persons.

Contrary to middle-class sensibilities, the right to a jury in civil cases provided by the Seventh Amendment and the Eighth Amendment protection against excessive bail and fines have not been incorporated.

The first eight Amendments to the Constitution provide a good backdrop for elucidating middle-class values and support for social justice. Underlying all of these rights and protections is a strong sense of the fairness proscribed in the American sense of justice. However, many questions and issues remain. If the Court's logic provides that incorporation follows from the provisions of the Fourteenth Amendment then it is puzzling to many Americans why the entire Bill of Rights has not been incorporated.

The Ninth Amendment, which provides that "[t]he enumeration in the Constitution, of certain rights, shall not be construed to deny or disparage others retained by the people," has largely been ignored because it is argued to be too vague to have authority. This

Amendment was important because of the argument forwarded by the Federalists that reasoned that by enumerating rights in a constitution any protections and liberties left unnamed would be lost. A more positive approach would have been for the Court to use the time since the passage of the Bill of Rights to enumerate these other rights on an ongoing basis. What comes immediately to mind is an explicit right to privacy.

Finally, the Tenth Amendment: "The powers not delegated to the United States by the Constitution, nor prohibited by it to the States, are reserved to the States respectively, or to the people." In *United States v. Darby* (1941) the Court argued that the Tenth Amendment is simply a truism. States' rights advocates use this Amendment to make their various arguments but the Supremacy Clause and the Necessary and Proper Clause make the Tenth Amendment all but meaningless except for those areas of jurisdiction the federal government would deem to grant the states. Originally, the Tenth Amendment was a concession given to appease Antifederalists (Wood 2009:71). In later decades, the Tenth Amendment evolved into an attempt to first protect slavery and then Jim Crow laws, which legalized discrimination against African-Americans. Currently, ultra-conservatives use the Tenth Amendment to resist federal programs.

Criminal Justice System Reforms: Law Enforcement, Corrections, and Juvenile Justice

The discussion that follows is not focused on class conflict per se but is meant to probe the important contributions to the conception of American justice that were motivated by middle-class culture in the mid-twentieth century. Opposition to these changes came regularly from the conservative establishment. With middle-class prominence, justice system restructurings of major substance were occurring that related, in part, to the Court's Constitutional reforms. Perhaps most notable in this respect was the society's dissatisfaction with law enforcement and policing practices.

It was not until the mid-nineteenth century that public police departments started to appear in large American cities. They were largely charged with keeping the peace, which often meant quelling strikes and political demonstrations. Police officers were given a great deal of discretion in how they dealt with the public and this treatment frequently had a rough, even deadly, edge. Police training at this time was generally nonexistent or was "on the job." Police officers generally had little education and were poorly paid. Added to the power inherent in their organizations and in the individual police officer, corruption, brutality, and a betrayal of public trust was common.

As the middle class became politically vigorous in the 1960s, their dissatisfaction with police practices became apparent. They wanted police officers that would protect them and their property, would be agreeable and responsive on a face-to-face basis, and were not corrupt and uneducated. Disagreeable contacts with the police were accentuated and reinforced by the violent treatment of Civil Rights and anti-war demonstrators viewed commonly on television and reported in the press. The police also had a well-deserved reputation of harsh biases toward racial and ethnic minorities.

By the mid-1960s the federal and local governments and the American Bar Association were responding to this public dissatisfaction with the formation of investigative commissions. Four of the most important commissions were:

National Advisory Commission on Civil Disorders (1967)
President's Commission on Law Enforcement and the Administration of Justice (1967)
National Advisory Commission on Criminal Justice Standards and Goals (1973)
American Bar Association's Standards Relating to Urban Police Function (1973)

All of these commissions came to similar conclusions and made analogous recommendations. "They pointed out the critical role police officers play in American society, called for careful selection of law enforcement officers, and recommended extensive and continuous training. The reports also recommended better police management and supervision, as well as internal and external methods of maintaining integrity in police departments" (Bohm and Haley 2010:156).

Other investigations from a variety of sources, pointed out similar problems. One of the more conspicuous investigations that focused specifically on police corruption was the Knapp Commission's investigation of the New York Police Department (1972). Wide-ranging corruption and abuse received national and international attention and did much to direct the society's awareness to policing reforms.

As a result of demands for policing improvements, three changes especially standout as reflections of middle-class values and desires.

First, there was the development of "community policing," where the focus of police efforts was to work with the community to solve problems. This was a major change from the traditional police-as-crime-fighters. In working closely with the community, police officers came into daily and continuous contact with community members and groups, thus developing personal relationships and knowledge of the community they patrolled.

Second, police professionalization undertook to improve the demeanor of police officers as they interacted with community members and organizations. Friendly officers who showed respect for citizens did much to improve community-police relations.

Third, police professionalization also emphasized more training and higher education, which did much to move police officers into the middle class. In this manner, police contacts with middle-class Americans were easier and on an equal footing. In the mid-1960s the average education for police officers was less than a high school education. Today, that average is approaching two years of higher education and many departments are now recruiting college-educated candidates.

In this same period, middle-class society also pushed for major reforms in the correctional system, especially reforms in prisons and jails. Presently, we think of American corrections as being decidedly punitive with harsh sentencing and overpopulated facilities driven by a huge illicit drug problem. While this is largely accurate and suggests that middle-class reforms in the 1970s fell far short, it is nonetheless true that the old dungeons and failing jails of the nineteenth and twentieth centuries were critically examined at mid-twentieth century and steps were taken to rectify many abuses.

The single event that came to symbolize the need for correctional reform in the public's mind was the Attica prison riot in 1971. After the riot had been suppressed by elements of the New York State Police and prison correctional officers, resulting in the deaths of nine hostages and twenty-eight inmates, a New York State Special Commission on Attica produced an investigative report that was highly critical of New York State prison authorities and Governor Nelson A. Rockefeller.

Like most of the prisons of its time (and today), Attica was grossly overpopulated. A prison designed for 1,200 inmates, Attica housed about 2,225 inmates at the time of the riot. Among many deficiencies, inmates received one shower a week and one roll of toilet paper per month. Food was usually cold and vermin-invested. Medical care was almost nonexistent.

Just as television coverage and press reports greatly influenced the attitudes of Americans regarding the Civil Rights Movement and anti-war sentiments surrounding the Vietnam War, so too did extensive television coverage of Attica affect public opinion regarding the American correctional system. Of the many results stemming from the demands for prison reform during this period, some have become institutionalized. This includes professional training of correctional officers, access to the courts and legal services for inmates, access to good medical services, and procedural due process in prison when inmates are accused of rule violations. "Probably the most important case in this area is *Wolff v. McDonnell* (1974). In *Wolff*, the Court held that although inmates facing a loss of good time for a rule infraction are not entitled to the same due process protections as in a criminal trial, such inmates are entitled to (1) a disciplinary hearing by an impartial body, (2) 24 hours' written notice of the charges, (3) a written statement of the evidence relied on and the reasons for the disciplinary action, and (4) an opportunity to call witnesses and present documentary evidence" (Bohm and Haley 2010:443–444).

Other important changes included greater freedom of speech (*Procunier v. Marinez* 1974), greater religious freedom (*Cooper v. Pate* 1964), and adequate medical care (*Estelle v. Gamble* 1976). In general, the courts, with public support, ended their "hands-off policy" when it came to prison conditions and began placing specific correctional institutions under court order to change poor prison conditions. Many of these rulings have come under a violation of the Eighth Amendment's prohibition of cruel and unusual punishment (Bohm and Haley 2010:445–446).

In accordance with middle-class values of fundamental fairness, we also find significant juvenile justice reform in the mid-twentieth century. While the old system of *parens patriae* (the court acting as parent) begun in the early twentieth century was itself largely a product of middle-class concerns regarding the treatment of juvenile delinquents, by midcentury it was becoming increasingly clear that this system was full of abuse and lacked fairness. Two important Court cases dealt significantly with juvenile issues.

In *Kent v. United States* (1966) the Court made a ruling regarding a juvenile charged with housebreaking and rape who had been transferred to adult court for trial without any due process protections. The Court ruled that when a juvenile was to be transferred to adult court, he or she had the right to a full hearing with the assistance of counsel. Furthermore, the juvenile's attorney must have full access to social records used in the determination, and the judge was required to state in writing the reasons for the transfer (Champion 2005:357).

Following *Kent*, the Court announced a year later in *In re Gault* (1967) that it was giving juvenile defendants additional due process protections. "This landmark case established a juvenile's right to have counsel, to confront and cross-examine accusers, to have protection from self-incrimination, and to have adequate notice of charges when there is the possibility of confinement as a punishment" (Champion 2005:349).

Underlying all of these extensive reforms were middle-class values of fundamental fairness and due process. When viewed together as a whole, these reforms do compellingly make up a Due Process Revolution, an attitude, tone, and change that helped to fulfill the promise to those early common Americans who supported a Revolution with a vision of a progressive republican government.

Notes

1. "[A] wide gap exists in the United States between people who retain strong religious beliefs, adhere to the traditional family, possess unquestioned loyalty to their country, dislike immigration, denounce pornography, and are suspicious of cultural relativism and those . . . who have accepted the basic axioms of feminism, support principles of multiculturalism, express cosmopolitan values, and place a high priority on civil liberties. . . . Upper-middle-class people who have prospered in the speculative 1980s and 1990s appear to be disproportionately represented on the liberal side, and those lower-middle-class Americans who still believe in savings accounts and family-oriented neighborhoods find themselves on the traditional side" (Wolfe 1998:13, 14).
2. The *Slaughter-House Cases* consolidated three similar cases: *The Butchers' Benevolent Association of New Orleans v. The Crescent City Live-Stock Landing and Slaughter-House Company; Paul Esteben, L. Ruch, J.P. Rouede, W. Maylie, S. Firmberg, B. Beaubay, William Fagan, J. D. Broderick, N. Seibel, M. Lannes, J. Gitzinger, Jo.P. Aycock, d. Verges, The Live-Stock Dealers' and Butchers' Association of New Orleans, and Charles Cavaroc v. The State of Louisiana, ex rel. s. Belden, Attorney-General; The Butchers' Benevolent Association of New Orleans v. The Crescent City Live-Stock Landing and Slaughter-House Company.* Error to the Supreme Court of Louisiana.
3. The freedom of assembly was incorporated in 1937 in *De Jonge v. Oregon;* the right to petition the government was incorporated in *Hague v. CIO* (1939); the free exercise of religion was incorporated in *Hamilton v. Regents of the University of California* (1934); and the establishment clause was incorporated in *Cantwell v. Connecticut* (1940).

9

Class Conflict in the Early Twenty-First Century

When U.S. households are ranked according to how much wealth they hold, they form a lopsided picture.

- *The bottom 40 percent of all households have only about 1 percent of all the wealth in the nation.*
- *The top 1 percent of all households have nearly 30 percent of all the wealth; the top 5 percent, 55 percent of the wealth; and the top 20 percent, 80 percent of the wealth*

(Quadrini and Rios-Rull 1997:22).

Class conflict in American society is an ongoing turmoil that invades numerous facets of social existence. Differences in class have affected the standard of living and life chances across the breadth of American history. The volume of class conflict in the early twenty-first century has been amplified by a number of important trends and events. In the past three decades Americans have become increasingly aware of the growing wealth and income disparity between elite and common people. Presently, the richest 1 percent of Americans receives about 25 percent of the national income (Noah 2010:1). "In 2004, the last year for which good estimates are available, the top 1 percent owned 34.3 percent of all marketable wealth" (Wolff 2007, Table 2. in Domhoff 2010[1967]:11).

Since 1980 and the election of Ronald Reagan, class inequality in wealth and income has increased to an unsurpassed historical high. Not since the Gilded Age has the divergence in wealth and income between the top tier and common people been so extreme (Phillips 2002; Noah 2010; Domhoff 2010[1967]). In the current presidential campaign (2012) wealth and income disparities have become a central issue reflected in the debate over which class should bear the greatest tax burden to alleviate the growing national deficit.

The escalating wealth and income gaps have been well and widely covered by media sources, thus keeping the issue in front of the American people. Notable in this media coverage is the *New York Times* series and subsequent book, *Class Matters* (2005). In the opening chapter, Janny Scott and David Leonhardt (2005:2) observe;

> [C]lass is still a powerful force in American life. Over the past three decades it has come to play a greater, not lesser, role in important ways. . . . At a time when the country is increasingly integrated racially, the rich are isolating themselves more and more. At a time of extraordinary advances in medicine, class differences in health and life span are wide and appear to be widening . . . most do not see a level playing field. They say the very rich have too much power.

Scott and Leonhardt (2005:5) continue by noting that "new research on mobility, the movement of families up and down the economic ladder, shows there is far less of it than economists once thought and less than most people believe." It has been the promise of mobility that has driven the American Dream, but in the past three decades common Americans have either remained in place or have slipped backward in their standard of living. Class antipathy has mounted as middle and working class Americans watch an enormous transfer of wealth into the upper class.

A good deal of the current attention focused on the wealth/income imbalance was initiated in 2001 and 2003 as a result of tax cuts given to wealthy Americans by the Bush Administration and the Republican-controlled Congress. These tax cuts, having been established with a sunset provision, were scheduled to end in 2010. As they approached their termination, Republicans refused to extend tax cuts for the middle class and benefits for the long-term unemployed unless tax cuts for the wealthy were extended. In a compromise, the tax cuts for all Americans were extended for two years expiring at the end of 2012—the current presidential campaign year.

Consequently, the tax and inequality issues have become central disputes between Democrats and Republicans and their presidential candidates. President Obama has argued that the tax cuts for the wealthiest American should be allowed to expire while retaining tax cuts for middle- and working-class Americans. Additionally, the President is advocating that wealthy Americans—those making one million dollars a year or more–should pay a standard tax rate of 30 percent. Democrats have made much of the fact that presidential candidate and multimillionaire, Mitt Romney, is taxed at a rate of 15 percent and that Warren Buffett, one of the wealthiest men in the world, pays a tax rate that is lower than his secretary's (the "Buffett Effect").

On April 12, 2012, as reported by *USA Today* (Jackson 2012), Vice President Biden further publicized this dispute by his reference to "The Romney Rule." "The (Mitt) Romney Rule says the very wealthy should keep the tax cuts and loopholes they have, and get an additional new tax cut every year that is worth more than what the average middle-class family makes in an entire year." Candidate Romney, who recently published his income tax returns, pays a lower income tax rate than many middle-class Americans.

For their part, Republicans accuse Democrats and the president of perpetuating class warfare. Republicans argue for their wealthy patrons that wealth and income are fairly earned and that tax breaks for the wealthy stimulate the economy, thus benefiting everyone. Identifying wealthy Americans as "job creators," the rich are praised and depicted as patriotic. This advocacy for the well-heeled has been extended to corporations, and Republicans have consistently advocated for lower corporate taxes and for corporate subsidizes like those afforded the oil industry.

Coincidental to the 2012 presidential campaign has been the appearance of the Occupy Wall Street Movement in the early fall of 2011. Although a nebulous movement with no elected or appointed leaders and professing a wide range of political and social positions, the movement's focal concerns are perhaps best identified by its slogan—"We are the 99%"—a slogan that specifically separates common Americans and their plight from the American elite. This slogan and the movement's central positions reveal concerns about social and economic inequality, the greed and corruption of corporations, and the undue influence of corporations on government policy.

Gaining momentum, the Occupy Wall Street Movement rapidly spread to cities and towns across the country. On October 9, 2011, barely a month after Occupy Wall Street first appeared in New York City, the Columbia Broadcasting System (CBS) reported that the movement had spread to twenty-five cities. The movement's longevity finally led to police interventions forcing these groups, who were commonly camped in various city parks, to disperse. This led to violent clashes between police and demonstrators that were especially alarming in Oakland, California, where hundreds of people were arrested.

Because of the extensive media coverage given the Occupy Wall Street Movement, class conflict-based discussions have become common in the media, educating many Americans on issues of which they had only a passing knowledge. The Occupy Wall Street Movement has gained widespread sympathy and support. Early polls showed a substantial support by Americans for the movement. A CBS poll in late October of 2011 found that 43 percent agreed with the views of the Occupy Wall Street movement whereas 27 percent disagreed (Montopoli 2011). Also in October of 2011 a *Time* news poll found that twice as many respondents (54 percent) were favorable to the Occupy Wall Street movement compared to the 27 percent favorable response to the Tea Party movement, a right-winged grassroots movement that has had a significant effect on the Republican Party (Shahid 2011). The effect of these movements may be witnessed in the summer and fall of 2012 as tax issues, anticipating the November election, are developed by the presidential candidates, their respective parties, and the media.

Also coincidental to the current presidential campaign are major labor disputes in Wisconsin, Ohio, Indiana, and elsewhere. As the Great Recession of 2008 has reduced state revenues, governors and lawmakers have looked for various ways to deal with their increasing deficits. In Wisconsin the Republican governor offered the Wisconsin Budget Repair Bill, which, among its many provisions, took away the right of public employees to collectively bargain for their pensions and health care benefits (Sulzberger 2011).

Reactions to the legislation and its subsequent passage have been considerable. In an attempt to keep Republicans from passing the bill, Democratic state senators initially left Wisconsin denying a legislative quorum (Zernike and Saulny 2011). Lasting for several months, large demonstrations consisting of union members, university students, and other sympathetic citizens ensued, in the beginning occupying the state senate building. The AFL-CIO and other opponents of the law filed lawsuits in an attempt to block the law's implementation. All of these measures failed to prevent the bill's passage.

Opposition to the law led to a partially successful attempt to recall six Republican Senators, three Democratic senators, and the Republican governor. Two of the Republican senators were defeated and the governor faced a recall challenge in June 2012. The governor collected over twelve million dollars for his election effort, half coming from big and corporate donors from outside the state, a record for a Wisconsin governor's race (Davey 2012).

In a very similar situation, occurring at almost the same time as the Wisconsin conflict, the Republican-dominated Ohio legislature passed anti-union legislation that was signed into law by their Republican governor. It provoked the same anger from public union members and their supporters as witnessed by their counterparts in Wisconsin. However, Ohio unions and their followers were able to repeal the law by a public vote of 62 percent to 38 percent in November of 2011 (Tavernise 2011).

In the neighboring state of Indiana the campaign against public employee unions has been extended to all union workers, public and private. Indiana had outlawed collective bargaining for its public employees in 2005 resulting in hundreds losing their jobs, especially those with many years of seniority as they were the employees receiving the highest wages (Greenhouse 2011). The Republican-controlled Indiana legislature then passed a right-to-work law signed by its governor in early 2012 (Schneider and Sikich 2012). This followed a similar action by the New Hampshire legislature in 2011 that was vetoed by its Democratic governor, a veto that the Republican-controlled legislature did not have the votes to override.

Other states, including Maine, Michigan, and Missouri, have similar pending legislation (Greenhouse 2012). The state option to right-to-work laws, passed as part of Taft-Hartley's repeal of the Wagner Act in 1947, prohibits union contracts from requiring employees to join the union. It allows and encourages employers to hire nonunion workers who will work for lower wages and fewer benefits. Historically such laws have destroyed most unions even though union workers, on average, receive substantially better compensation than nonunion workers.

The American public has largely supported the efforts of public union workers in Wisconsin and other states. A *USA Today*/Gallup Poll (Keen and Cauchon 2011) found that 61 percent of Americans said they would oppose the kinds of union restrictions that had been passed in Wisconsin, in contrast to 33 percent who said they would support them. Similarly, a *New York Times*/CBS Poll (Tapscott 2011) found that 60 percent of Americans opposed restricting collective bargaining with 33 percent supporting restrictions.

More generally, Americans perceive the larger class conflict in their society. A recent Pew Research Center survey, which has received considerable media coverage, found that two-thirds (66 percent) of Americans recognize class conflict in their society, exceeding the tensions perceived between races and between immigrants and the native-born. The greatest recognition in the perception of inequality has been among white middle-class persons making between $40,000 and $75,000 annually. Seventy-one percent of this same group now recognizes class conflict between wealthy and common Americans (Morin 2012; also see Tavernise 2012).

It seems certain that the class tension in American society has been aggravated by the Great Recession of 2008. A recent study at the School of Public and Environmental Affairs at Indiana University discusses in stark terms the social and economic stresses experienced by common Americans (Seefeldt et al. 2012). After four and a half years of recession and slow recovery the country is still registering an unemployment rate of just under 8 percent. More telling, perhaps,

> The Great Recession has left behind the largest number of long-term unemployed people since records were first kept in 1948. More than four million Americans report that they have been unemployed for more than 12 months. Although the official rate of unemployment is declining, much of this apparent progress is attributable to the fact that many adults are giving up on the search for a job. The more telling indicator of an economy's job-producing performance, the ratio of the number of employed people to the number of working-age adults (the "jobs-to-people" ratio), has improved only slightly since the Great Recession ended in June 2009. If the long-term unemployed lose their unemployment insurance benefits before the economy produces enough well-paying jobs to approach full employment, the ranks of the "new poor" will steadily swell between now and 2017 (Seefeldt et al. 2012:5).

The Indiana study notes that as of 2010 there are 46.2 million Americans (15.1 percent of the population) officially living in poverty. "The proportion of people living in poverty has increased by 27% between the year before the onset of the Great Recession (2006) and 2010" (Seefeldt et al. 2012:5). As state and federal governments face increasing deficits they are making cutbacks in the safety net that affects the standard of living of common Americans and their families (Seefeldt et al. 2012:31–35).

Class and Justice: A Conclusion

This discussion began with an understanding that justice generally refers to "fairness," and that just societies, in the American sense, must necessarily distribute that fairness equally. In a just society the law not only applies to all equally, but the law itself arises from the consent of the people it embraces. As such, justice implies that people have access to governance. For most, this means the right to vote but, by extension, also means that a citizen, being equal under the law, may also pursue public office in an equal manner as other citizens. A just society also provides and guards social and individual rights for all its members. The freedom of speech, therefore, is not a privilege of some but a right of all, and the society should institutionalize processes to guarantee that freedom. More difficult, perhaps, justice as fairness means that the resources of the society are shared equitably, if not equally; for if not, can justice truly exist? Can a person of modest means receive the same justice as the person of great wealth unless the institutions of justice take steps to maintain fairness?

In discussing the subject of American justice, two points are conceded. First, that justice is substantially defined relative to some authority (e.g., the Constitution and the law). And second, that justice does not exist in any state of perfection. While seemingly apparent, we must nonetheless ponder these two qualifications because Americans especially and firmly believe that justice arises naturally as one's due from divine and natural sources and they are disappointed when this standard falls short.

Americans are often heard to say that they live in a society that, for all its faults, is the most just society in the world. With this nationalistic passion, any critical discussion of justice in American society is difficult to pursue. Beard discovered this in 1913 with the publication of his book *An Economic Interpretation of the Constitution of the United States*, and Zinn (1995 [1980]) much later with his work *A People's History of the United States: 1492–Present.*

In the American case, we find that justice has a number of roots, perhaps most notably from Anglo-Saxon history where a just society was formulated over time through the composition and compilation of documents that outlined social and personal liberties. More immediately, American justice has been delineated in the Founding documents, especially the Declaration of Independence and the Constitution of the United States, including particularly the Bill of Rights and the Fourteenth Amendment. In this respect our most immediate sense of justice comes largely from the Founders' written documents. Nonetheless, their sense of justice was restricted in two vital ways. First, in that women, slaves, Native Americans and other minorities, and the propertyless were excluded to varying degrees from a just society. Second, justice was also restricted by the Founder's sense of rank, their discernment of the inherent superiority of the gentry, which meant that justice would be defined to protect elite interests (property and power) and, in their minds, the welfare of the country. These restrictions on justice were not found so much in the documents themselves, but in their application by executive, legislative, and judicial authority.

Because of the American gentry's appreciation of exclusion and rank, the meaning of justice was diminished by social status and class divisions, just as it was also devalued by discrimination on the basis of gender, slave status, ethnic origin, religion, and sexual preference. While we choose to view American justice in this text through a prism of social class conflict, it would be incorrect to portray this perspective as somehow whole. American justice is relative to different cultural groupings and conditions and is thus some distance from its encompassing ideal.

From the ground level, where common citizens stand, justice and its inference of "fairness" means that this standard applies to all citizens equally. More specifically, this is often translated to mean equality under the law, equality of opportunity, and equal access to the decision-making processes. With less simplicity, justice also includes a sense of equity, righteous retaliation, and economic parity. Equity thus refers to what people feel is their due (their "rights") when justice comes into question. Usually this is answered by reference to the Founding. Through Fourteenth Amendment incorporation of the Bill of Rights many of these liberties and protections have become less ambiguous.

Justice as retaliation is illustrated by the criminal justice system. The difficulty with this facet of justice is related to the sheer numbers of people who are officially accused and charged and the fact that the overwhelming numbers are poor and of minority status. On this point the question of whether a just society can exist with income and wealth inequality is starkly made.

Economic equality in a just society is commonly interpreted in America to mean that all should have equal access to the same opportunities; a person is free to pursue "happiness" within the limits of the law. With this notion of justice each person should succeed relative to their abilities and even though the result will be an unequal distribution of wealth, resources are nonetheless shared. Commonly called a meritocracy, its flaws make it the weakest link in the justice chain. Excessive wealth has compromised justice in all its facets. While a degree of redistribution and leveling would go a long way in creating a more just society, an absolute equality has not been ideologically required.

The obstacle is not just that the elite do not want to give up a fair share of their wealth to taxes but that their sense of justice is different, a difference that has its roots in the struggle to define the nature of our republic. The conservative republicanism to which they subscribe strongly stipulates their right to rule and to preserve their wealth. This ideology of conservative republicanism necessarily creates a justice contrary to that desired at ground level. In this conservative republicanism, those with wealth are believed to have special merit. This merit, it is believed, lifts the individual up a hierarchal scale where standards of privilege modify and exceed the justice asserted by a more progressive republicanism.

These differences in republican ideology not only result in different standards of justice but necessarily divide the society socially by class. In earlier American history the conflict between social classes was expressed by discontentment and violence. This raw clash continued through the creation and adoption of the Constitution and through the first century of labor unrest when this conflict began to institutionalize itself in various movements and organizations. With industrialization, especially after the Civil War, when the industrial economy was becoming dominant, the Democratic Party could no longer contain the discontentment of common Americans whether laborer or farmer, and open dissent and violent clashes escalated. American capital resisted social and political reform and escalated the conflict to dangerous levels. By the end of the nineteenth century the American elite were beginning to realize that reforms were necessary if business was going to prosper and the conservative republic was going to survive. Through various political and economic reforms, expanded suffrage, western expansion, and a sense of investment in governance, common American discontentment was moderated and channeled into legitimate social structures by the mid-twentieth century.

Into the nineteenth-century conflict arrived a growing middle class that was generally strong on progressive republican values but conservative in the actions they were willing to employ and tolerate in a system in which they were successfully invested. The middle class was not new to social reform having been involved in many social-reform movements. During the Progressive Era the middle class supported moderate reforms like Social Security and became further acquainted with and invested in the underlying ideology and political beliefs of the republic. Snubbed and ridiculed by their upper-class counterparts and more closely related to labor and agriculture, the middle class had sympathies with democratic reforms, including the direct election of the Senate (1913), the prohibition of alcohol (Eighteenth Amendment in 1919), and suffrage for women (Nineteenth Amendment in 1920). These political reforms were major accomplishments and implied a key change in cultural dominance, reflecting a more middle-class way of life.

As the middle class grew in size and wealth, their cultural and political hegemony quietly began to have profound effects on the American polity, steering governance moderately in a progressive republican direction. These changes were symbolically represented by the incorporation of the First Amendment in 1925 and followed by the Constitutional Revolution (1937) and the recognition by the Court that human rights, at least in some cases, might trump property rights.

In 1954 *Plessey* was overturned, ushering in racial integration, a salient cultural change. This was followed in the 1960s and 1970s by the Due Process Revolution that strengthened the protections that citizens had from governmental abuses. This was accompanied by major reforms in law enforcement and correctional practices and substantial reforms in the juvenile justices system. All of these and numerous other social changes reflected a middle-class sense of progressive republican justice.

Although these significant changes have been followed recently by a substantial backlash from the elite-backed conservative movement, it seems unlikely that this fundamental progressive republican shift, witnessed mainly in the twentieth century, will be lost. It seems just as likely that this historical class conflict over the nature of our republic will continue into the future.

References

Appleby, Joyce. 2001. "The Social Consequences of American Revolutionary Ideals in the Early Republic." In *The Middling Sorts: Explorations in the History of the American Middle Class,* edited by Burton J. Bledstein and Robert D. Johnston, 31–49. New York, NY: Routledge.

Applegate, Debby. 2001. "Henry Ward Beecher and the 'Great Middle Class': Mass-Marketed Intimacy and Middle-Class Identity." In *The Middling Sorts: Explorations in the History of the American Middle Class,* edited by Burton J. Bledstein and Robert D. Johnston, 107–124. New York, NY: Routledge.

Amar, Akhil Reed. 1998. *The Bill of Rights. Creation and Reconstruction.* New Haven, CT: Yale University Press.

Beard, Charles A. 1963[1913]. *An Economic Interpretation of the Constitution of the United States.* New York, NY: The Free Press.

———. 1943[1915]. *Economic Origins of Jeffersonian Democracy.* New York, NY: The Free Press.

Bledstein, Burton J. and Robert D. Johnston (eds.). 2001. *The Middling Sorts: Explorations in the History of the American Middle Class.* New York, NY: Routledge.

Blumin, Stuart M. 1989. *The Emergence of the Middle Class: Social Experience in the American City, 1760–1900.* New York, NY: Cambridge University Press.

Bohm, Robert M. and Keith N. Haley. 2002. *Introduction to Criminal Justice* (6th edition). New York, NY: McGraw-Hill.

Brands, W. H. 2000. *The First American: The Life and Times of Benjamin Franklin.* New York, NY: Anchor Books.

Bridenbaugh, Carl. 1950. *The Colonial Craftsman.* New York, NY: New York University Press.

Brinkley, Douglas. 2010. *Witness to America: A Documentary History of the United States from the Revolution to Today.* New York, NY: Harper.

Brown, Roger H. 1993. *Redeeming the Republic: Federalists, Taxation, and the Origins of the Constitution.* Baltimore, MD: John Hopkins University Press.

Carneiro, Robert. 1970. "A Theory of the Origin of the State." *Science* 169:733–738.

Champion, Dean John. 2005. *The American Dictionary of Criminal Justice* (3rd edition). Los Angeles, CA: Roxbury.

Christman, Henry. 1945. *Tin Horns and Calico.* New York, NY: Holt.

Conrad, Clay S. 1998. *Jury Nullification: The Evolution of a Doctrine.* Durham, NC: Carolina Academic Press.

Dahl, Robert A. 2003[2002]. *How Democratic Is the American Constitution?* (2nd edition). New Haven, CT: Yale University Press.

Davey, Moncia. 2012. "Recall Election for Wisconsin Governor Who Battled Unions." In *New York Times*, http://www.nytimes.com/2012/03/31/us/wisconsin-approves-recall-election-for-governor.

Diamond, Jared. 1997. *Guns, Germs, and Steel: The Fates of Human Societies.* New York, NY: W. W. Norton.

Domhoff, G. William. 2010[1967]. *Who Rules America? Challenges to Corporate and Class Dominance* (6th edition). Boston, MA: McGraw-Hill.

———. 1983. *Who Rules America Now? A View for the '80s.* Englewood Cliffs, NJ: Prentice-Hall.

———. 1978. *The Powers That Be: Processes of Ruling Class Domination in America.* New York, NY: Random House.

———. 1978. *Who Really Rules? New Haven and Community Power Reexamined.* New Brunswick, NJ: Transaction Books.

———. 1975. *Bohemian Grove and Other Retreats: A Study in Ruling-Class Cohesiveness.* New York, NY: Harper Torchbooks.

———. 1972. *Fat Cats and Democrats: The Role of the Big Rich in the Party of the Common Man.* Englewood Cliffs, NJ: Prentice-Hall.

———. 1970. *The Higher Circles: The Governing Class in America.* New York, NY: Vintage Books.

Dray, Philip. 2010. *There is Power in a Union: The Epic Story of Labor in America.* New York, NY: Doubleday.

Dubofsky, Melvyn and Dulles, Foster Rhea. 2010[1949]. *Labor in America: A History* (Eighth edition). Wheeling, IL: Harlan Davidson, Inc.

Durkheim, Emile. 1982[1895]. *The Rules of Sociological Method.* New York, NY: The Free Press.

Ellis, Joseph J. 2004. *His Excellency George Washington.* New York, NY: Alfred A. Knopf.

Erikson, Kai T. 1966. *Wayward Puritans: A Study in the Sociology of Deviance.* New York, NY: John Wiley & Sons.

Evans, Mark. 2009. "Populist Socialism Reconsidered." In http://www.sonic.net/-doretk/ ArchiveARCHIVE/Mark%20EVANS/PopulistSocialism.html.Farrand, Max (ed.). 1966[1911]. *The Records of the Federal Convention of 1787, Vol. II.* New Haven, CT: Yale University Press.

Ferguson, E. James. 1961. *The Power of the Purse: A History of American Public Finance 1776–1790.* Chapel Hill, NC: University of North Carolina Press.

Gordon-Reed. 2008. *The Hemingses of Monticello: An American Family.* New York, NY: W. W. Norton.

Foner, Eric. 2010. *The Fiery Trial: Abraham Lincoln and American Slavery.* New York, NY: W. W. Norton & Co.

Gouldner, Alvin W. 1970. *The Coming Crisis of Western Sociology.* New York, NY: Basic Books.

Greenhouse, Steven. 2011. "In Indiana, Clues to Future of Wisconsin Labor." In *New York Times*, http://www.nyltimes.com/2011/02/27/business/27collective-bargain.

———. 2012. "A Gathering Storm Over 'Right to Work' in Indiana." In *New York Times*, www.nytimes.com/2012/01/03/business/gathering-storm-over-right-to-work-in-india

Gusfield, Joseph R. 1986[1963]. *Symbolic Crusade* (2nd edition). Urbana-Champaign, IL: University of Illinois Press.

Harris, Marvin. 1977. *Cannibals and Kings: The Origins of Cultures.* New York, NY: Random House.

Hoffert, Robert W. 1992. *A Politics of Tensions: The Articles of Confederation and American Political Ideas.* Niwot, CO: University Press of Colorado.

Horkheimer, Max. 1982. *Critical Theory.* New York, NY: Seabury Press.

Irons, Peter. 1999. *A People's History of the Supreme Court.* New York, NY: Viking Press.

Jackson, David. 2012. "Biden: 'Romney Rule' favors rich." In *USA Today*, http://www.content.usatoday.com/communities/theoval/post/2012/04/biden-romney-rule-favors-r.

Johnson, Allen W. and Timothy Earle. 1987. *The Evolution of Human Societies: From Foraging Group to Agrarian State.* Stanford, CA: Stanford University Press.

Keen, Judy and Dennis Cauchon. 2011. "Public Favors Union Rights." In *USA Today*, http://www.usatoday.com/printedition/news/201110223/lawisconsinpoll23-start.

Keller, Morton. 2007. *America's Three Regimes: A New Political History.* New York, NY: Oxford University Press.

Kennedy, Edward M. 2009. *True Compass.* New York, NY: Twelve.

Konvitz, Milton R. 2001. *Fundamental Rights: History of a Constitutional Doctrine.* New Brunswick, NJ: Transaction Publishers.

Kuo, David. 2006. *Tempting Faith: An Inside Story of Political Seduction.* New York, NY: The Free Press.

Lash, Kurt T. 2009. *The Lost History of the Ninth Amendment.* New York, NY: Oxford University Press.

Lee, Richard B. 1990. "Eating Christmas in the Kalahari." In *Anthropology: Contemporary Perspectives* (6th edition), edited by Phillip Whitten and David E. K. Hunter. 154–157. Glenview, IL: Scott Foresman.

Lenski, Gerhard. 1966. *Power and Privilege: A Theory of Social Stratification.* New York, NY: McGraw-Hill.

Levy, Leonard W. 1999. *Origins of the Bill of Rights.* New Haven, CT: Yale University Press.

Lynd, Staughton. 2009[1967]. *Class Conflict, Slavery, and the United States Constitution.* New York, NY: Cambridge University Press.

Main, Jackson Turner. 1961. *The Antifederalists Critics of the Constitution 1781–1788.* Chapel Hill, NC: University of North Carolina Press.

Marshall, John. 2000[1803–1807]. *The Life of George Washington.* Indianapolis, IN: Liberty Fund.

Matthews, Rick A. 2006. "Ordinary Business in Nazi Germany." In *State-Corporate Crime: Wrongdoing at the Intersection of Business & Government.* edited by Raymond J. Michalowski and Ronald C. Kramer, 116–133. New Brunswick, NJ: Rutgers University Press.

McCullough, David. 2001. *John Adams.* New York, NY: Simon & Schuster.

McDonald, Forest. 1986. "A New Introduction." In *An Economic Interpretation of the Constitution of the United States* by Charles A. Beard (1963[1913]), vii–xl. New York, NY: The Free Press.

———. 1979[1965]. *E Pluribus Unum. The Formation of the American Republic 1776–1790.* Indianapolis, IN: Liberty Press.

———. 1958. *We the People: The Economic Origins of the Constitution.* Chicago, IL: University of Chicago Press.

Michalowski, Raymond J. and Ronald C. Kramer (eds.). 2006. *State-Corporate Crime: Wrongdoing at the Intersection of Business and Government.* New Brunswick, NJ: Rutgers University Press.

Miller, John C. 1988[1960]. *The Federalist Era 1789–1801.* Prospect Heights, IL: Waveland Press.

Mills, C. Wright. 2002[1951]. *White Collar: The American Middle Class.* New York, NY: Oxford University Press.

———. 2000[1959]. *The Sociological Imagination.* New York, NY: Oxford University Press.

Montopoli, Brian. 2011. "Poll: 43 percent agree with views of "Occupy Wall Street." In *Political Hotsheet* CBS News, http://www.cbsnews.com/8301-503544_162-20125515-503544/poll-43-percent-agree-with.

Morin, Rich. 2012. "Rising Share of Americans See Conflict Between Rich and Poor. Pew Research Center. http://www.pewsocialtrends.org/2012/01/11/rising-share-of-americans-see-conflict-betwee.

Moskowitz, Marina. 2001. "Public Exposure: Middle-Class Material Culture at the Turn of the Twentieth Century." In *The Middling Sorts: Exploration in the History of the American Middle Class,* edited by Burton J. Bledstein and Robert D. Johnston, 170–184. New York, NY: Routledge.

New York Times (ed.). 2005. *Class Matters.* New York, NY: Times Books.

Noah, Timothy. 2010. "The United States of Inequality. Introducing the Great Divergence." In *Slate.com* (Sept. 3). http://www.slate.com/.

Nolan, Patrick and Gerhard Lenski. 2009[1970]. *Human Societies: An Introduction to Macrosociology* (11th edition). Boulder, CO: Paradigm Publishers.

Philips, Kevin. 2002. *Wealth and Democracy: A Political History of the American Rich.* New York, NY: Broadway Books.

Priest, Dana and William M. Arkin. 2010. "Top Secret America." In *Washington Post* (July 19).

Quadrini, Vincenzo and Jose-Victor Rios-Rull. 1997. "Understanding the U.S. Distribution of Wealth." In *Federal Reserve Bank of Minneapolis Quarterly Review* 21, no. 2:22–36.

Rakove, Jack N. 1996. *Original Meanings: Politics and Ideas in the Making of the Constitution.* New York, NY: Vintage Books.

Raphael, Ray. 2001. *A People's History of the American Revolution: How Common People Shaped the Fight for Independence.* New York, NY: Perennial.

Rawls, John. 1999[1971]. *A Theory of Justice.* Revised Edition. Cambridge, MA: Harvard University Press.

Rayback, Joseph G. 1959. *A History of American Labor.* New York, NY: Macmillan.

Rosen, Jeffrey. 2006. *The Supreme Court: The Personalities and Rivalries that Defined America.* New York, NY: Times Books.

Rosenman, Samuel. 1950. *The Public Papers & Addresses of Franklin D. Roosevelt, Vol. XIII.* New York: Harper.

Ryerson, Richard A. 1978. *The Revolution is Now Begun: The Radical Committees of Philadelphia, 1765–1776.* Philadelphia, PA: University of Pennsylvania Press.

Schneider, Mary Beth and Chris Sikech. 2012. "Indiana becomes Rust Belt's first right-to-work state." In *The Indianapolis Star,* http://www.usatoday.com/ news/ nation/story/ 2012-02-01/indiana-right-to-work-bill/529163.

Scott, Janny and David Leonhardt. 2005. "Shadowy Lines That Still Divide." In *Class Matters,* published by *New York Times.* New York, NY: Times Books.
Seefeldt, Kristin, Gordon Abner, Joes A. Bolinger, Lanlan , and John D. Graham. 2012. "At Risk: America's Poor During and After the Great Recession." Bloomington, IN: School of Public and Environmental Affairs, Indiana University.
Shahid, Aliyah. 2011. "Occupy Wall Street movement is twice as popular as the Tea Party: Time poll." In *New York Daily News,* http://articles.nydailynews.com/2011-10-13/news/ 3029344_1_tea-party-wall-street-move.
Shogan, Robert. 2004. *The Battle of Blair Mountain: The Story of America's Largest Labor Uprising.* New York, NY: Basic Books.
Sulzberger, A. G. 2011. "Wisconsin G.O.P. Plans to Work Without Democrats." In *New York Times,* http://www.nytimes.com/2011/02/22/us/22wisconsin.
Tapscott, Mark. 2011. "CBS News/New York Times Survey Oversampled Union Households." In *Washington Examiner,* http://washingtonexaminer.com/blogs/beltway-confidential/2011/03/cbs-newsnew-york-times-survey-oversampleed-union-households.
Tavernise, Sabrina. 2011. "Ohio turns back a Law Limiting Unions' Rights." In *New York Times,* http://www.nytimes.com/2011/11/09/us/politics/ohio-turns-back-a-law-limiting-unions-rig.
———. 2012. "Survey Finds Rising Perception of Class Tension." In *New York Times,* http://www.nytimes.com/2012/10/12/us/more-conflict-seen-between-rich-and-poor-survey.
Volpe, Andrea 2001. "Cartes de Visite Portrait Photographs and the Culture of Class Formation." In *The Middling Sorts: Explorations in the History of the American Middle Class,* edited by Burton J. Bledstein and Robert D. Johnston, 157–169. New York, NY: Routledge.
Wilentz, Sean. 1982. "On Class and Politics in Jacksonian America." *Reviews in American History* (December). Baltimore, MD: Johns Hopkins University Press.
Woodrell, Daniel. 1998. *Tomato Red.* New York, NY: Henry Holt.
Wolfe, Alan. 1998. *One Nation, After All: What Middle-Class Americans Really Think About: God, Country, Family, Racism, Welfare, Immigration, Homosexuality, Work, The Right, The Left, and Each Other.* New York, NY: Viking.
Wolff, Edward. 2007. *Recent Trends in Household Wealth in the United States: Rising Debt and the Middle-Class Squeeze.* Annandale-on-Hudson, NY: Levy Economics Institute.
Wood, Gordon S. 1998[1969]. *The Creation of the American Republic 1776–1787.* Chapel Hill, NC: University of North Carolina Press.
———. 2009. *Empire of Liberty. A History of the Early Republic, 1789–1815.* Oxford, England: Oxford University Press.
Zakaria, Fareed. 2003. *The Future of Freedom: Illiberal Democracy at Home and Abroad.* New York, NY: W. W. Norton.
Zernike, Kate and Susan Saulny. 2001. "Wisconsin Bill Advances, Then Stalls." In *New York Times,* http://www.nytimes.com/2011/02/26/us/26states.
Zinn, Howard. 1995[1980]. *A People's History of the United States.* New York, NY: HarperCollins.

Index